AF581226

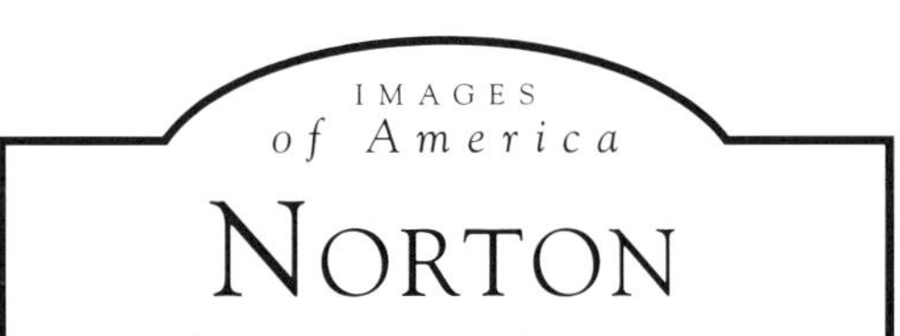
IMAGES
of America
NORTON

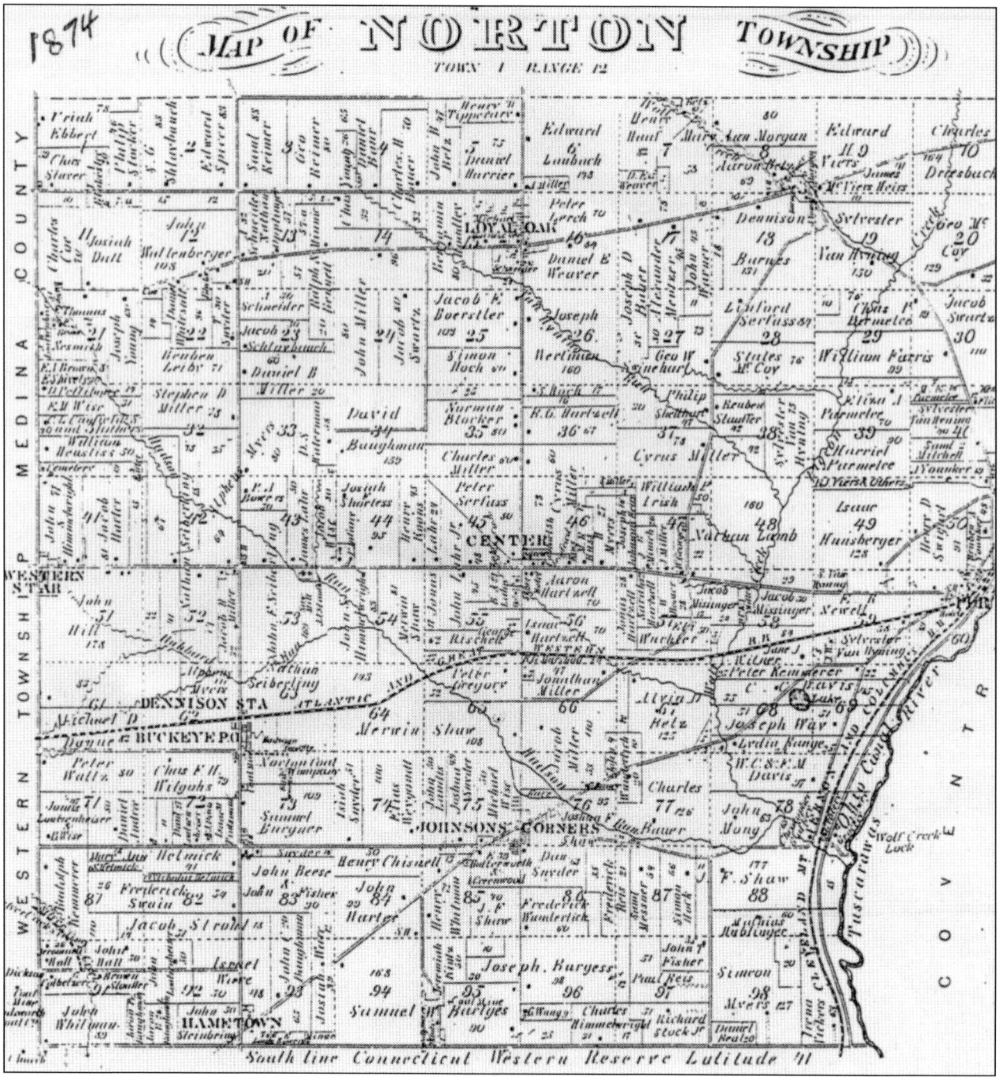

1874 MAP OF NORTON TOWNSHIP
TOWN 1 RANGE 12

Surveyed by Joseph Darrow in 1810, Norton Township became Town 1, Range 12 in the Western Reserve, a portion of land claimed by the Colony of Connecticut—and later, by the State of Connecticut—in what is now mostly part of the northeastern region of Ohio. Norton was named after Birdsey Norton, one of the original landowners of the township. (Courtesy of *Combination Atlas Map of Summit County, Ohio.*)

ON THE COVER: In the early part of 1900s, the McCoy family poses for a photograph at their 86-acre home at 3215 Clark-Mill Road. Pictured here are, from left to right, (first row) Norm Miller, George McCoy, Amelia Falor McCoy, Norm Miller and his sons Ervin (being held) and Ernest McCoy; (second row) Myrtle McCoy and her husband Henry Zeisick, and Elsie McCoy Miller. The farm was known for its dairy, hay, and geese. (Courtesy of Norm Kendall.)

IMAGES
of America

NORTON

Lisa Ann Merrick

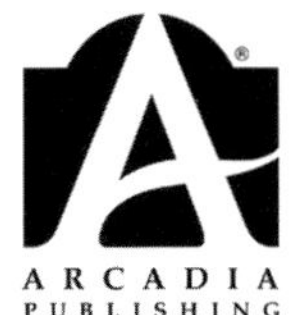

ISBN 978-1-4671-1441-7

Published by Arcadia Publishing
Charleston, South Carolina

Printed in the United States of America

Library of Congress Control Number: 2015931844

For all general information, please contact Arcadia Publishing:
Telephone 843-853-2070
Fax 843-853-0044
E-mail sales@arcadiapublishing.com
For customer service and orders:
Toll-Free 1-888-313-2665

Visit us on the Internet at www.arcadiapublishing.com

I dedicate this book to my father, Archer J. Merrick, and to my mother, Janet A. Boots Merrick, who brought me to Norton and to the Norton Historical Society.

Contents

ACKNOWLEDGMENTS

This photographic history of Norton showcases many images that have not been previously published. It includes images and research on places and people from around the 1800s up to the present. Looking around every nook and cranny of Norton, I tried to include as many families, businesses, and school images of historical interest as possible.

Without the vast records, scrapbooks, genealogies and photographs donated to the Norton Historical Society, Biery House and Museum made available to me, this book may not have come to fruition. The society had an idea for a book to be published for years, and I decided to take it on as a personal mission, hopefully one of which the community will be proud.

I want to extend a special thank-you to our museum curator and my friend, Patricia Snyder, for lending her support and guidance through the entire process.

I would like to thank my brother Christopher Merrick of CM Graphics and Kathie Schaffner at Power Graphics for being patient with my requests for help. Thanks especially to Ann Campbell for computer tutorials to help streamline my efforts.

Thank you Janean Skiles Ray, Kim Nevling Zita, Kelly Holderbaum, and Claude Collins for promoting interest and digging for facts. Thank you Maggie Abbott for hunting down images, and John Janovec Jr. for his hours of research regarding our town founder.

I would also like to thank Rodger Ramsthaler, Chuck Miller, William Blackburn, Dr. Robert Hemphill, Virginia Swain Knox, Betty Bodo, Denise Emery, Stephanie Whims, Christine Daniel, Tim Brenner, Wayne Pressler, Lori Lewis Pfahler, Mauri O'Brodo, Mike and Marcia Lucas, Weldon "Shot" Bauer, Crystal Noel Bassett, Karen Merlo, and June Witchey Patera for taking the time to either meet with me or sending materials to me for this publication.

To all of the above, a heartfelt thanks.

Unless otherwise noted, all images are courtesy of the Biery House and Museum.

INTRODUCTION

Norton was originally a part of Wolf Creek Township, which consisted of present-day Norton and Copley in Summit County and Wadsworth, Sharon, Guilford, and Montville in Medina County. Norton was organized in 1816 with an election held that April, with Henry Van Hyning Sr. and Salmon Warner selected to be the first justices of the peace. Philemon Kirkham was elected town clerk, and Nathan Bates, Jacob Miller, and Abraham Van Hyning were elected trustees. In 1818, Norton Township was organized.

History notes that Norton was founded on some of the finest land and was recognized as an agricultural community dotted at one time with various large farms. The land is diverse, including areas of sandy loam, which makes the optimum soil for agricultural purposes. Included in this area are the muck areas in the eastern portion of the township.

The coal industry was important. In 1825, the first mine was opened in the southwest section, with hundreds of thousands of tons mined near the hamlet of Sherman (Dennison Station) by the Nypano Railroad.

Within Norton, there were seven small hamlets, which still remain enclosed within the city as a reminder of the founding citizens and their unique small communities. The hamlets within the community making up Norton each had their own industries, churches, schools, and stores. The hamlets are as follows: Norton Center, Western Star, Loyal Oak, Hametown, Sherman (Dennison Station), Johnson's Corners, and New Portage. New Portage was wiped out by an epidemic of black plague, or tongue fever, in 1826–1827.

The very early pioneer residents of Norton found that there were numerous obstacles to subsistence in the region. First, they had to have a roof over their heads, in addition to a few acres of cleared land to grow the absolute necessities to live by and feed the few animals they brought with them.

As soon as they had shelter and food, many early settlers set up some kind of small business; the income of which enabled them to live a bit easier. Sawmills, gristmills, tanneries, and blacksmith shops were the most important of the early industries in the village.

The first sawmill was built by Thomas Johnson at Johnson's Corners in 1823. Early settlers were able to bring logs they cleared from their farms and have them converted into lumber to build barns and houses. Johnson also built the first gristmill around 1830. The second sawmill was built by Hezekiah Ward on Hudson Run in the northwest corner of the township. In 1837, Nathan Seiberling built a large sawmill farther down Hudson Run.

Around 1830, the first tannery was opened in Western Star, operated by Lebbens Hoskinson, along with the first blacksmith shop opened by Samuel Baker.

These first industries provided Norton-area residents with vital services. The proprietors and operators of these early businesses had to be men of considerable mechanical ingenuity, as they did not have a machine shop or parts facility available. Machinery had to be kept in operation with whatever they could improvise.

Nathan Seiberling settled in Norton and brought with him some German mechanical ingenuity when he started his first sawmill and tried a new kind of saw: a geared muley saw. It was designed to cut much faster than the saws used by other mill operators.

Two of Nathan Seiberling's grandsons, Frank A. and Charles W., were born in the Seiberling home in Western Star, and after serving an apprenticeship with their father, John Seiberling, struck out in the industrial world for themselves. In 1898, Goodyear Tire and Rubber Company was organized by these brothers and grew to become one of the largest rubber companies in the world.

North of Loyal Oak, on Reimer Road, was another man growing up to be destined to head one of the largest companies in the world. Edwin J. Young was born in 1857, the son of Charles Young, who had come to Loyal Oak area from Pennsylvania. Young's enthusiasm and determination served him well as he became the manufacturer of injectors, valves, paper products, salt, and matches with his Ohio Match Company.

Many creeks and streams run through the township, including Wolf Creek, Pigeon Creek, Van Hyning Run, Hudson Run, Silver Creek, and Hubbard Run.

The principal production of the township included wheat, oats, corn, livestock, and coal. Fine thoroughbred cattle were bred in the township, as well as draft horses.

The great Scioto Trail, also known as the Great Trail, ran partially through the township. This trail was used by the first inhabitants as a path for warfare, trade, and migration. The trail struck the township near the northeast corner of lot 20, crossed Wolf Creek, passed down the west side of Wolf Creek bottoms, and made a straight cut to Johnson's Corners. From there, it took a southwesterly course nearly identical to Wooster Road.

The early settlers had to rely on stagecoaches until 1827, when the Ohio Canal was completed, providing settlers with a naval route north and south. New Portage was a station stop on the Erie and Cleveland, Akron, Columbus, railroads, and in 1905 an electric trolley line was extended from Barberton through Norton to Wadsworth and was used for many years as a means to travel over northern Ohio on connecting lines.

Early settlers in Norton took part in the Revolutionary War, including Hinsdale Bates, Samuel Baker, Phineas and Silas Bronson, Alexander Griswold, Cato Mead, Thomas McNeil, Henry VanHyning, and Hosea Wilcox.

Norton's military roll of honor in the Civil War has an impressive number of young men of which to be proud. Over 115 men served in the Union army, and many brothers served together, including Bakers, Betzes, Dagues, Fergusons, Seiberlings, Millers, Loutzenhisers, Ebers, Bennetts, Blockers, Bears, Henshues, Knoxes, Powerses, Wrights, Waltzes, Wares, and Youngs.

Today, Norton boasts a highly rated school system and quality fire, police, and service departments. The city has 10 parks within its border, and organized youth sports are available to all age groups. Many clubs are active, including Kiwanis, Women's Club, Norton Historical Society, Lions Club, and various garden clubs. There are Boy and Girl Scouts, and the 4-H is active as well.

Each year, Norton hosts its cider festival in late September and early October, which began in 1988. The festival is held at the Columbia Woods Park, which can accommodate large crowds in an idyllic setting. Visitors can enjoy cider tastings, contests, concerts, rides, and a pancake breakfast.

One

Families, Homesteads, and Fascinating Folks

As early as 1810, some of the first purchases of land in Norton were made by James Robinson and John Cahow of Maryland. The general rush of settlers found their way through a trackless forest; among them were Philemon Kirkham, Seth Lucas, Lyman and Nathan Bates, Joseph Holmes, Elisha Hinsdale, Ezra Way, Joseph D. Humphrey, and Abraham and Henry Van Hyning. The families of Benjamin Hoadley, William George, and Charles Miller arrived in 1816. The years 1817–1818 brought more pioneers who helped to form the foundation for the hamlets of Norton. Much of their time was spent in cutting roads, clearing the land, and helping each other build houses. The first death was Patty O'Brien, age two, and the first marriage was that of James Robinson and Lois Bates. Miles Clark became the first doctor. Edwin J. Young, who was born in the Loyal Oak area in 1857 to an early Pennsylvania settler, became interested in the design of injectors. The enthusiasm and determination with which he worked served an important part in the phenomenal growth of companies in Wadsworth. His companies manufactured injectors and valves, paper products, salt, and matches, and the Ohio Match Company was destined to become the largest match plant in the world.

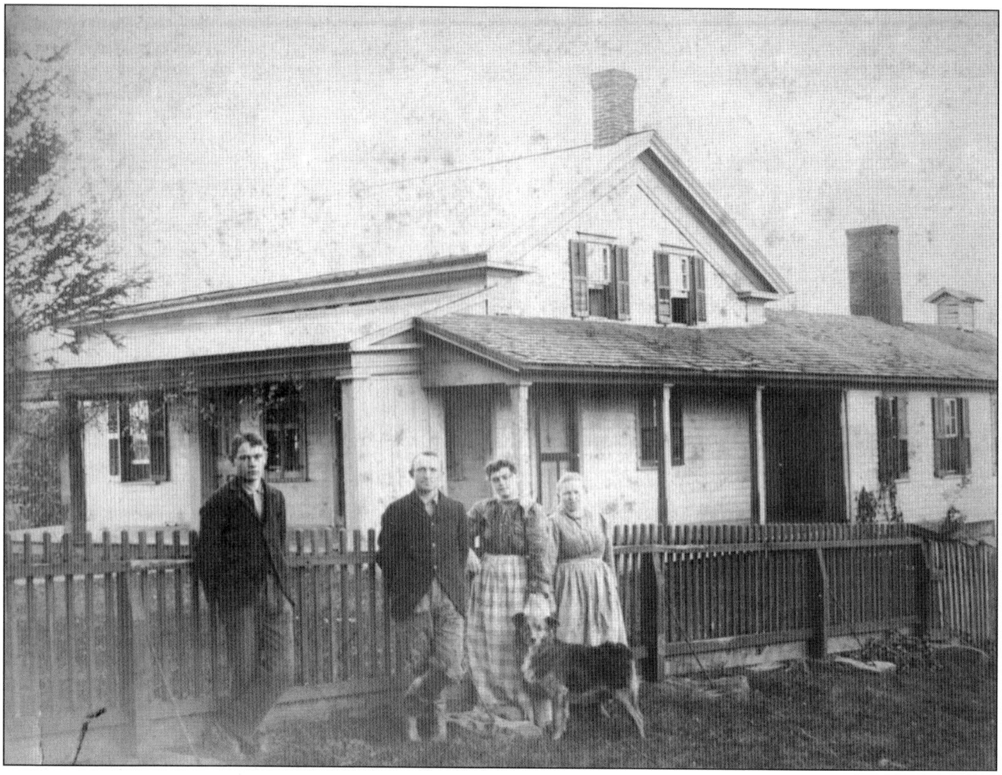

Pictured here at the Miller homestead at 3500 Hametown Road are, from left to right, Albert Miller, Charles O. Miller, Pearl Stimson Miller, and Harriet "Hattie" Miller. The Miller family farm was purchased by Stephen and Mary Ann Musser Miller from her parents, David and Mary Read Musser. (Courtesy of Chuck Miller.)

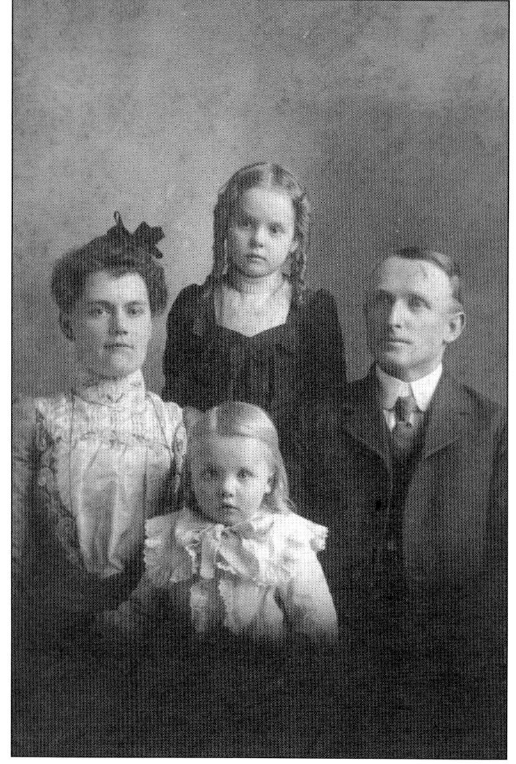

In 1902, the Charles O. Miller family sat for this photograph. From left to right are Pearl, Thelma, Clarence (center), and Charles. Charles and Pearl were married in 1895, and memories abound for family who visited them at the homestead. The family cabin on the property had a carbine lighting system, and the artesian well provided a steady stream of ice-cold water. They hosted a husking bee in late fall, redolent with good things: cider, cookies, ham, eggs, bacon, goldfish, and the flowers in their grandmother's garden. (Courtesy of Chuck Miller.)

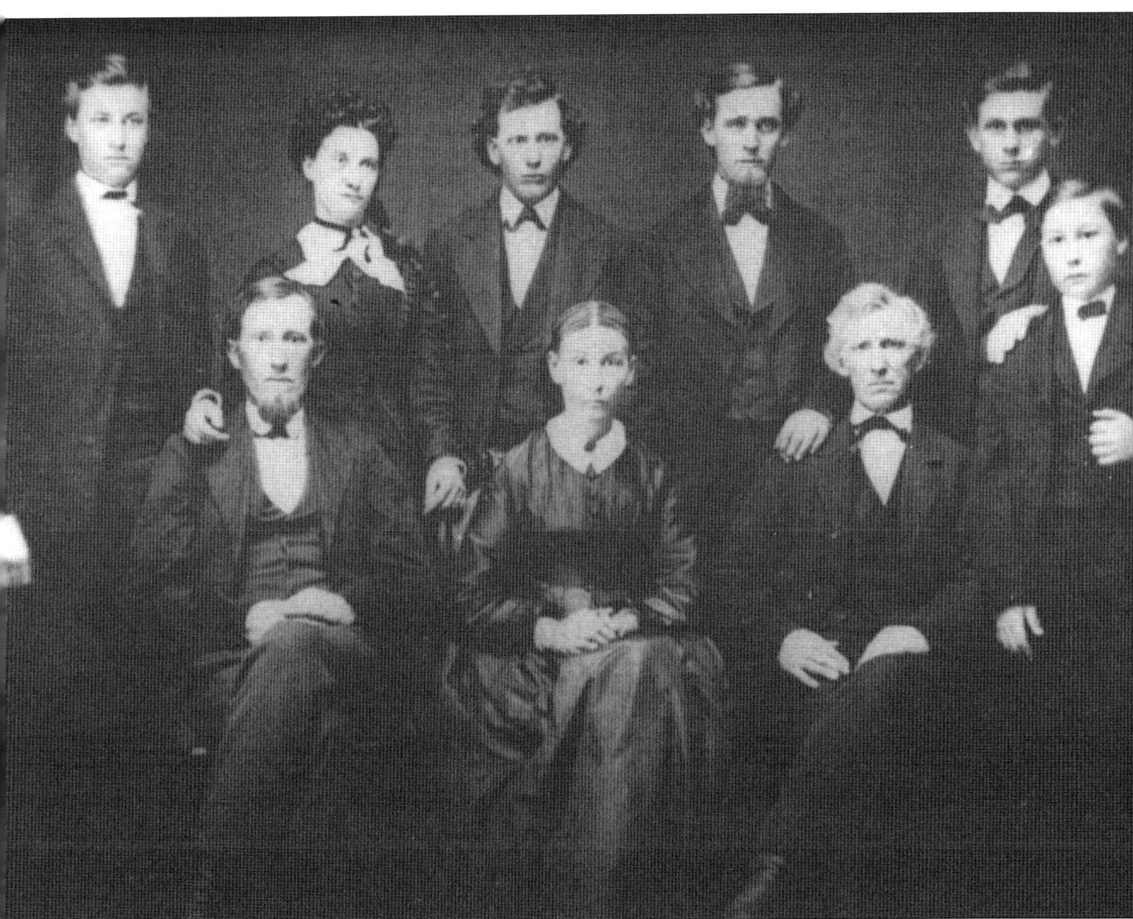

One of the oldest families of Norton are the VanHynings. Henry VanHyning settled here in 1816, and eight generations of his descendants have made Norton their home. Suffering from extreme hardship, as with many families that came to the Western Reserve, they trudged through forests with family members and livestock, forged rivers, and faced the elements. Henry Sr., who lived to the age of 102 and is buried in Norton Center Cemetery, served as one of the justices of the peace, and Abraham VanHyning was an elected trustee in 1816. Pictured here around 1870 is the Sylvester VanHyning family; from left to right are (first row) Henry, Melissa Hollister VanHyning, and Sylvester; (second row) Homer, Hannah VanHyning Betz, Perry, and Sylvester Jr. Sylvester was said to have been a careful farmer, giving attention to the most improved methods of agriculture and stock raising. He died on July 1, 1885, of paralysis at the age of 79. His wife, Melissa, died on November 2, 1903, of dropsy at the age of 82.

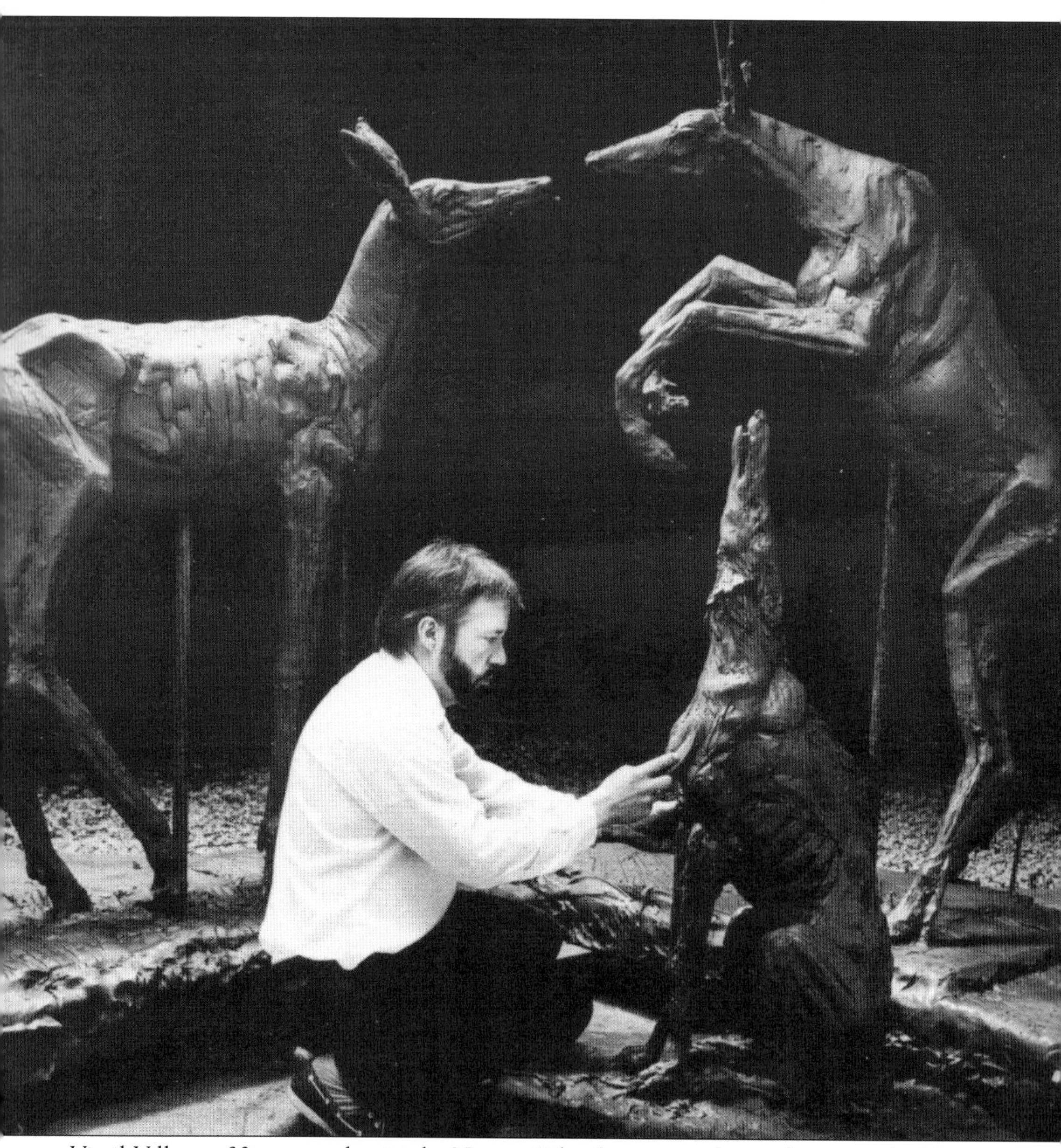

Virgil Villers, a 30-year teacher in the Norton School system and an inductee in the Norton School Hall of Fame, is shown here sculpting *Moon Magic*. It is a piece made of clay that was later cast for a mall in North Carolina. The idea is based on the folk legend that animals of different species interact and can talk to one another once in a blue moon. Villers has an extensive resume, which includes master's and bachelor's degrees, broad teaching experience, numerous exhibitions, multiple awards, and several installations in public and private collections. What most impacted his career were the North American Sculpture Exhibition award, the Palm Desert Art in Public Places exhibition, the O.C. Barber competition for Lake Anna, in neighboring Barberton, and the Northeast Ohio Competition for the main sculpture in the amphitheater at Akron Children's Hospital. (Courtesy of Virgil Villers.)

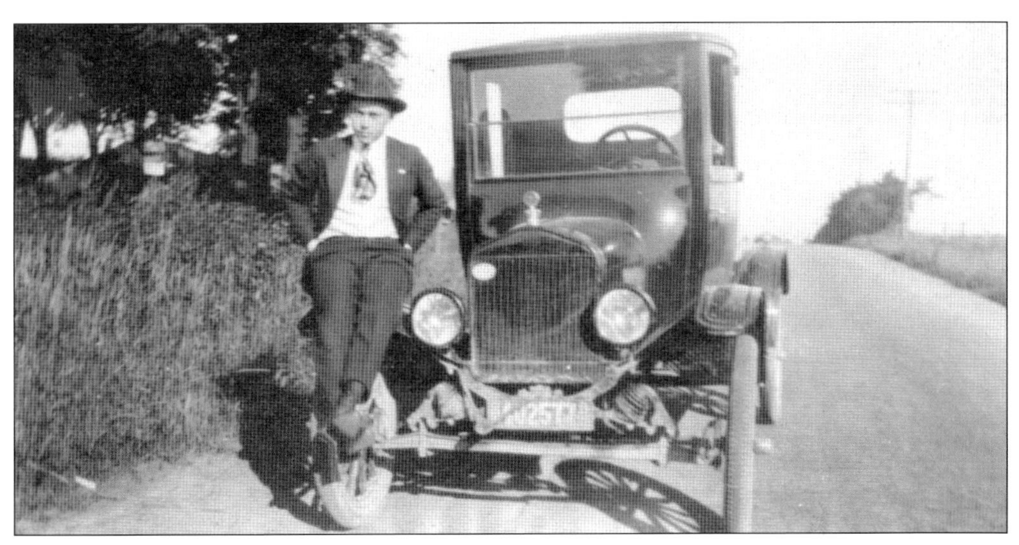

Clarence A. Miller purchased his first car, a 1921 Ford Coupe Model T, with a promissory note for $150. His father, Charles O. Miller, was his cosigner. (Both, courtesy of Chuck Miller.)

$ 150 00/100 May 10 1923

Ninty Days after date we promise to pay to the order of H C Gross

one Hundred + Fifty ——— Dollars

Without defalcation, value received, with interest.

And further, we do hereby empower any Attorney of any Court of Record within the United States or elsewhere, to appear for and after one or more declarations filed, confess judgment against us as of any term for the above sum, with costs of Suit and Attorney's commission of the 1 percent, for collection and release of all errors, and without stay of execution and inquisition and extension upon any levy on real estate is hereby waived and condemnation agreed to and the exemption of personal property from levy and sale on any execution hereon, is also hereby expressly waived, and no benefit of exemption be claimed under and by virtue of any exemption law now in force or which may be hereafter passed.

Witness ______ hand and seal

Clarence A. Miller (SEAL)

Chas O Miller (SEAL)

No. 3941

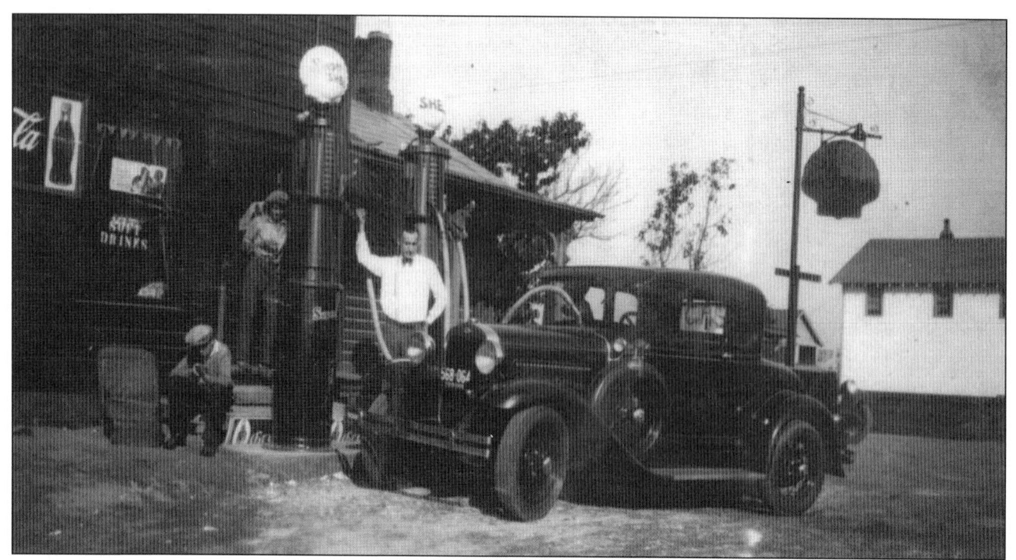

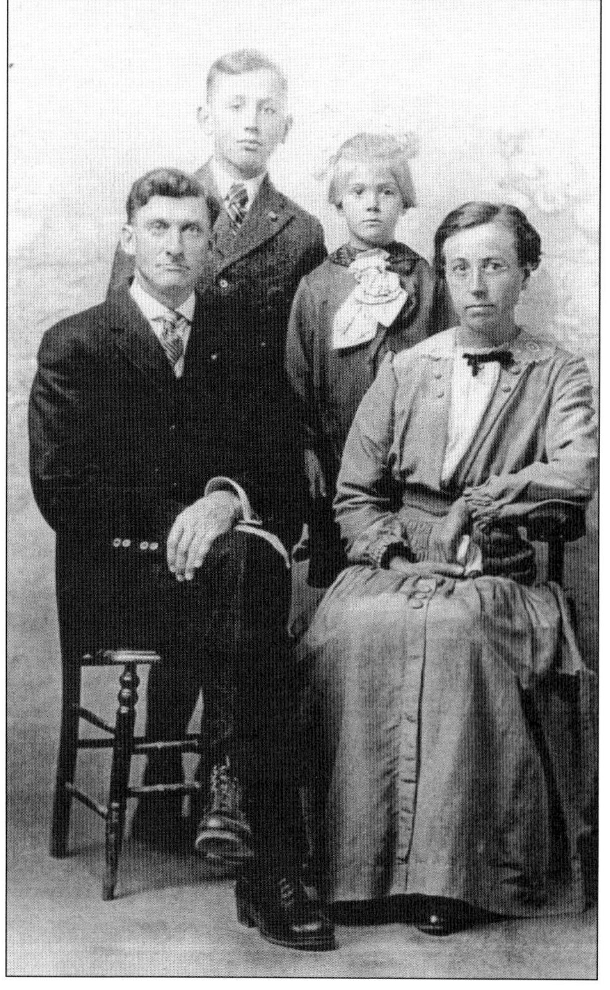

Ed and Edith McQuiston came to Norton from Medina County around 1916. They tended the John Wieser farm, which was located where Route 76 crosses Cleveland-Massillon Road. The road today is called Grenfall, and the farm encompassed 88 acres. After having left Norton for a period of time in 1928, they returned, but farming was out of the question, as they had sold all of their farming equipment. Ed eventually opened a neighborhood grocery store and gas station on Norton Avenue. (Courtesy of Alice McQuiston.)

Pictured here from left to right are Ed McQuiston, Myron Skinner, Alice McQuiston, and Edith McQuiston. Skinner was raised by the McQuistons. (Courtesy of Alice McQuiston.)

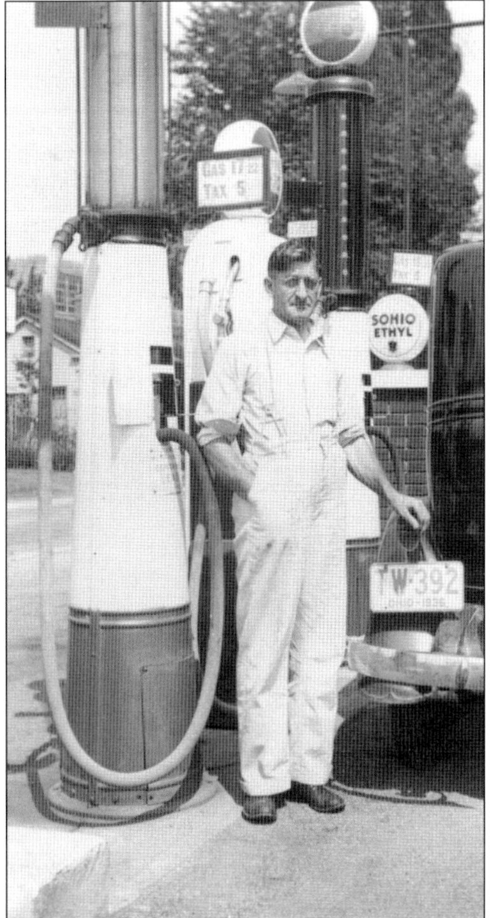

Ed McQuiston is shown here at his general store and gas station in Norton Center. In those days, schoolchildren flocked to the store at noon. McQuiston's scoops of ice cream were said to be especially generous at only 5¢ each. Store hours meant long days, seven days a week. The business was a fixture in Norton all through the Great Depression and into the 1940s. McQuiston died in 1952.

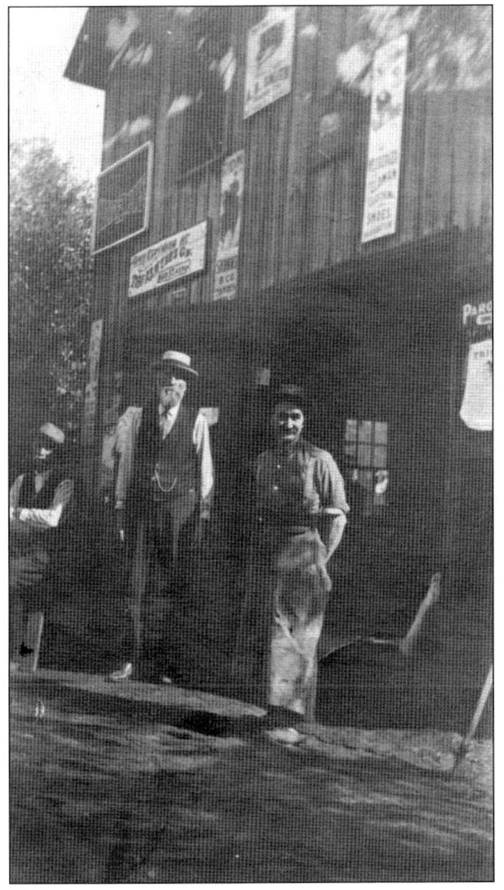

Jacob Flickinger (right), pictured here with Dan Betz to his immediate left, was the blacksmith in Loyal Oak, having learned the trade from his father-in-law, Isaac Weyrick. Flickinger died from internal injuries at the age of 74, the result of being struck in the back by an automobile driven by Ruth Moore of Wadsworth. The accident happened in front of his home one week after he and his wife, Editha, celebrated their golden anniversary.

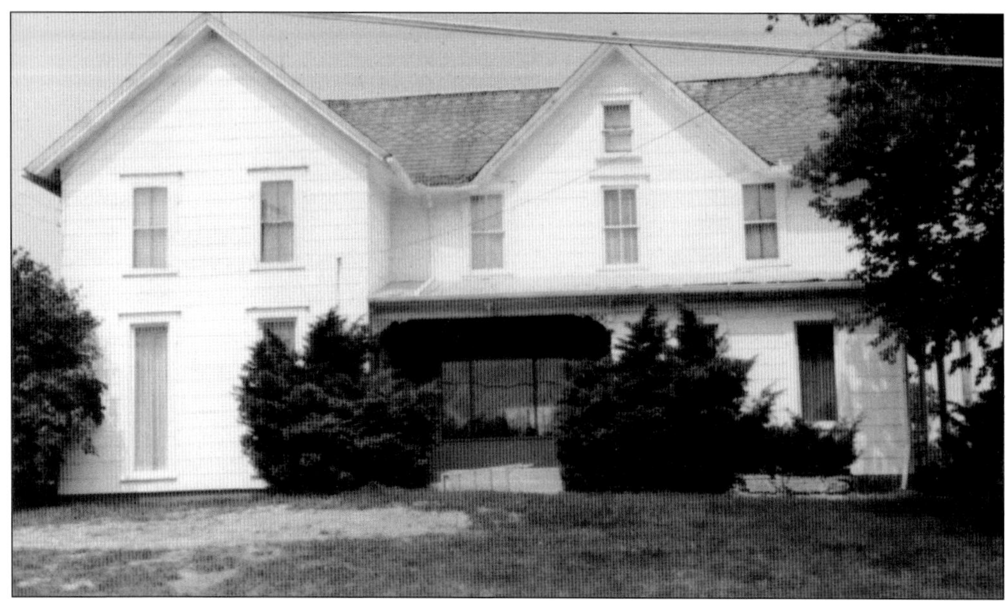

In 1858, Lot 17 was the home of Henry Sparhawk. The farmhouse had been built in 1853. Later known as the Bauer farm then the Edward P. Laubach farm at 2702 Akron-Wadsworth Road, it was comprised of 135 fine acres. Edward P. was born to Edward and Lavina (Dewatch) Laubach. Edward P. married Fietta E. Bauer, and they had two children, Mahlon George and Maude. Later, the farmhouse was used as a nursing home for World War II veterans. It was run by Lena Love Woodall as the Forest View Nursing Home.

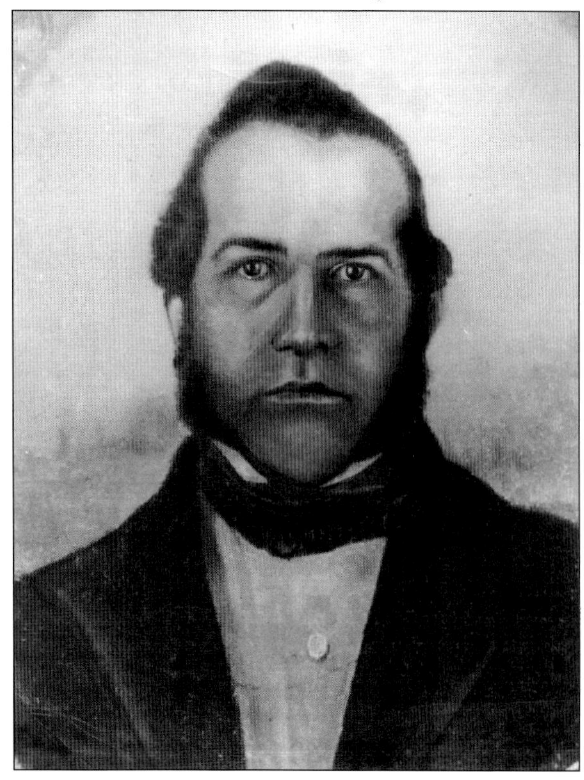

By means of a mule, a carpetbag, and an ax, Henry Gardner Sparhawk arrived in Norton around 1834. He acquired a farm close to his brother Ebenezer and built a log cabin on Lot 17. He was appointed Norton's constable and successfully incarcerated counterfeiters and horse thieves. Sparhawk married Lucy Chandler Baker in 1838 and erected a beautiful home for his family in Loyal Oak. Harvey Augustus Sparhawk, pictured here, was one of six children born to Henry and Lucy. Harvey resided in Norton Township and married Emma Jane Wolfe in 1871. (Courtesy of Stephanie Whims.)

John Himmelright and Mary Anna "Maria" Bachman Himmelright are pictured here with their three children, Raleigh (left), James, and Eva. James later married Effie Mae Dutt and continued the family farming tradition at the same homestead. (Courtesy of Christine Daniel.)

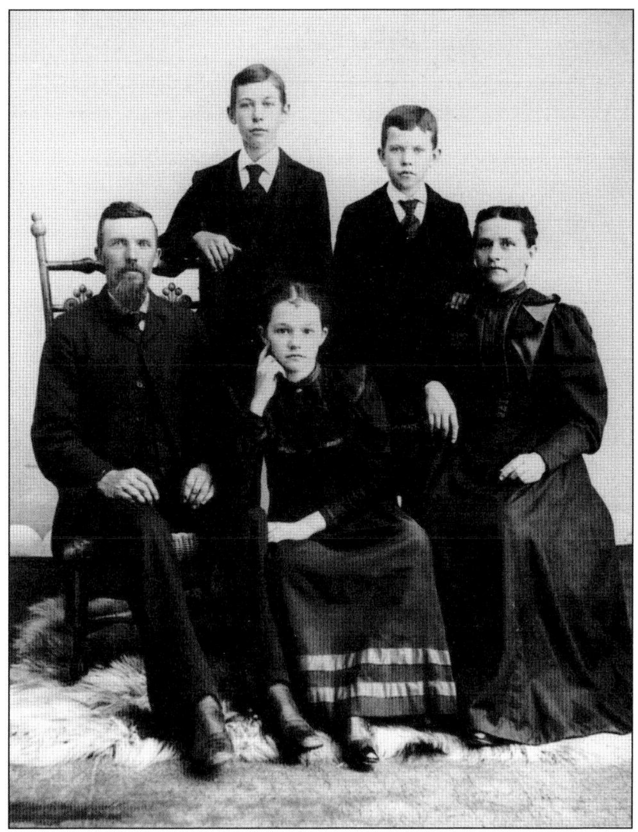

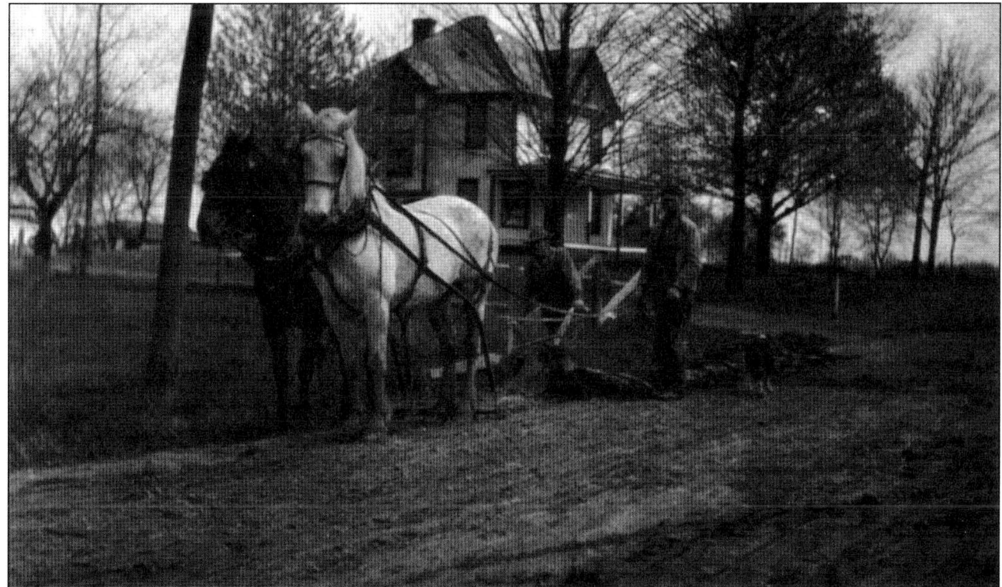

James and Effie Himmelright, along with other residents that lived along dirt roads, were tasked with maintaining ditches that ran alongside them. Pictured here around 1920 are James (left) and a hired hand digging a ditch in front of the Himmelright homestead at 4379 Greenwich Road. (Courtesy of Christine Daniel.)

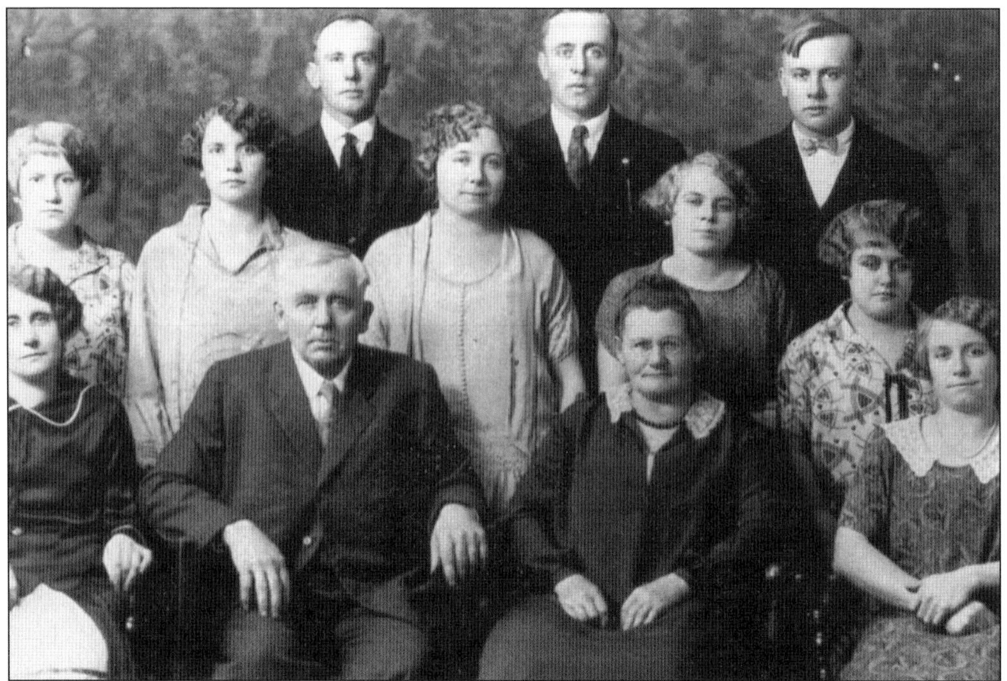

The William Daniel and Phoebe Viola Stimson Bauer family are shown here in 1925. From left to right are (first row) Celia L., William, Phoebe, and Blanche M.; (second row) Ruth, Grace F., Elva P., Nellie, and Ruby; (third row) Warren F., Joseph R., and Lloyd O. (Courtesy of Weldon [Shot] Bauer.)

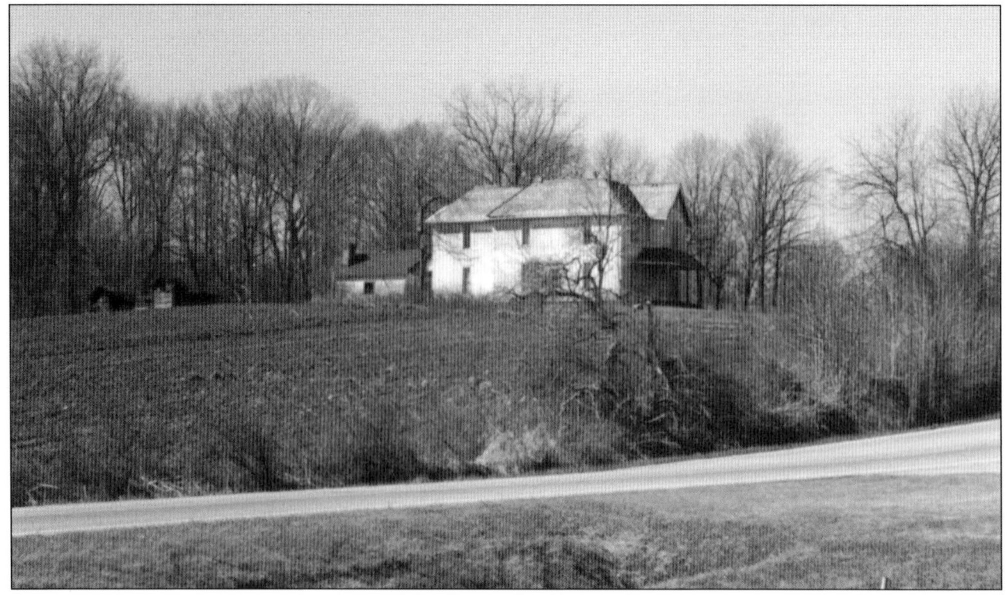

Daniel Bauer purchased this 151-acre farm near Loyal Oak on June 23, 1843, from Benjamin and Thoedatis Sanford for $1,800. Joseph Daniel Bauer, son of Daniel Bauer, built the house around 1885. The farm became the property of Edward Laubach, who married Fietta E. Bauer, Joseph's daughter. Presently, the farm on Akron-Wadsworth Road is still partially owned by family members.

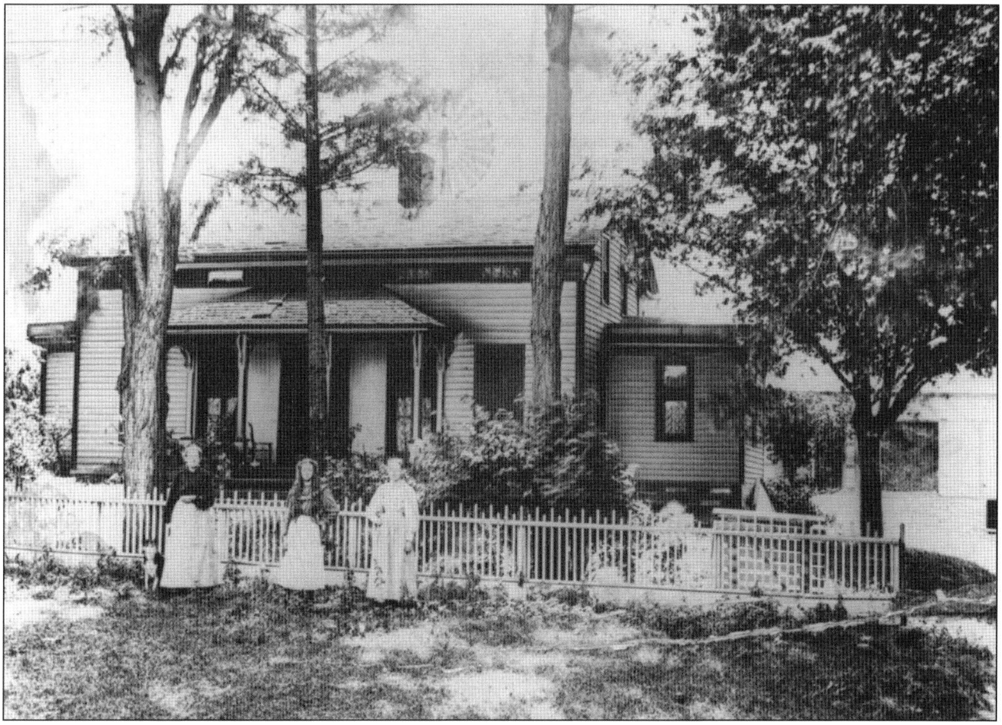

In 1910, from left to right, Julia Marie Fritz and her daughters Molly and Bessie Fritz pose in front of their early 1800s farmhouse at 4298 Akron-Wadsworth Road. The family, along with Julia's husband and son Harvey, lived with Julia's mother, Bessie May Swinhart. Julia Marie Swinhart, "Marie," the granddaughter of Julia Fritz, married Ellis Edward Frederick, and they inherited the farm and continued to operate it as a dairy after Julia's mother, Bessie, died in 1967. Ellis served in the Pacific theater in World War II and remained a first sergeant in the Army reserves. Today, the farm is still in the Frederick family; the 74 acres of fields are leased out, and the barn and silo still exist today. (Courtesy of Bob Frederick.)

On Norton maps from 1874 to 1883, the Beese family (pictured) lived on Lot 83, on Hametown Road. By 1891, the family must have moved on, as their name no longer shows up on any of the existing maps.

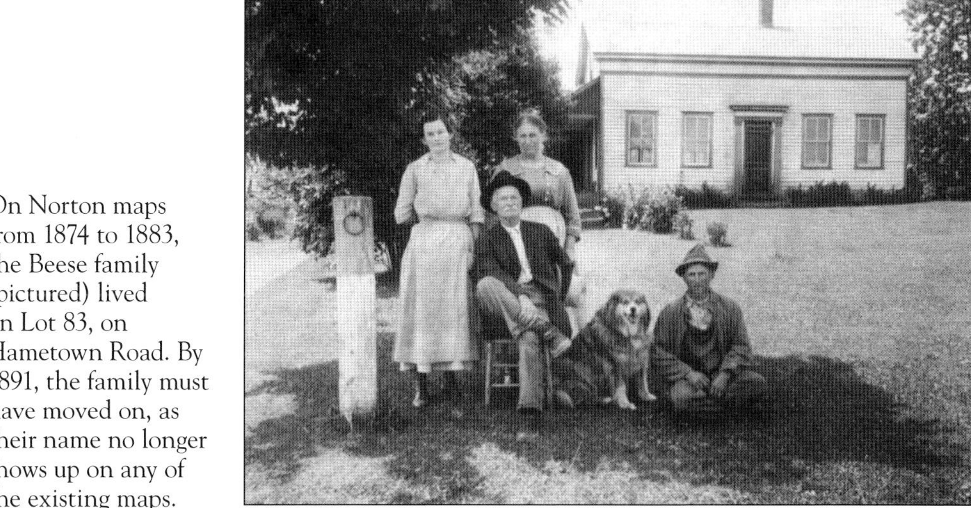

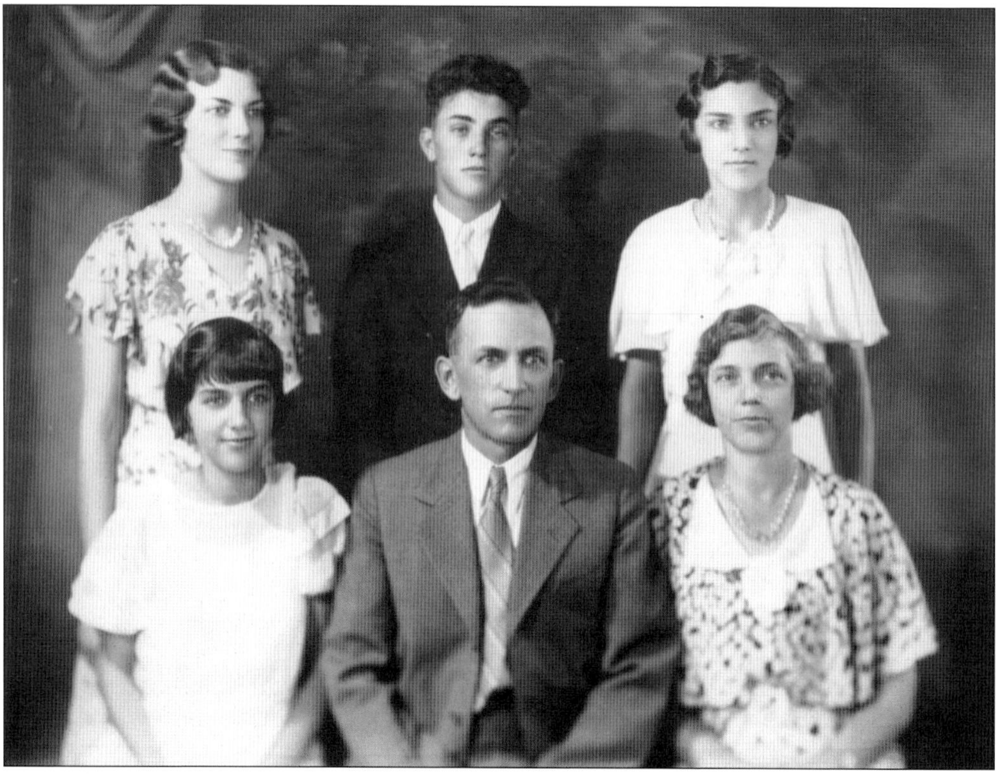

Pictured here is the Harris family; from left to right are (first row) Maude, Fred, and Pearl; (second row) Lillian, Kenneth, and Mildred.

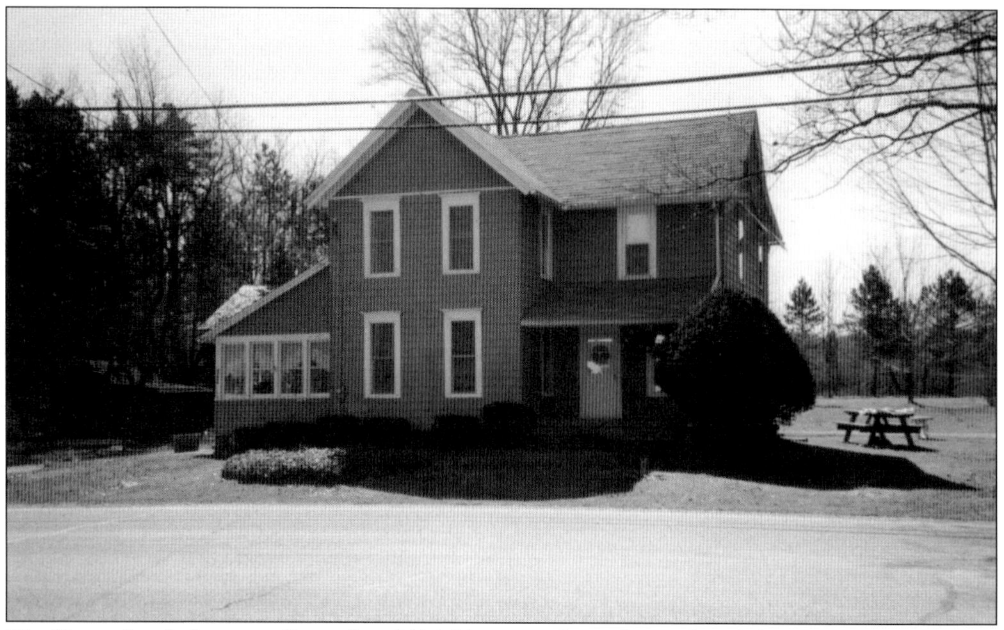

The Harris family farm is still stands at 3196 Akron-Wadsworth Road, and the original outbuildings are still on this five-acre property. The current owners plan to recreate the farmstead as a mirror image of the original, including traditional livestock.

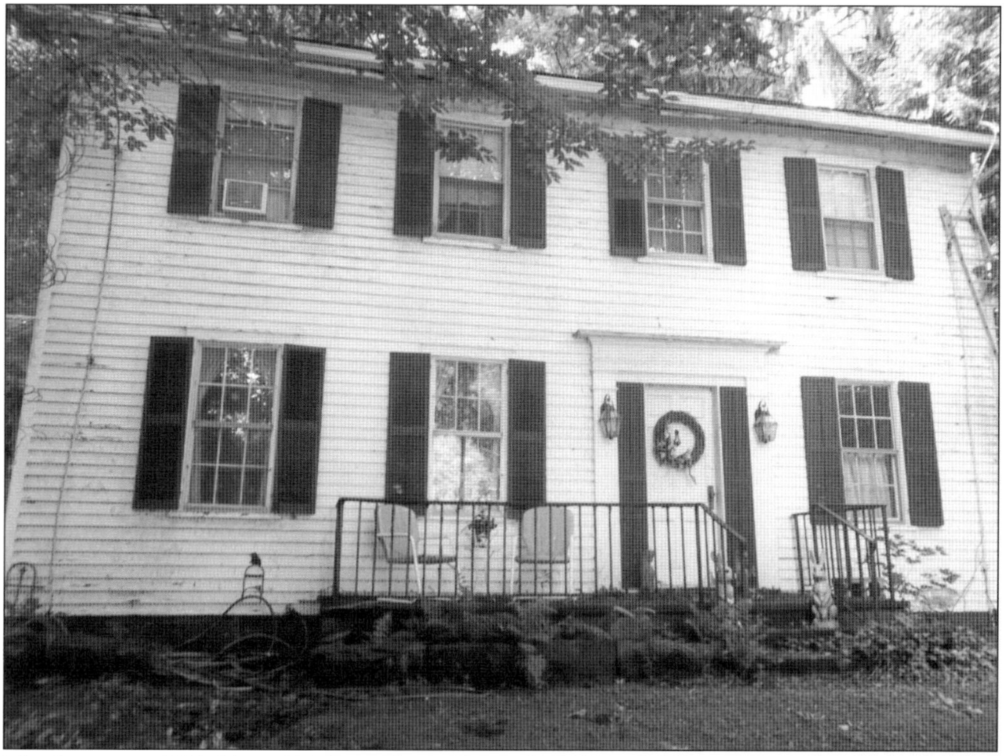

This home, at 1684 Akron-Wadsworth Road, was built by Robert Moore in 1850 and sits below the 30–40 foot Wintergreen Ledges and its cold freshwater springs and cave-like structures. The house has a slate roof, beams of hand-hewn oak, basement walls of large blocks of stone cut from the ledges, and pine and poplar floors. Beginning in 1947, Paul D. Suloff, his wife Hazel, and their children Jane, David, and Paul Jr. occupied the home. Paul Sr. worked for the Goodyear Tire and Rubber Company for 52 years and was licensed and trained to pilot blimps for the firm. He flew solo from Cleveland to Boardman, Ohio, for the Goodyear Zeppelin Corporation. This flight made him eligible for a National Aeronautical Association license, pictured below. Note that this document was signed by Orville Wright. Later, Suloff became a designer of conveyor belts for coal and ore mines, and he flew gliders and piloted a balloon across the Swiss Alps. Hazel was artistic, and she created pottery, sculptures, needlework, poetry, and paintings.

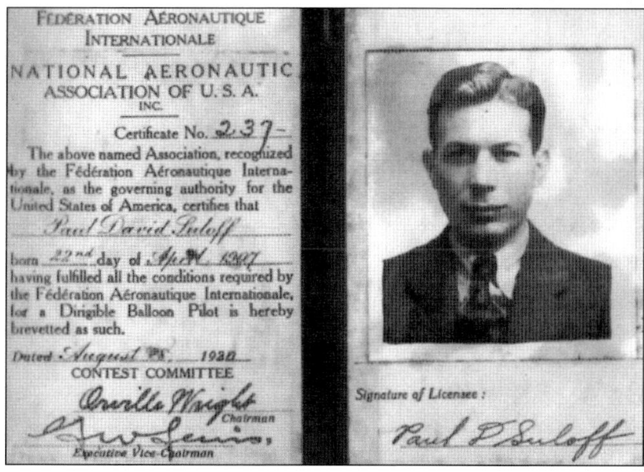

FÉDÉRATION AÉRONAUTIQUE INTERNATIONALE

NATIONAL AERONAUTIC ASSOCIATION OF U.S.A. INC.

Certificate No. 237

The above named Association, recognized by the Fédération Aéronautique Internationale, as the governing authority for the United States of America, certifies that

Paul David Suloff

born 22nd day of April 1907

having fulfilled all the conditions required by the Fédération Aéronautique Internationale, for a Dirigible Balloon Pilot is hereby brevetted as such.

Dated August [illegible], 1930

CONTEST COMMITTEE

Orville Wright, Chairman

Executive Vice-Chairman

Signature of Licensee: Paul D Suloff

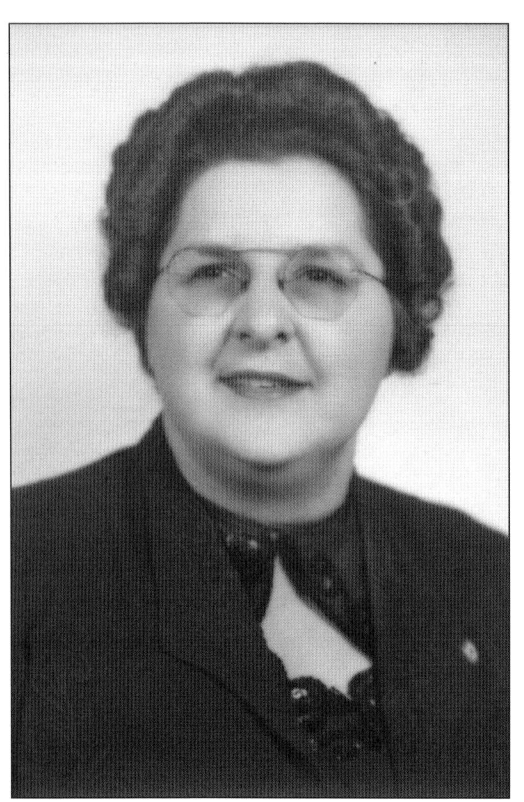

Times were hard for plumber George Wiese and his wife, Geraldine, during the Great Depression. George worked his plumbing business out of their home at 2845 Akron-Wadsworth Road while Geraldine took a job at the Diamond Match Company. She made $15 a week working 10-hour shifts. Geraldine would help George load the truck with heavy pipe and fittings as he headed out with his toolbox, which he carried on his shoulder. He began his plumbing business with a desk in the dining room before moving to a bedroom downstairs, which later became an office. Finally, in 1979, Wiese purchased property a few miles west of the homestead, and established a freestanding business, which meant more service and a larger staff to serve the community. Wiese Plumbing and Heating was up and running at 3807 Akron-Wadsworth Road. Today, the store is run by George and Geraldine's son James Wiese, who employs approximately 20 people and has a fleet of a dozen vehicles servicing residential and commercial properties. (Both, courtesy of Wiese Plumbing.)

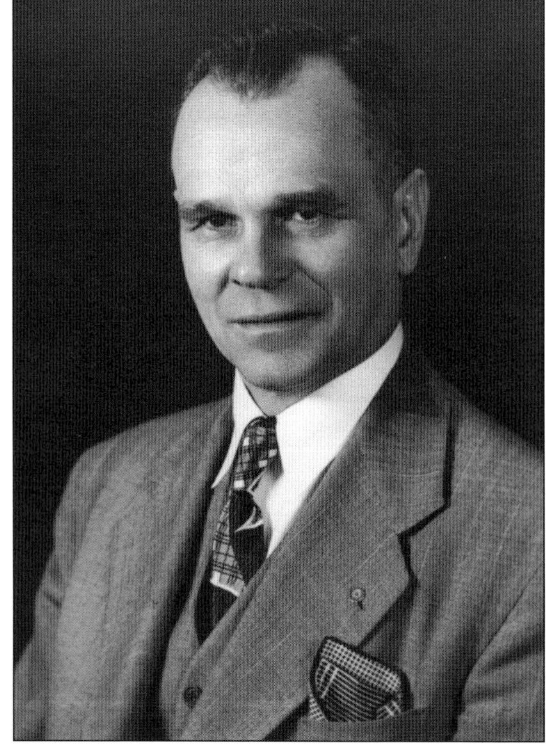

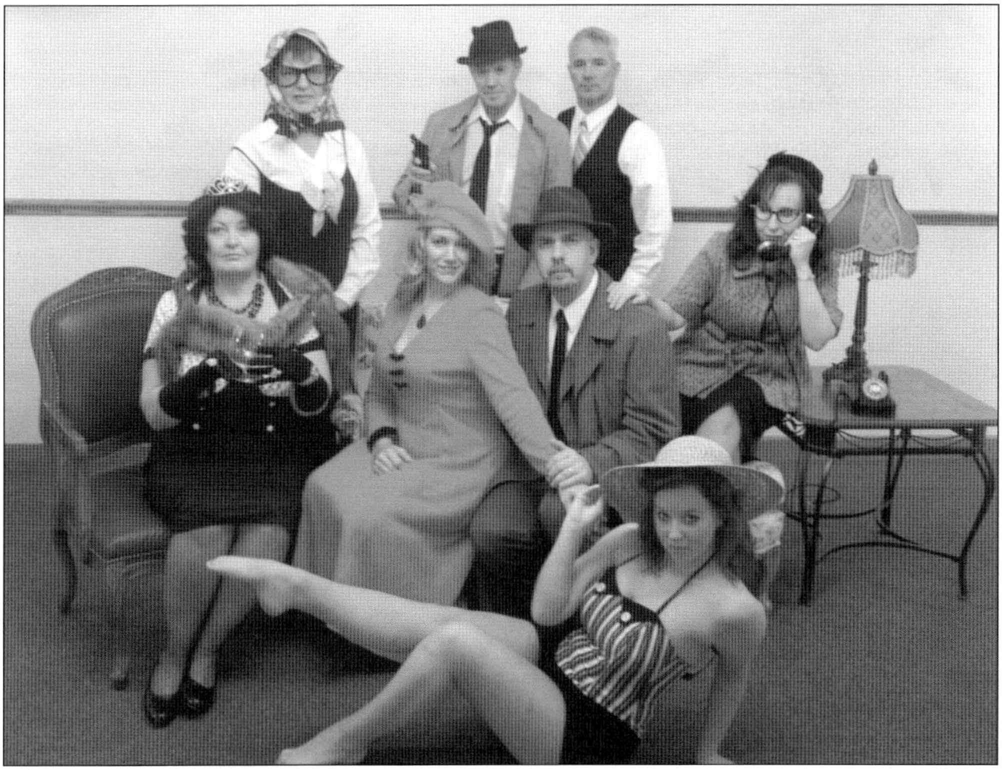

In the play *Kill Me, Deadly*, Charlie Nickels's client, millionaire widow Lady Clairmont, is murdered, and her most prized possession, a red 300-carat Bengal diamond, is missing. Nickels's search for the killer and the stolen diamond takes him on a tour of 1940s Hollywood, as recreated by Norton's Wolf Creek Players in 2013. Pictured here from left to right are (first row) Cori Gleason; (second row) Karen Rose, Maureen Davis, Jim Trenta, and Leslie Manna; (third row) Sherry Clark, Charlie Shook, and Scott Davis (Courtesy of Donna Rizor Longfellow.)

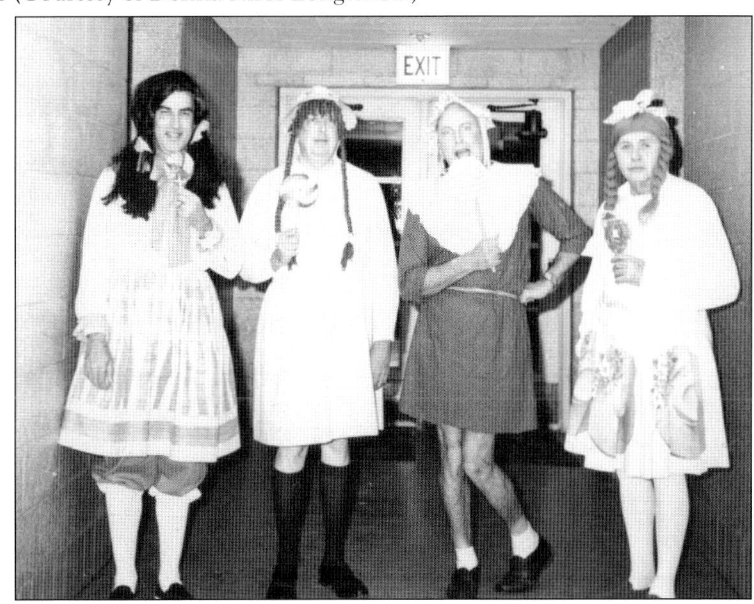

On November 29–30, 1968, an annual variety show was put on by members of the Norton Kiwanis Club. That year, they put on a play called *Smiles*, directed by George Hayden. Posing from left to right as the "Playthings" are John Henning, Leon Sanders, Bill Bantz, and Clarence Miller.

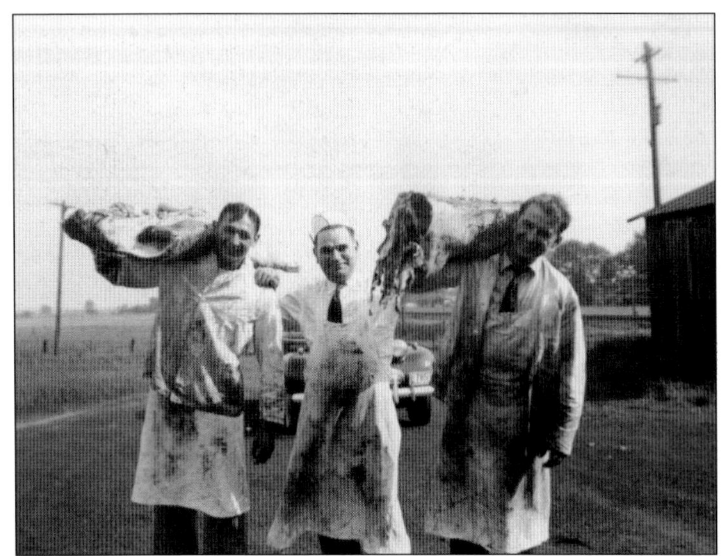

Sherman Provision, at 4002 Johnson Road, was a slaughterhouse until recently, when meats began being processed off the premises. In 1945, the slaughterhouse supplied meat for two grocery stores in Akron. Pictured in the center is owner Mike O'Brodo around 1948. The other two men are unidentified. (Courtesy of Sherman Provision.)

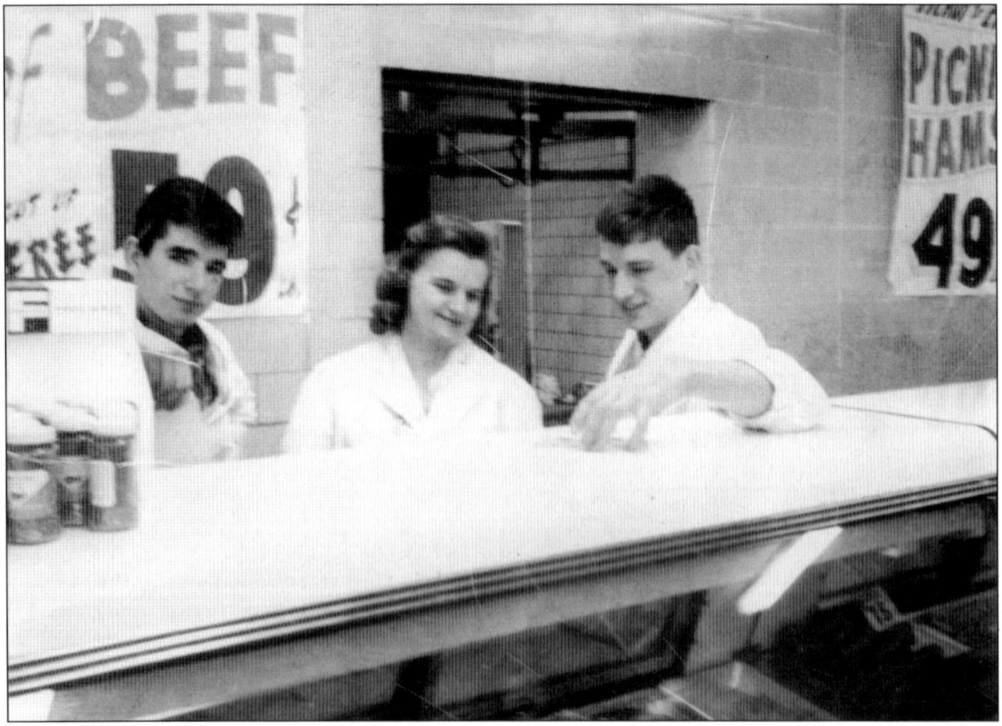

In 1950, a retail shop was opened that specialized in meats and international groceries geared to European clientele. Owners Mike O'Brodo, who was Serbian, and his wife, Josephine (known as "Sophie"), who was Hungarian, shared a common interest in providing the best they could to others looking for ingredients and products from Eastern Europe. Sophie ran the retail store in Sherman Provision and took care of responsibilities in the home they owned next door. Today, the business is thriving, with most of the original structures in place and some of the older equipment still in use. The shop is currently owned by Michael O'Brodo and his wife, Mauri. Pictured here in 1966 are, from left to right, Michael, Sophie, and David O'Brodo. (Courtesy of Sherman Provision.)

William "Bill" Blackburn, who was drafted in 1945, served on the 11,000-ton aircraft carrier the USS *Cowpens* during World War II. Blackburn, pictured here, was a seaman first class, and his ship sailed to Guam and the island of Okinawa to transport servicemen. (Courtesy of William Blackburn.)

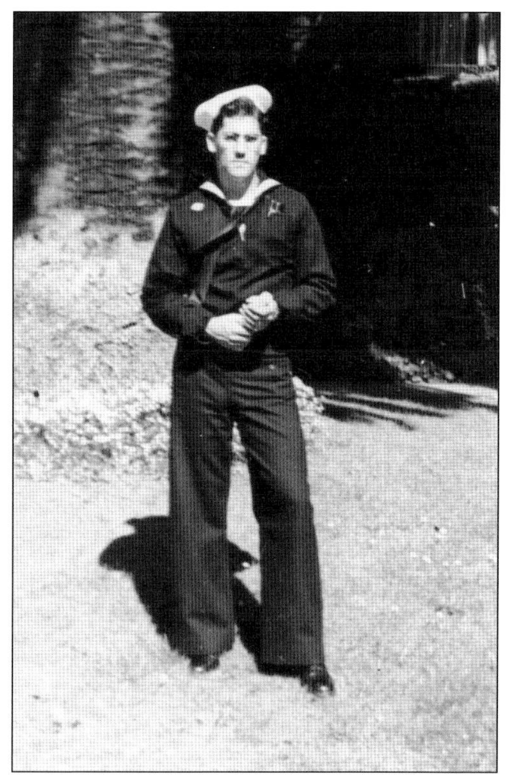

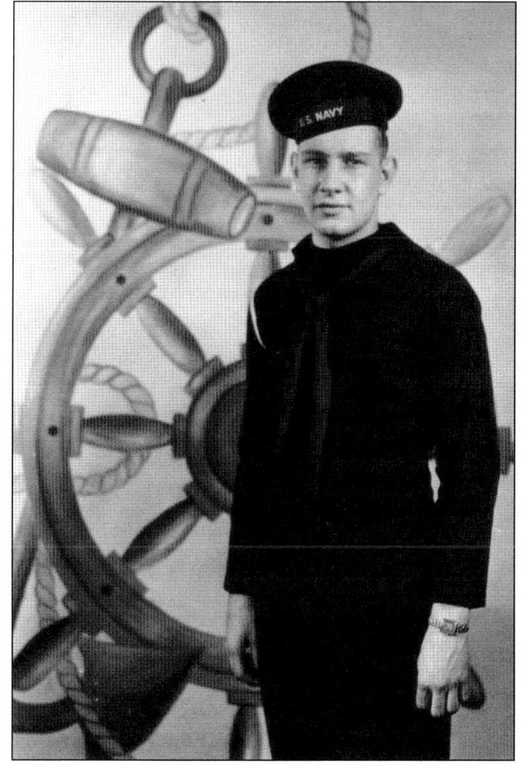

In May 1943, his third year of high school, Bob Hemphill left school due to the wartime pressure to enlist and applied to the Naval Academy and other training facilities to enter officers' training. He was drafted in 1944 and discharged in 1945 as a naval cadet. Hemphill continued his education and graduated with a medical degree from the University of Louisville, Kentucky, in 1948. He returned to service in 1949 as a lieutenant and continued medical training at City Hospital and the Cleveland Clinic before being called up in 1952 for the Korean War. It was not until 1969 that Dr. Hemphill received his high school diploma.

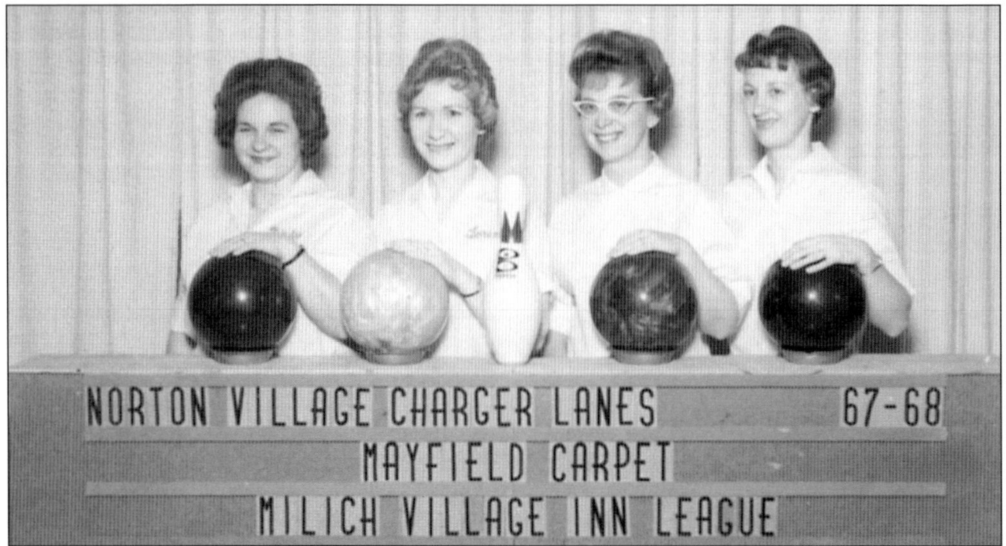

Pictured here at Charger Lanes around 1967–1968 are, from left to right, Marilyn Rinehart, Lorena Skiles, Pat Robinette, and Pat Cornell. Charger Lanes, located at 1213 Norton Avenue, advertised housewife leagues with a free childcare from 9:00 a.m. to 4:00 p.m. In 1964, the general manager was Robert Spratt. The business offered a supper club, snack bar, billiards, and 32 automatic games. (Courtesy of Janean Skiles-Ray.)

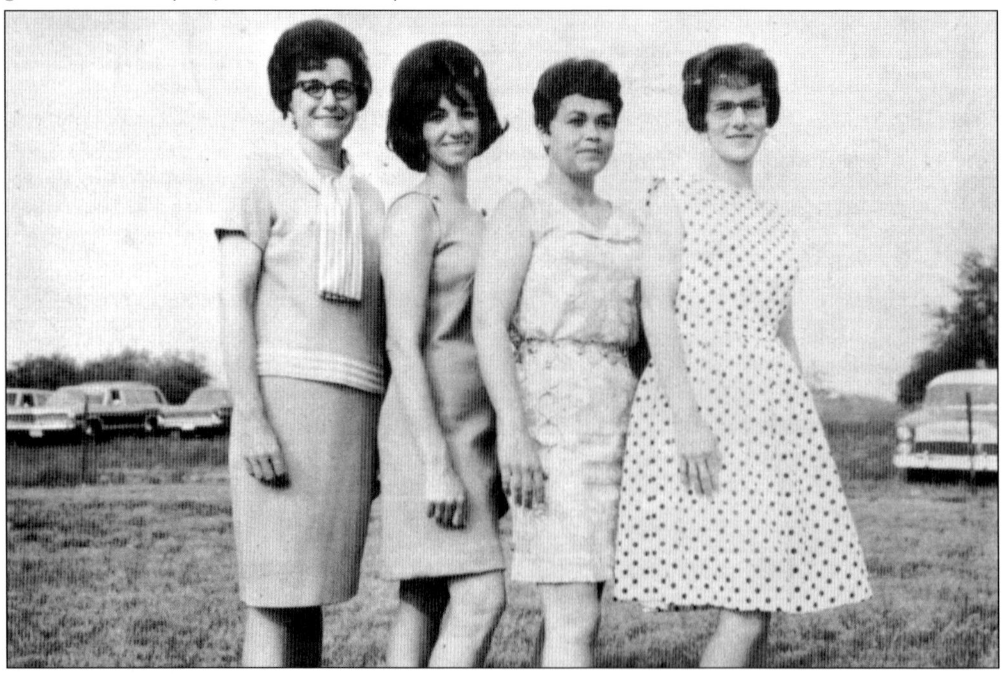
In 1960, Norton Little League was conceived and competed against four major teams. The played their games at the new Howell Field in Norton under the direction of Martin Howell. Four minor teams were added to the league in 1961. In 1965, another playing field was created and named Edison Field, honoring the Ohio Edison Company for their generosity. In this 1968 photograph are the Norton Little League Mother's Club officers. From left to right are Mae Irwin (president), Pat Winans (secretary), Jean Withrow (vice president), and Doris Munka (treasurer).

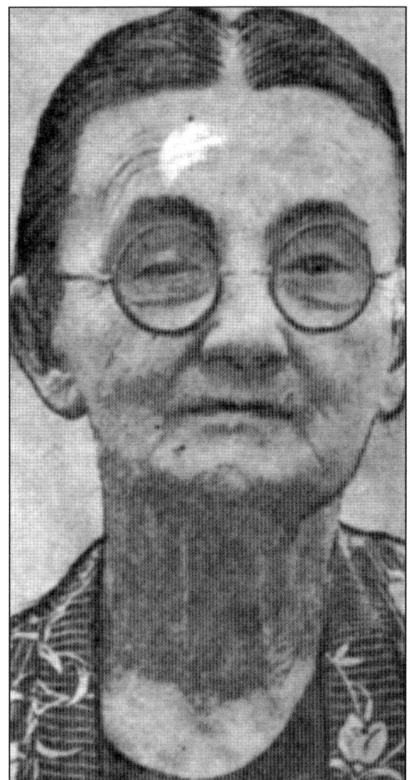

In February 1934, Sarah Editha Weyrick Flickinger had a hard time keeping up with the 116 individuals in her family. She and her husband, Jacob, had 14 children, who produced 51 grandchildren and 24 great-grandchildren. They were the largest family in the history of Loyal Oak. At the age of 78, Editha was still entirely self-supporting, living alone, and performing all of her own housework and chores.

The Jacob and Sarah Editha Flickinger family are pictured here from left to right (first row), Ethel, Fred, and Edith; (second row) Ada, Editha, Norman, Lula, Jacob, and Cora; (third row) Clarence, Artie, John, Charles, Ella, and George. The 14th child not pictured, Lloyd, died in infancy.

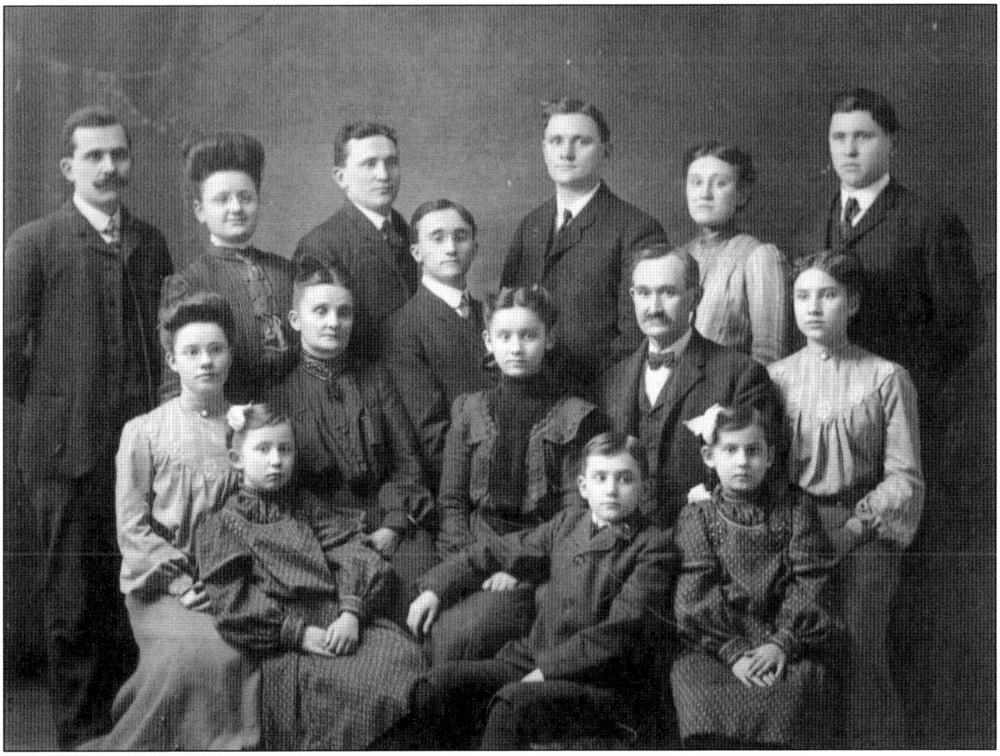

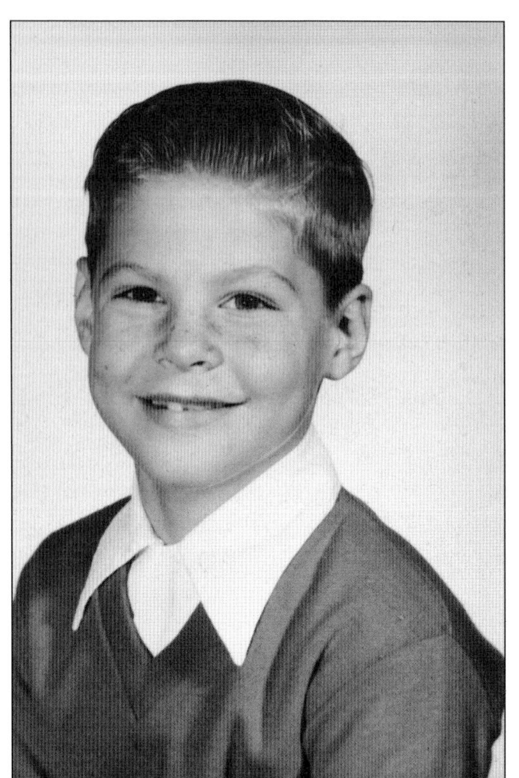

Pictured here is James "Jim" Hodge, who graduated from Norton High School in 1973. Hodge went on to graduate from West Point and was commissioned a second lieutenant in the US Army Transportation Corps. He completed a 34-year Army career, rising to the rank of major general, and was awarded the Bronze Star and the Distinguished Service Medal for action in Operation Iraqi Freedom. Indoctrinated into the Transportation Corps Hall of Fame in 2014, Hodge recently was selected as president of the Institute for Defense and Business in Chapel Hill, North Carolina. (Courtesy of James and Michelle Hodge.)

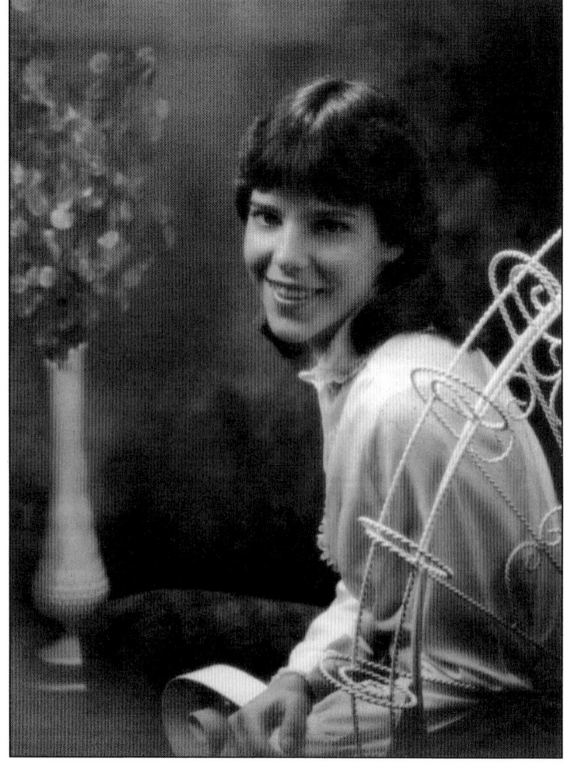

Lisa Kohler, a 1984 Norton High School graduate, began her career at the University of Toledo with a bachelor's degree in biology and went on to the Medical College of Ohio in Toledo. A pathology residency at the University of Pittsburgh was to follow and then her forensic fellowship at the Medical College of Virginia. Since 2001, Dr. Kohler has been the chief medical examiner for Summit County, having worked for the office since 1998. (Courtesy of Dr. Lisa Kohler.)

The Nathan and Catherine Seiberling home on Greenwich Road is one of the most well-known locations in the community. The couple traveled from Pennsylvania to settle in the township in 1831, and their son Gustavus stayed on the family farm and became one of the most influential men in Western Star Village. Formerly, the home was owned by Cloyd Seiberling and Ellis Seiberling, and is presently owned by Chuck Seiberling. It continues to be a working farm to this day and hosts one of the most popular corn and vegetable stands in the area.

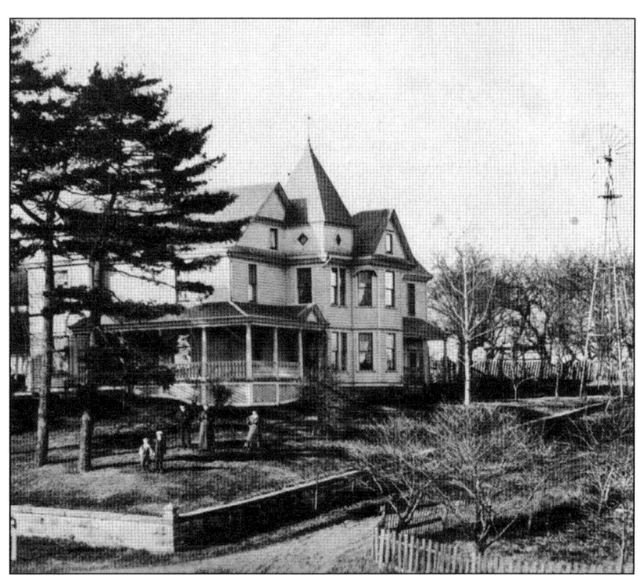

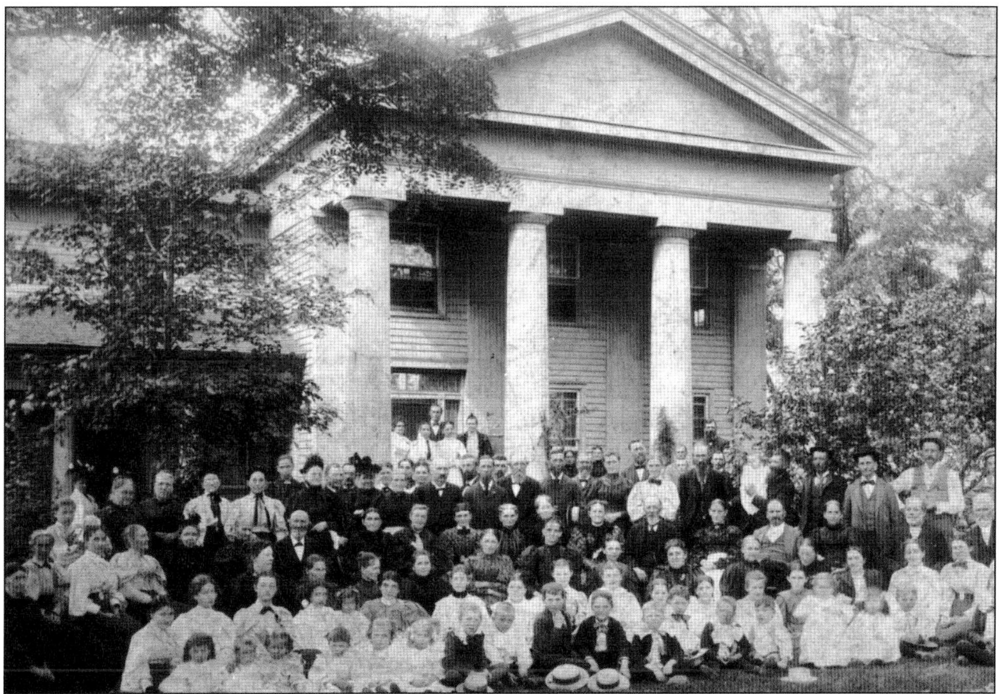

The "pillar home," as people in Norton identify this house on Greenwich Road in Western Star, is also the location of the birthplace of Charles Willard and Frank August Seiberling. These brothers were known for their many business ventures in Akron, Ohio, notably the Seiberling Tire and Rubber Company. Pictured here on August 19, 1896, students pose in front of the home during a reunion of those who attended Western Star Academy, likely a private school just to the west of this location.

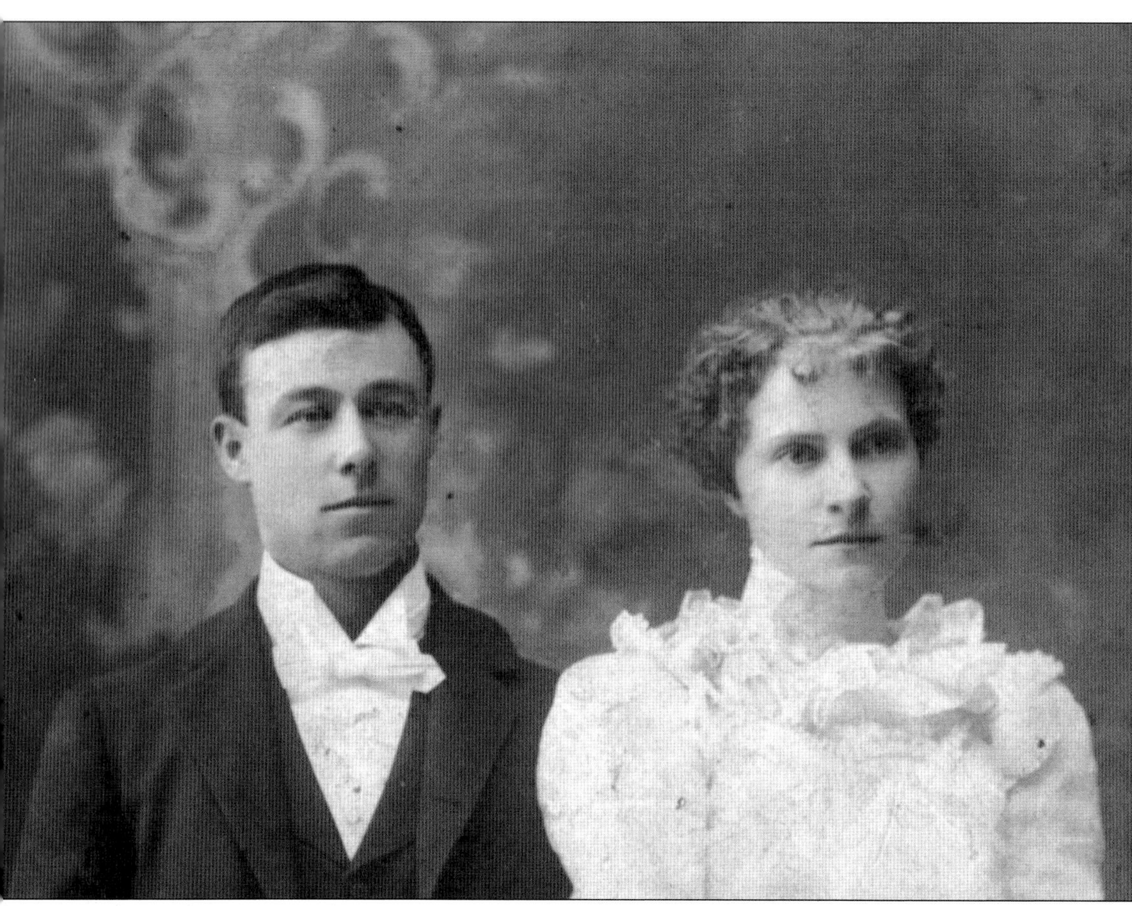

John Hoffman married Mary Ann Rogers in 1852, and one of their children, Alice, married Eugene Watson Cady when she was 16 and he was 21. Animosity flared between the Hoffmans and Cady with the young man's courtship of their young daughter. Years later, after having had six children, Alice was told by her doctor that another birth would probably kill her. Child number seven was born five years later, but Alice died along with their unnamed infant in 1886. Eugene arranged to have Alice and their infant buried in the same coffin at Norton Center Cemetery. He did not choose one of the available Cady family Lakewood Cemetery plots, nor was Alice buried in a Hoffman plot in Norton Center Cemetery, but in a nearby plot without a marker. Eugene later discovered that a large marker had been placed on Alice's grave identifying her as the daughter of John and Mary Hoffman, with the words "Erected by her Mother" engraved on the base. Enraged, Eugene had the bodies of his wife and their child exhumed and moved to Lakewood Cemetery in Akron. To this day, the marker stands in the cemetery as a silent sentinel guarding an empty grave. (Courtesy of Bud Theising.)

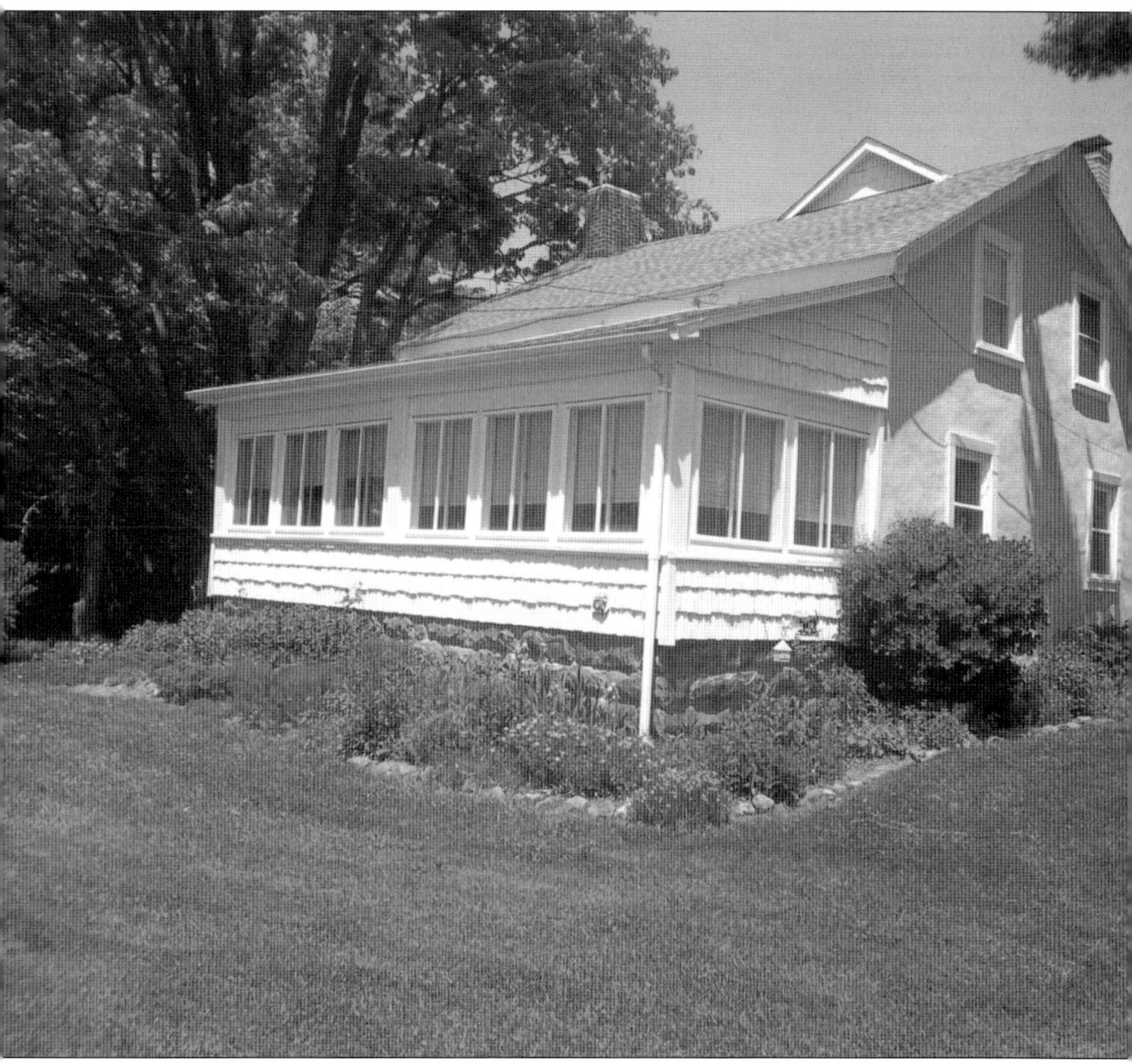

The 75-acre farm of John Benson Betz and his wife, Catherine "Katie" Weaver, was located at 3295 Reimer Road. They raised corn, wheat, oats, rye, timothy seed, and clover as well as cows, pigs, sheep, horses, turkeys, and chickens. The couple had six children, one of whom died after having lived only one year. It is said that their daughter Maude is buried on the property, their son Charles was gored by a bull and developed spinal meningitis and died of his wounds, and John and son Daniel fell off the barn roof, but both got up and walked away unscathed. John served in the Union army at the age of 19, as he wanted to get into the glamour and away from the farm. Described as six feet tall with grey eyes and dark hair, he joined Company G, 177th Ohio. He became ill while serving, was discharged, and came to be known as one of the best marksmen in Ohio, despite living constantly with his disability. After the deaths of John and Katie, the farm was taken over by the their son Daniel. (Author's collection.)

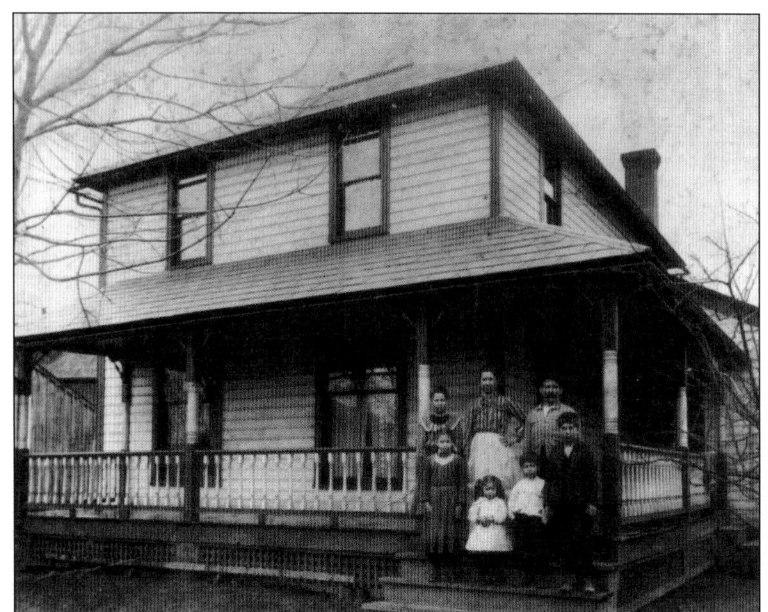

The Langguth family lived on the northwest corner of Wooster Road and Cleveland-Massillon Road in 1907. Jacob Langguth was a German immigrant that worked for Seiberling Rubber to support his family, which included, from left to right (first row) Clara, Madeline, Albert, and Bill; (second row) Bertha, Minnie, and Jacob. (Courtesy of Lori Lewis Pfahler.)

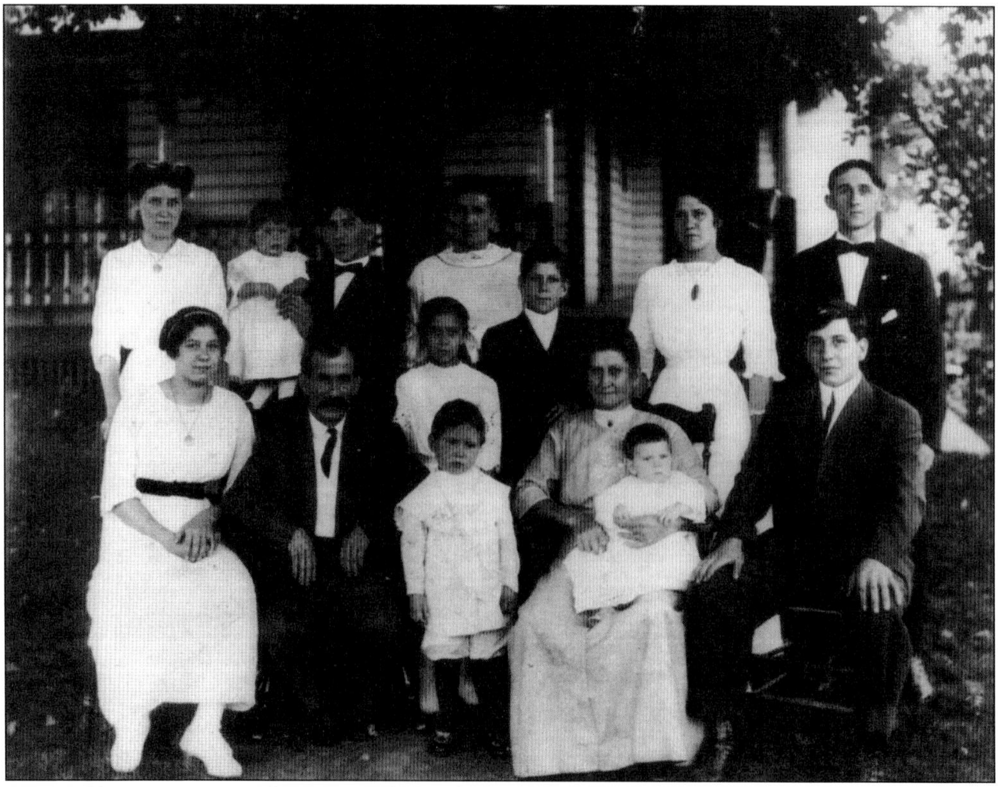

Pictured here in 1914 at the Langguth family farm in Johnson's Corners are, from left to right, (first row) Bertha Langguth, Jacob Langguth, Ebert Langguth, Minnie Schleedorn Langguth (holding Raymond Diesz), and Bill Langguth; (second row) Minnie and Albert Langguth; (third row) Theresa Ries, Jacob John Langguth (holding Alberta May Langguth), Creszenia Wolfa Schleedorn, Clara Langguth, and Edward Diesz. (Courtesy of Lori Lewis Pfahler.)

Located in the Western Star Cemetery is the grave of Revolutionary War soldier William Lampson (1761–1827). A patriot grave marking for Lampson and a cemetery dedication was held in the spring of 2009. Lampson served as a private in the Revolutionary War under Capt. David Wheeler in the Battle of Bennington. He also served in the War of 1812. He married Rachel Powell (1766–1813), and they had 12 children. (Right, painting by Gilbert Stuart, private collection of Pom Lampson; below, author's collection.)

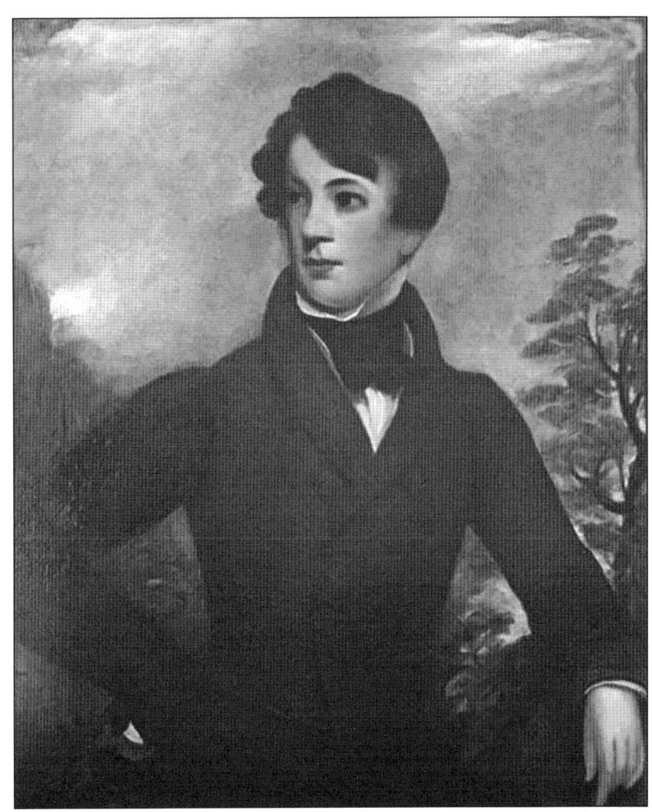

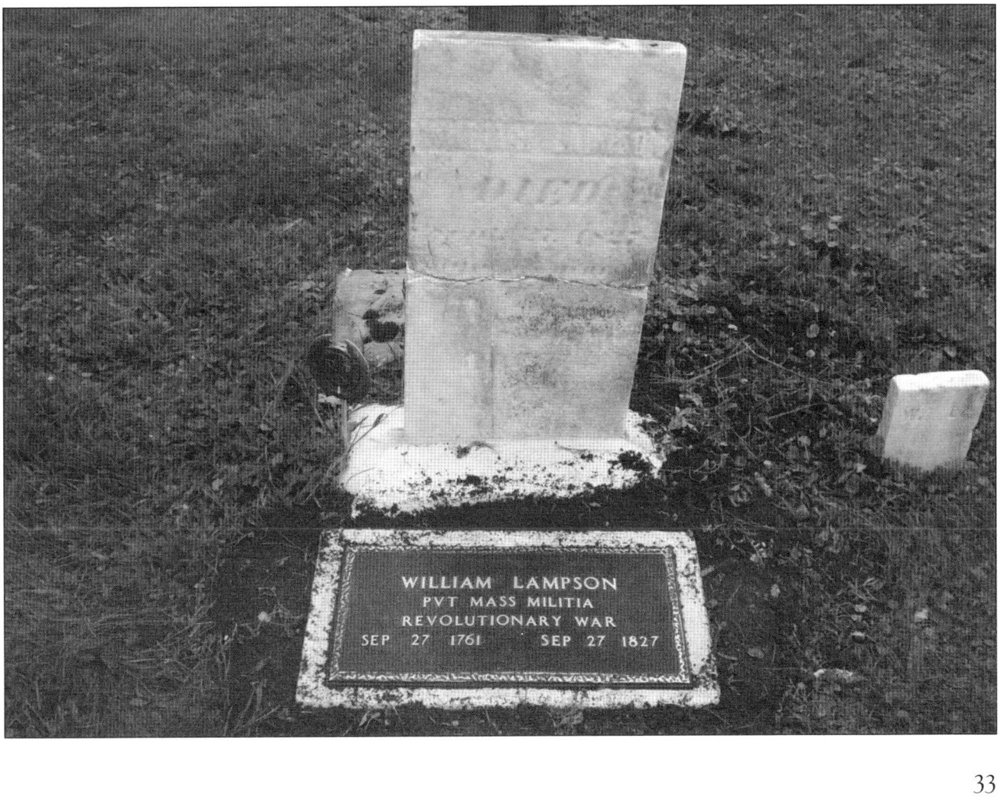

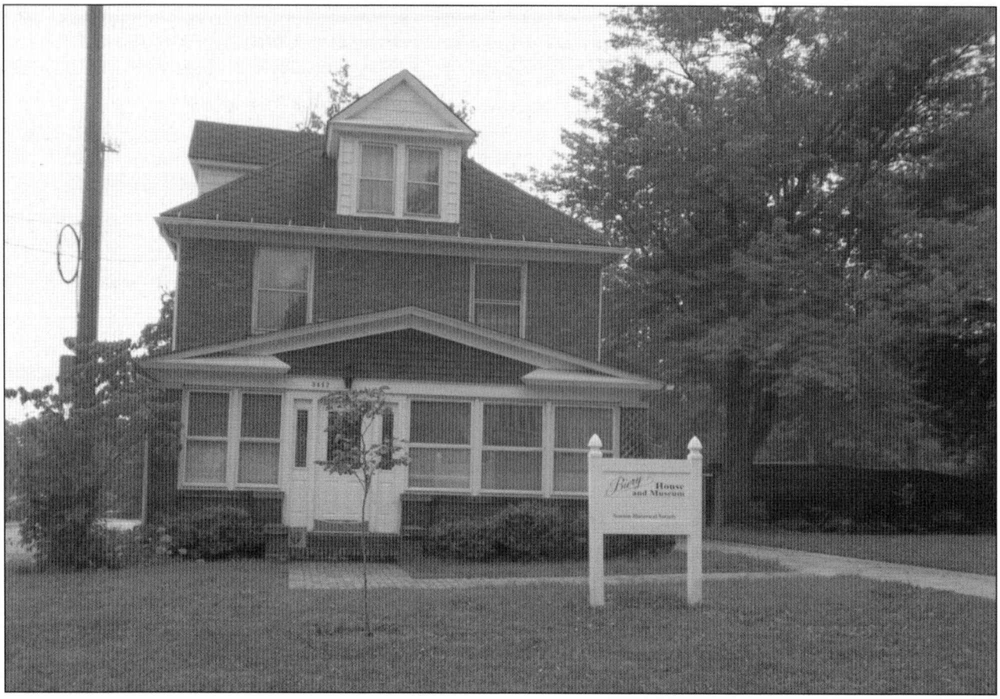

The Biery House and Museum, which is home to the Norton Historical Society, can be found at 3412 Greenwich Road. The City of Norton administration had the foresight to purchase this property and the 1912 farmhouse to be used as a museum for its residents. In earlier years, the museum was housed in a 1840s home just to the east. The area was cleared of the old home and the Beldick Motel to make way for the new fire station. (Author's collection.)

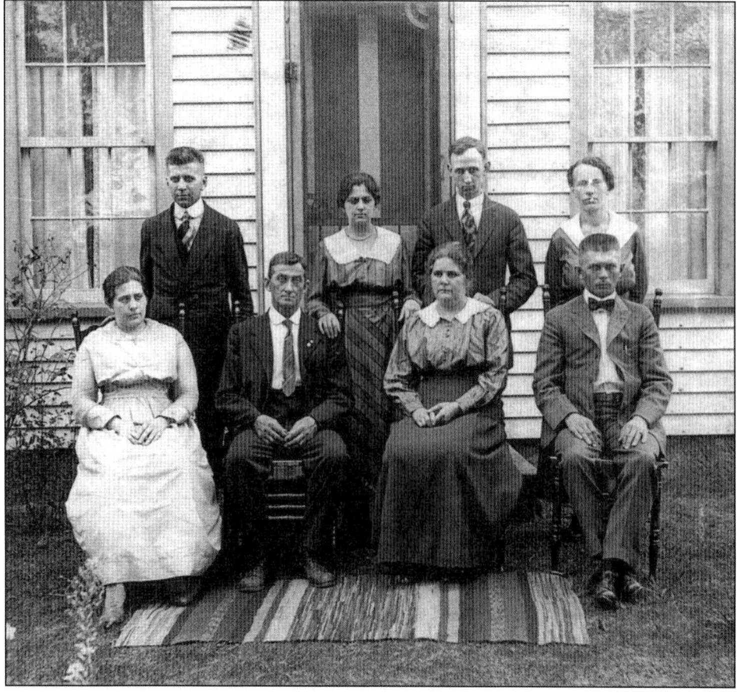

Builder of the Biery House and Museum Charles Biery is shown here with his family about 1930. From left to right are (first row) Grace Cowling Biery, Charles, Carrie Lower Biery, and Rollen Biery; (second row) Hobert Biery, Odessa Riley Biery, Sylvester Riley, and Mattie Biery (Rollen's wife). The brick farmhouse has been called a fortress because of its stone foundation and 18-inch wall construction with basket-weave wooden floors.

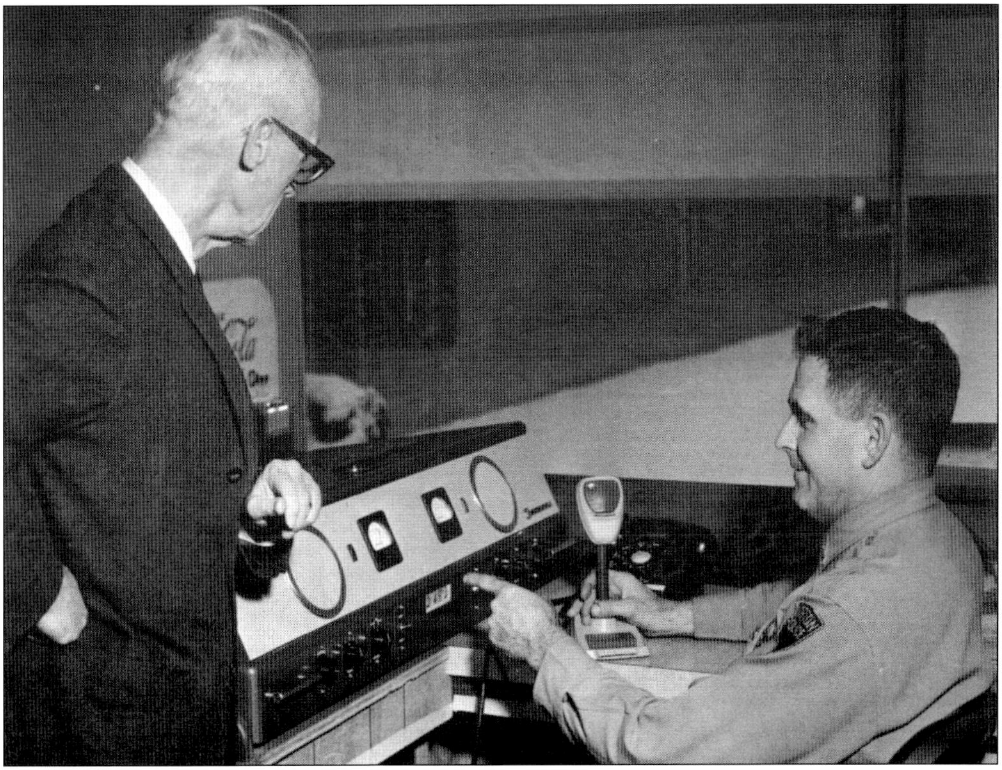

Norton Township had a one-man police force in the 1930s and 1940s, beginning with George Knecht, then Clarence Miller. Each officer provided his own car, had no office, served for minimal pay, and had no regular hours but was always on call. Fortunately, crime was minimal; there were few accidents and only a few domestic disputes, which were usually settled on the front porch. John Van Hyning replaced Clarence Miller in 1951. In 1961, Forest C. Diefendorff was appointed as the first chief of police. Pictured here in 1964 is Mayor Max W. Johnstone (left) with Chief Forest Diefendorff, inspecting the new base radio station.

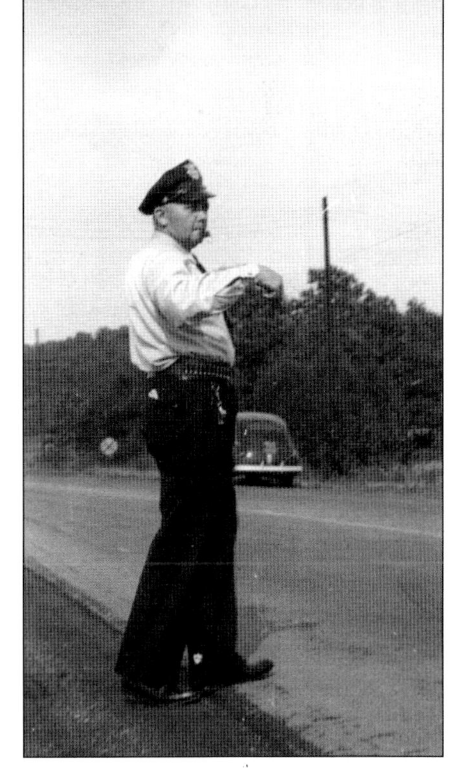

Clarence Miller is directing traffic at the scene of an accident at Akron-Wadsworth and Clark-Mill Roads in 1942. Miller worked at various shops over the years repairing Ford automobiles before being a garage service manager and salesman for Bertsch Motor Company. During World War II, he worked for PPG Industries in the chemical division, all the while continuing maintaining the farm at the family home on Hametown Road. (Courtesy of Chuck Miller.)

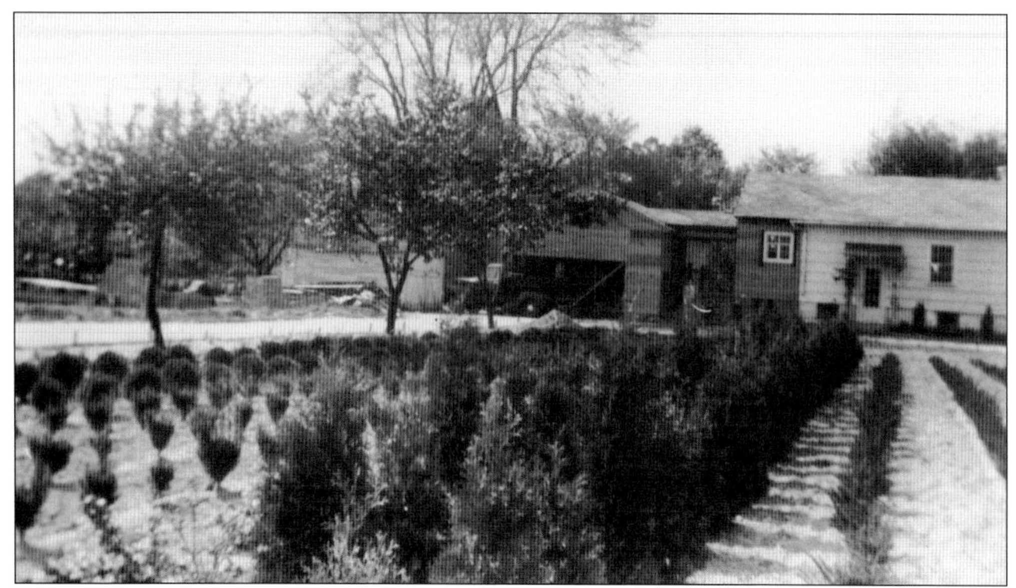

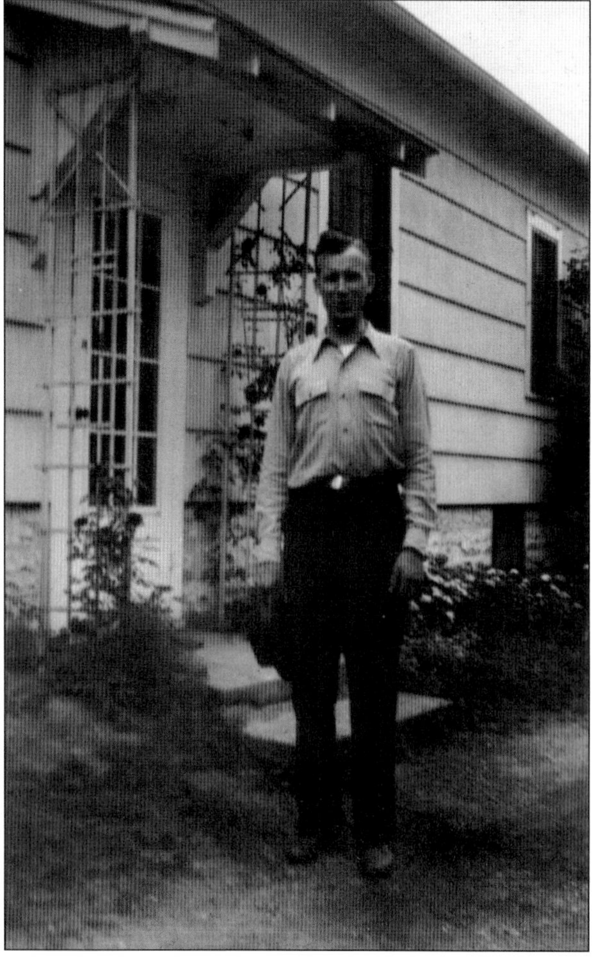

Leaving the US Navy after World War II and serving on the torpedoed ship USS *Thomas Stone*, Stanley Lucas sought to establish a new life and his own business. Lucas was born to Lithuanian immigrants, and he eventually met and married Helen Janickas, another Lithuanian from Akron in 1946. Obtaining a piece of property from his brother-in-law on Johnson Road, Lucas began planting trees of various varieties, and from there, Lucas Nursery was born. Lucas worked alone with assistance from relatives who had other jobs in Akron's factories with the booming postwar economy. Expansion of the business started in the 1960s with Eisenhower's interstate highway program and the purchase of 50 acres of farmland. Lucas Nursery and Landscaping would come to design and complete landscaping for B.F. Goodrich's world headquarters and the Seiberling factory in Barberton, along with the homes of Goodyear and Goodrich's chief executive officers. Stanley Lucas is pictured here posing next to his house in the 1940s. (Both, courtesy of Mike and Marcia Lucas.)

The Blackburn children pose for in front of the family country store, located just west of Loyal Oak, in 1928. Pictured here are, from left to right, (first row) Glenn, William, and Francis; (second row) Ethel and Carl. In 1923, their parents, Chester and Angeline, moved to Norton, where they owned and operated a store next to their house, selling grocery staples as well as motor oil and Sinclair gasoline. (Courtesy of William Blackburn.)

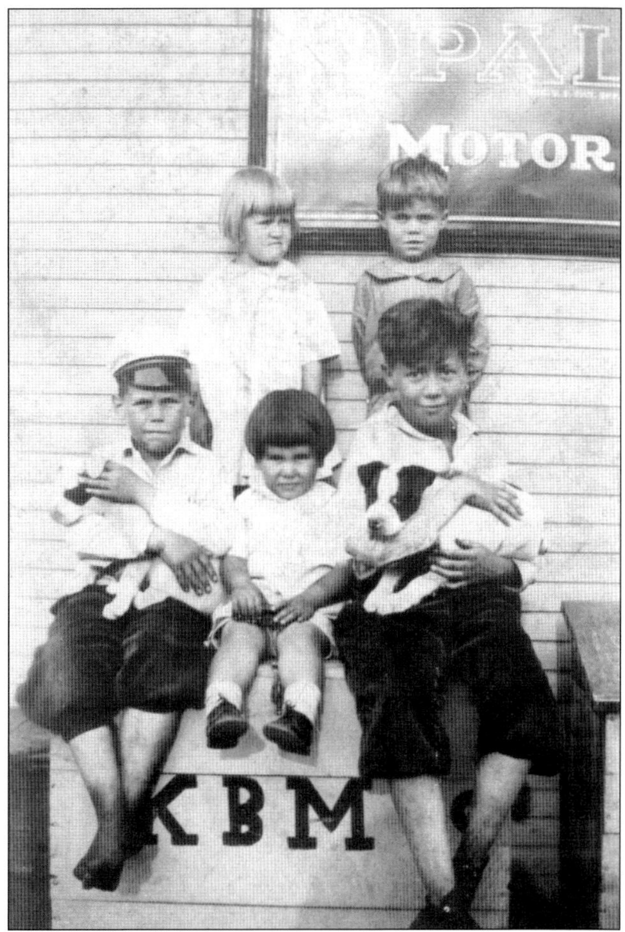

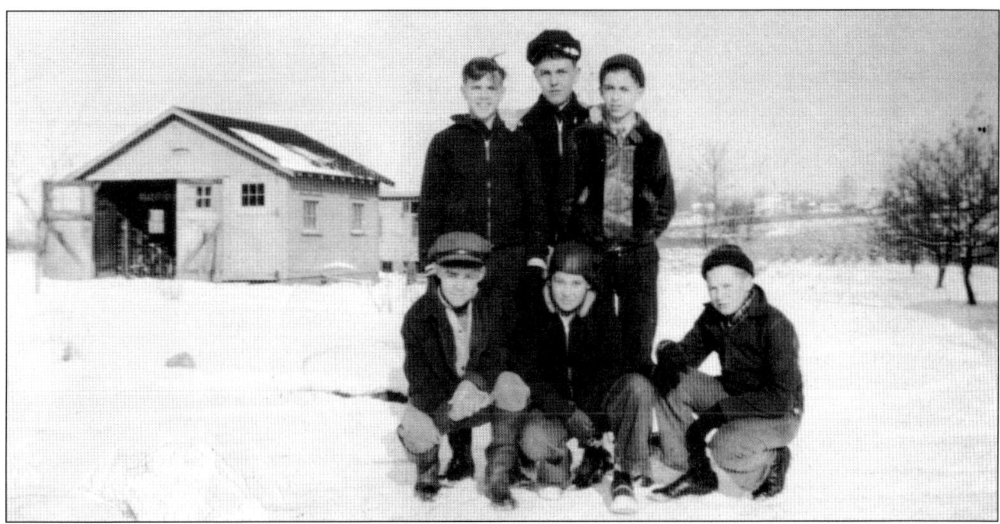

Some of the Loyal Oak boys got together for this winter photograph in 1938. Pictured here are, from left to right, (first row) Bob Hemphill and William and Carl Blackburn; (second row) Eddie Ault, Don Redhead, and Everett Diefendorff. (Courtesy of William Blackburn.)

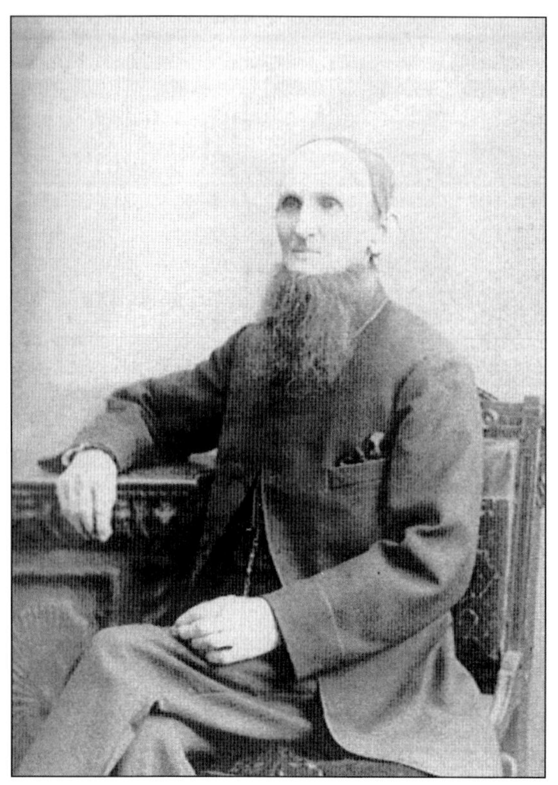

Nathan Oplinger, born in 1822, and Sobina Deiter, born in 1823, were joined in marriage on December 5, 1843. Their golden wedding anniversary was held at their daughter's home, and during the festivities, the following was read by William Oplinger of Wadsworth: "Nathan Oplinger and Sobina Deiter were joined in wedlock by Reverend William Gerhart in Moore Township, Northampton County, Pennsylvania where they lived with mother Oplingers parents for a year. On October 1949 they started in a one horse wagon over hill and dale for Ohio. As the iron horse was not at their service, it required a journey of 18 days to make the trip and reach their destination, Wadsworth, Ohio." In 1850, they purchased a house and lot of 17 acres and remained for 12 and a half years. In 1893, they moved once again to another home in Loyal Oak, where they lived out their days, Sobina died in 1894 and Nathan followed in 1898. (Both, courtesy of Crystal Noel Bassett.)

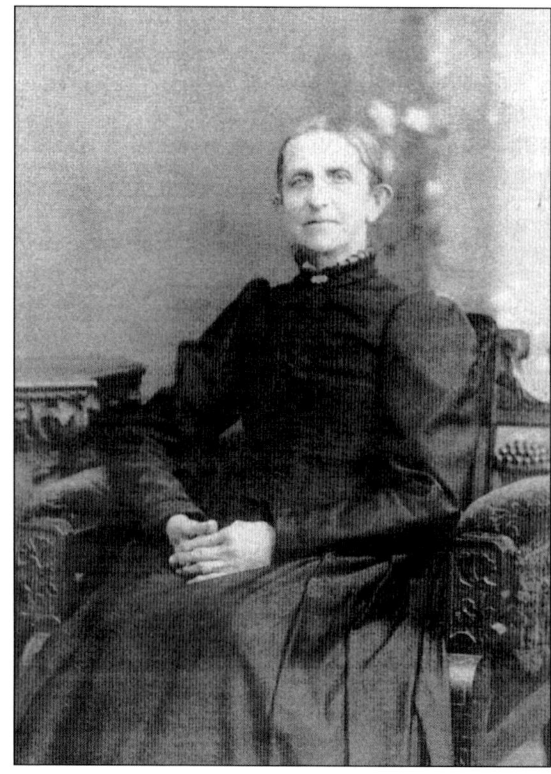

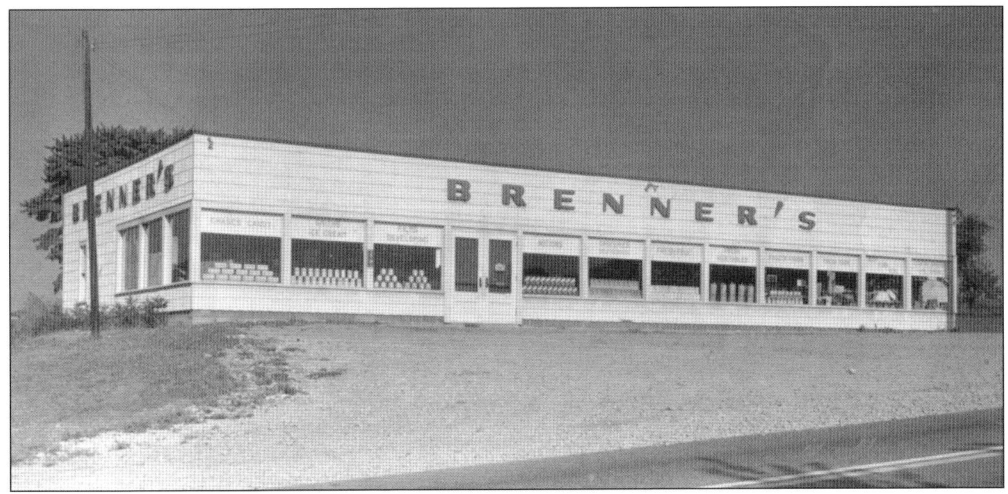

Starting as a fruit stand, and then a small store, in 1935, Brenner's became a large grocery and meat market built by Vernon T. Brenner, located at 2680–2682 Cleveland-Massillon Road. The larger building was erected in 1945 and catered to a large clientele until Route 21 changed the traffic patterns in Norton and severely cut back on patronage. In 1958, the building was being rented by a furniture dealer, and it caught fire and burned to the ground. The blaze was believed to be a work of arson. (Courtesy of Tim Brenner.)

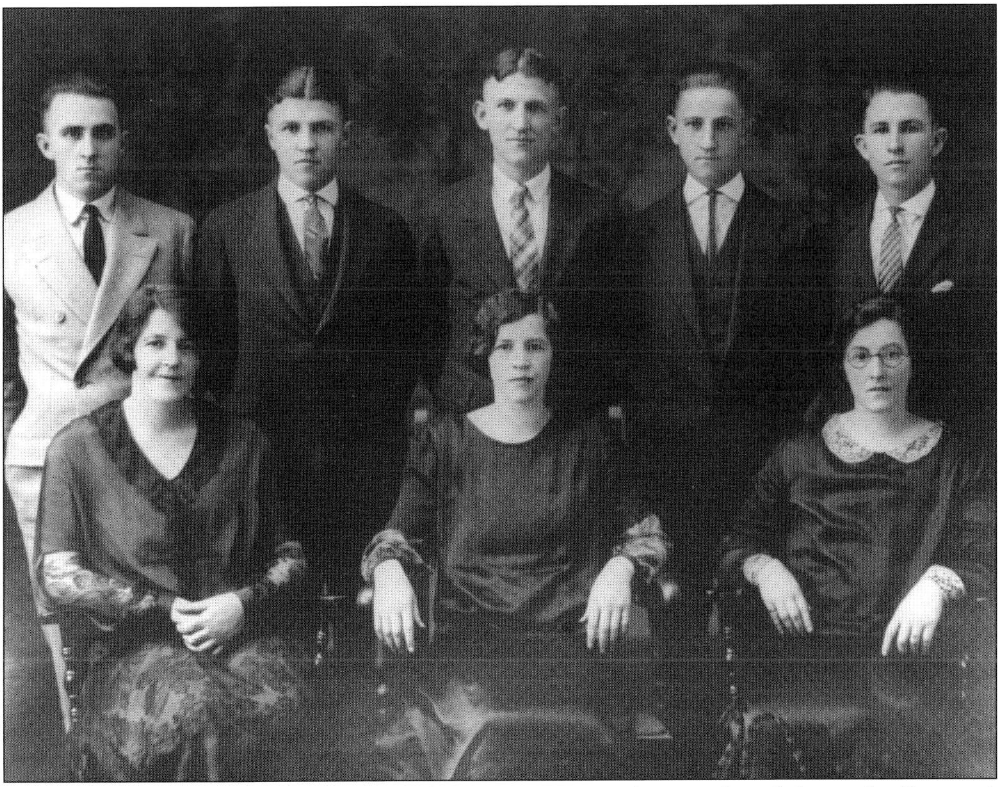

Shown here are the children of Lewis and Naomi Brenner. They are, from left to right (first row) Ellen, Cathryn, and Ruth; (second row) Willis, Dick, Charles ("Chick"), Daniel, and Vernon. (Courtesy of Tim Brenner.)

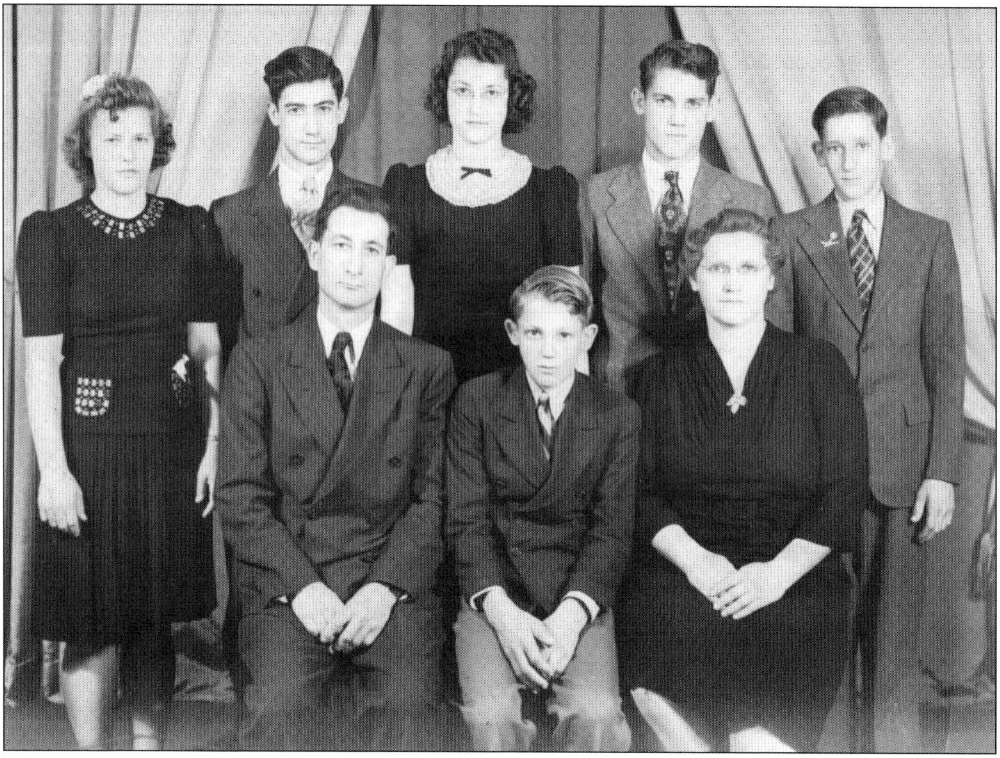

Pictured here around 1942 are, from left to right, (first row) Fred, Arthur, and Blanche Swain; (second row) Edith, Milford, Virginia, Ivan, and F. Melvin Swain. The Swain family resided on Medina Line Road south of Western Star. The homestead shown here on Medina Line Road no longer exists. It included a farmhouse, windmill, silo, barn, summerhouse, smokehouse, and pig enclosure. (Courtesy of Virginia Swain Knox.)

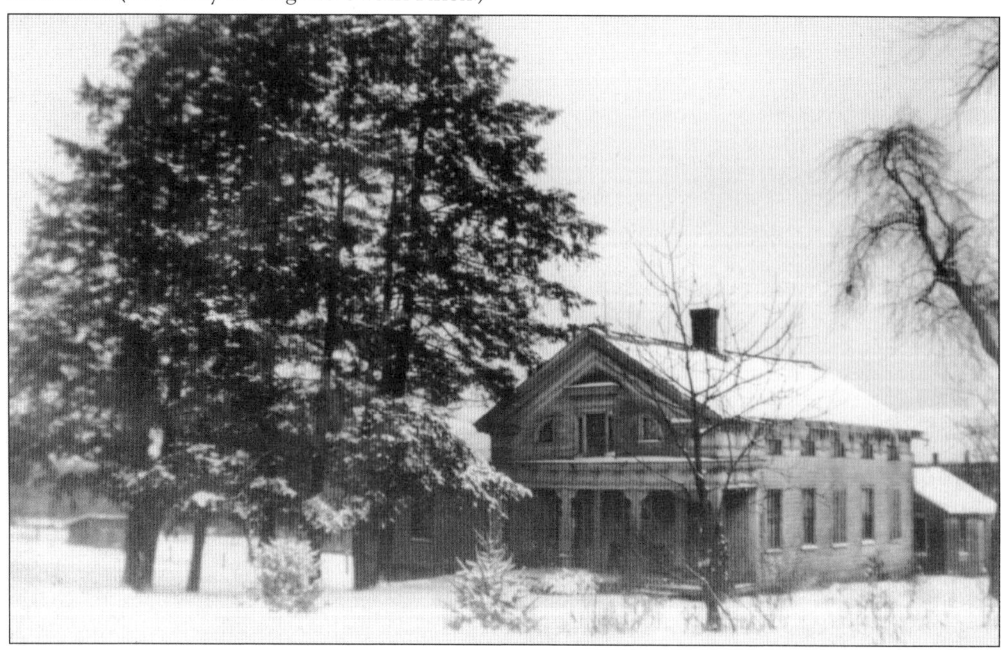

Willis A. Shelhart and Emma Grace Schneider Shelhart are shown here at their home at 3916 Cleveland-Massillon Road. They had three children: Myra, Alvin, and Leroy. Willis and Emma celebrated their golden wedding anniversary in 1933.

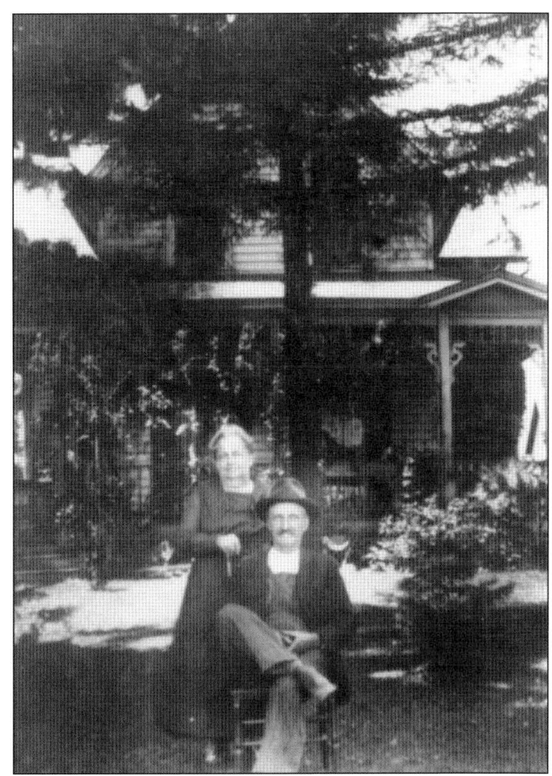

The Edwards family are pictured here from left to right: (first row) Lillian Harris, Margaret Edwards, Harold Edwards, Beulah Edwards, and Mildred Harris; (second row) Maude Edwards (holding Kenneth Edwards), James Edwards Jr., James Edwards Sr., Hattie Edwards, Paul Edwards, and Beulah Dasher; (third row) Serata Edwards, Fred Edwards, Emma Edwards, unidentified, Nora Dasher, Russel Edwards, and Helen ?.

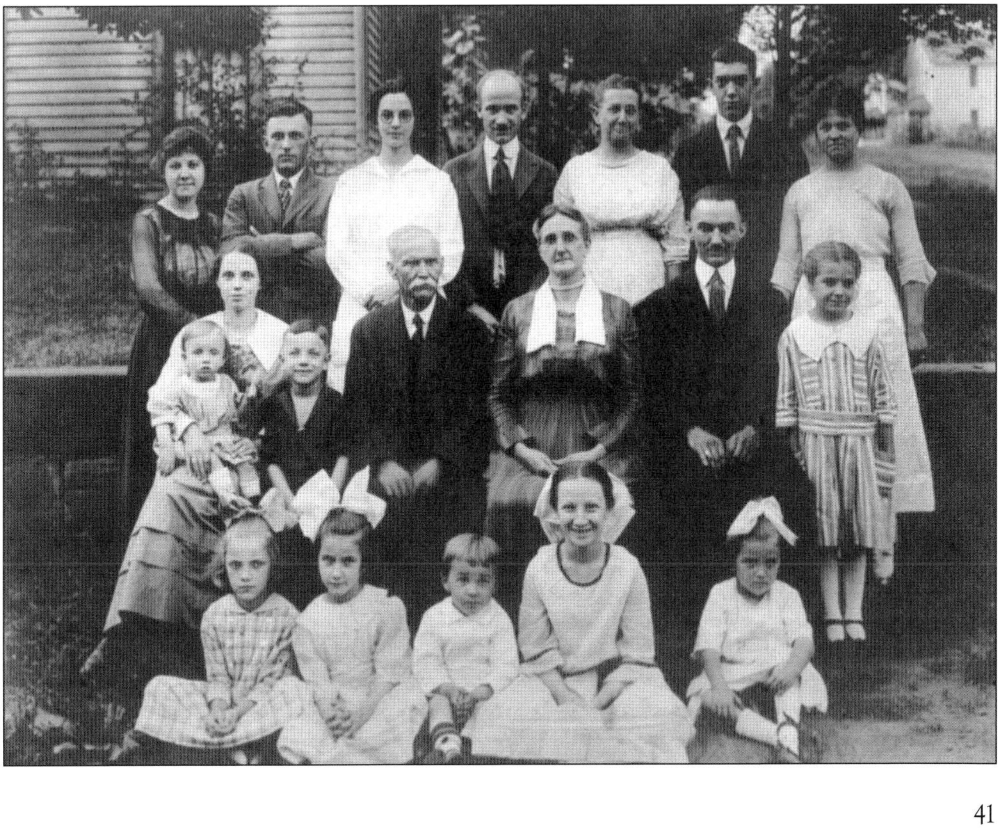

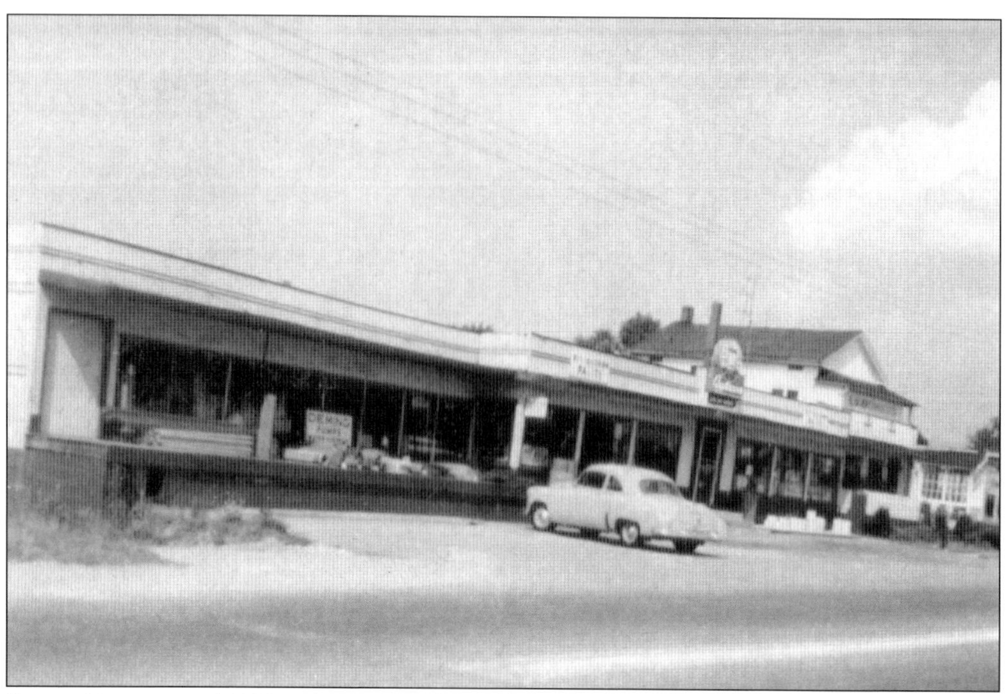

Pictured here around 1950 is the Mary and Francis Zurbuch's Loyal Oak Hardware Store, located at 3063 Akron-Wadsworth Road. Francis was known to loan tools to customers unable to make a purchase and would extend credit. For years, many customers attempted to pick up a coin on the floor of the hardware without success, as Francis had nailed it to the floor; he enjoyed a private laugh. Mary and Francis had two sons, Lowell and Claire, and the family lived in an attached home. (Courtesy of Lowell Zurbuch.)

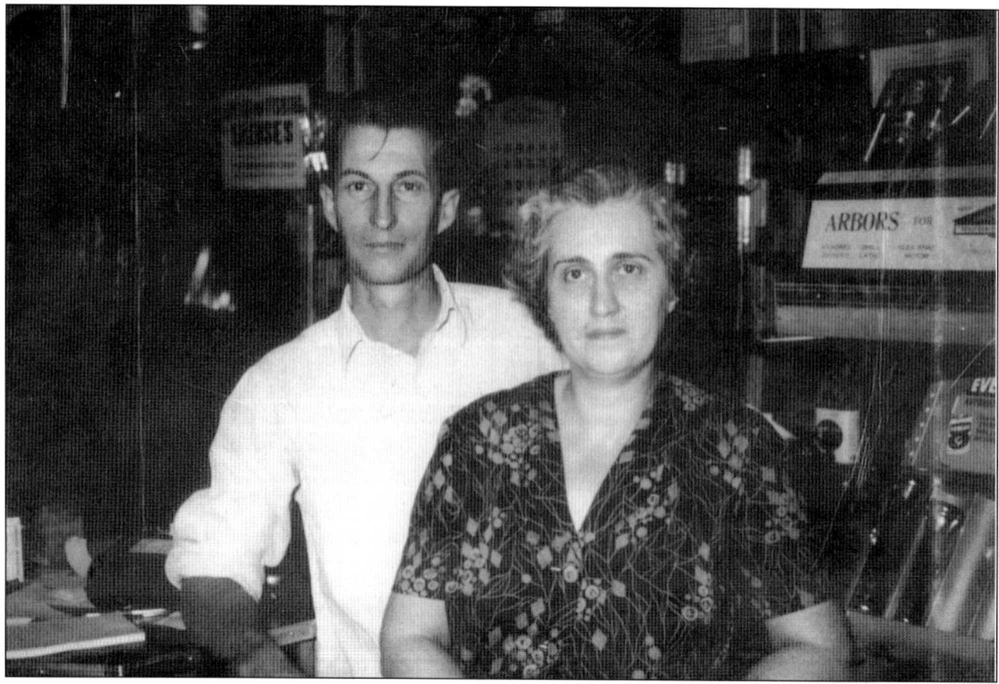

George C. Bennett made a financial success of himself with his ill-gotten gains by scamming farmers and mailing obscene printed matter. At one time, he was arrested, jailed, and fined $500. He lapsed into loose ways after becoming rich, contracted pneumonia, and died in 1874 at the age of 23. It is said that "he lay uneasy where he had been laid and he is still seen walking nights within God's acre which is his grave." He is buried in the Western Star Cemetery. (Courtesy of *Wadsworth Heritage*.)

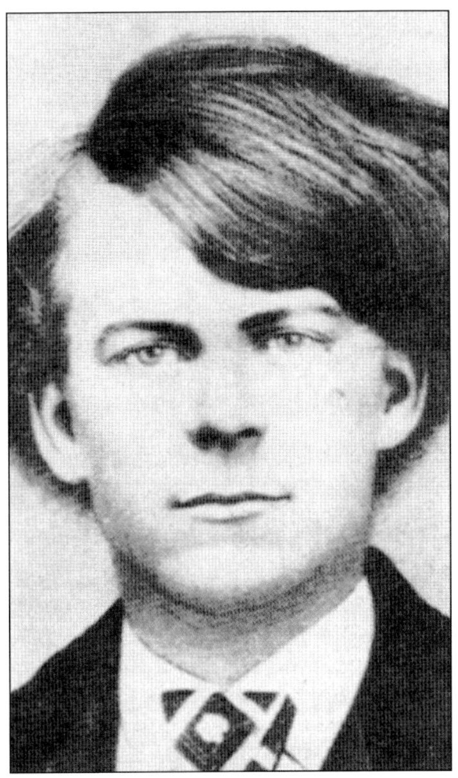

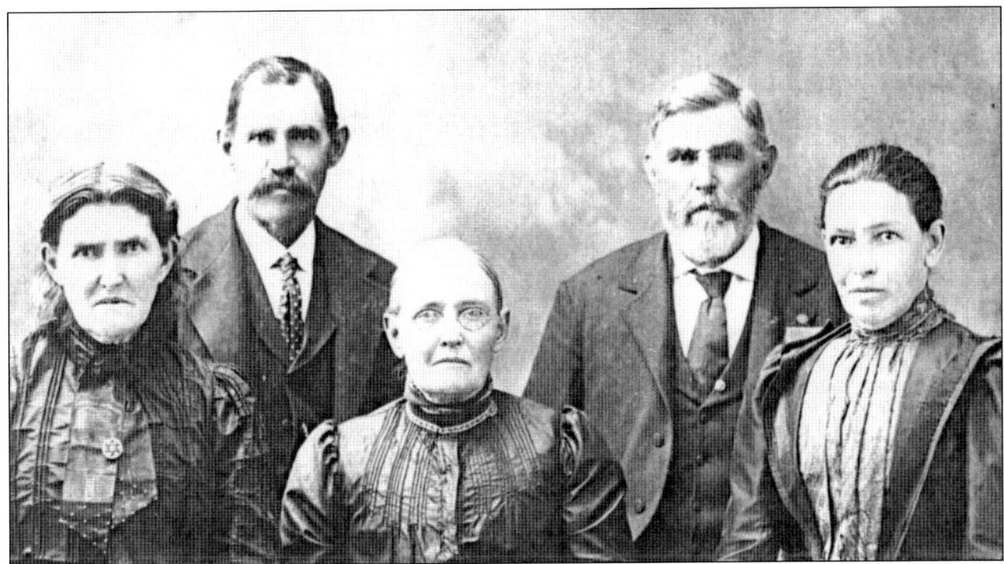

Four of the seven adult children from the union of Thomas Gilman Young and Rowena French Young are pictured here. From left to right are Olive Abigail Young Farr, Andrew Harvey (Phebe's husband), Phebe Ellen Young Harvey, Gilman McKendry Young, and Mary Alice Young Bird. At the tender age of 18, Rowena French, a young New Englander from Vermont and the daughter of Gideon French and Phoebe Carpenter, traveled to Ohio all alone. Her trek took six weeks, covering 800 miles by stage, canal, schooner, and on foot. Her courageous trek named her as one of the pioneer women of the Western Reserve.

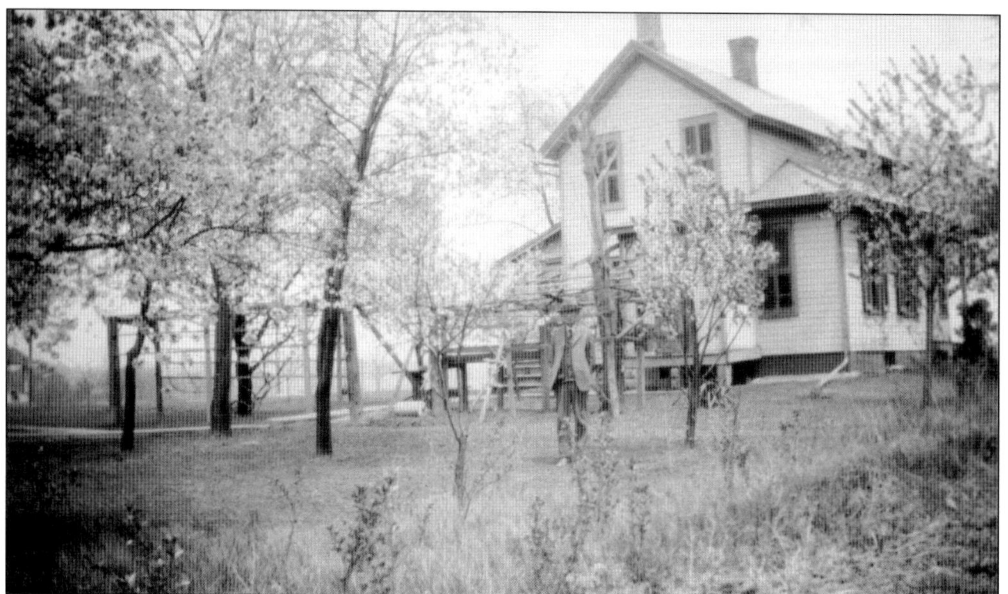

The unknown builder of this 1890 Colonial home stands at 4422 Cleveland-Massillon Road. Beginning in 1950, Fred and Vera Witchey lived at this home with their daughter June. This is where the Witchey Lightning Rod Company was started. Fred went places such as a US radar station in Nome, Alaska, where he installed rods in temperatures 70 degrees below zero and as high up as 980 feet on a smokestack for the Ohio Edison Company. Witchey would also install rods on houses, silos, and farms, as he was the only licensed lightning-rod installer in the state of Ohio. (Courtesy of June Witchey Patera.)

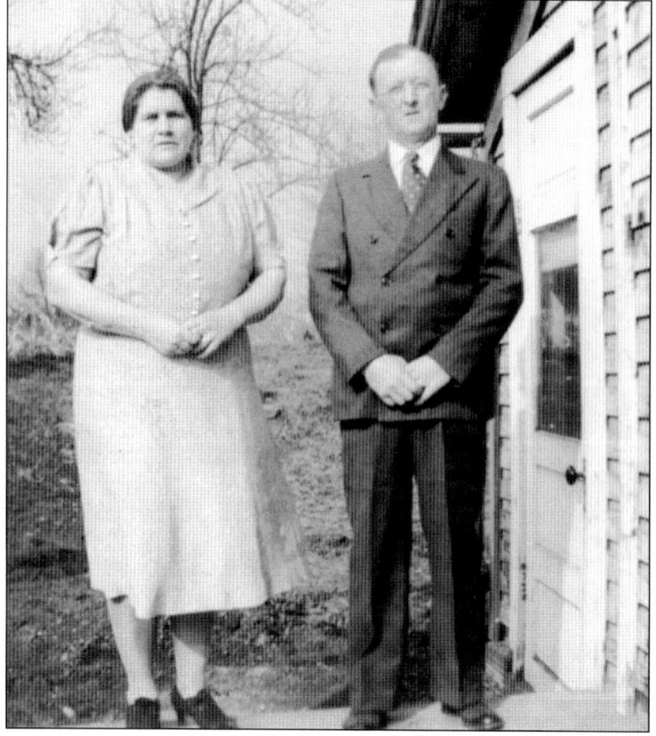

Walter Storm and Florence Frase Storm are pictured here at their home on Greenwich Road in Western Star. Walter, a former farmer, was a watchman for PPG Industries, and Florence was a homemaker. They had three children: Velma (Storm) Dohner, Carl, and Orrin. Both sons served in military during World War II. Carl was in the Army as a staff sergeant and Orrin served in the Navy as an engineman. (Courtesy of Gary Dohner.)

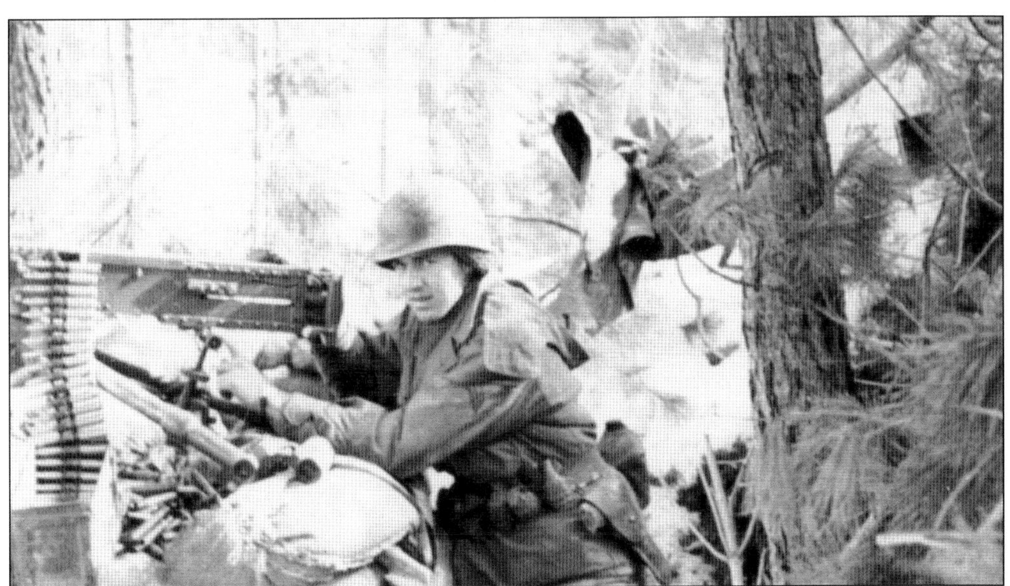

Rick Maier, formerly in the Marine Reserves, became a volunteer draftee into the US Army, where he completed Airborne Ranger training. During his tour of Korea, he was decorated six times and wounded twice. In this photograph from 1951, Maier, a sergeant, and his troops were engaged in a month-long battle of Heartbreak Ridge, just a few miles north of the 38th Parallel. After the war, he became the assistant dean of the University of Akron, obtained a master's degree, and pursued doctoral studies, becoming a teacher in the Barberton School system. He was elected president of the teachers association in 1961. (Courtesy of Rick Maier.)

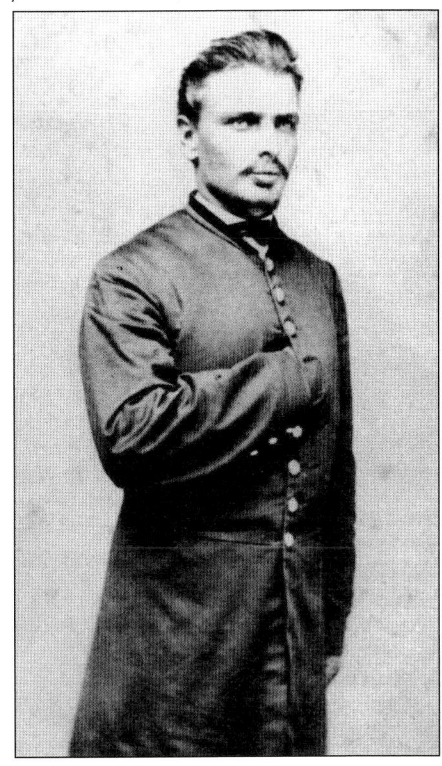

Norton native and Union army officer Myron T. Wright served in the Civil War in Company D, 29th Ohio. In 1862, he was wounded while fighting against Stonewall Jackson's Shenandoah Valley campaign and wounded again in the Battle of Peach Tree Creek in July 1864. He was later struck in the heel by a musket ball, which proved to be a fatal blow. His foot was amputated and became infected, and he died less than three weeks later. (Courtesy of *Buckeye Blood: Ohio at Gettysburg*.)

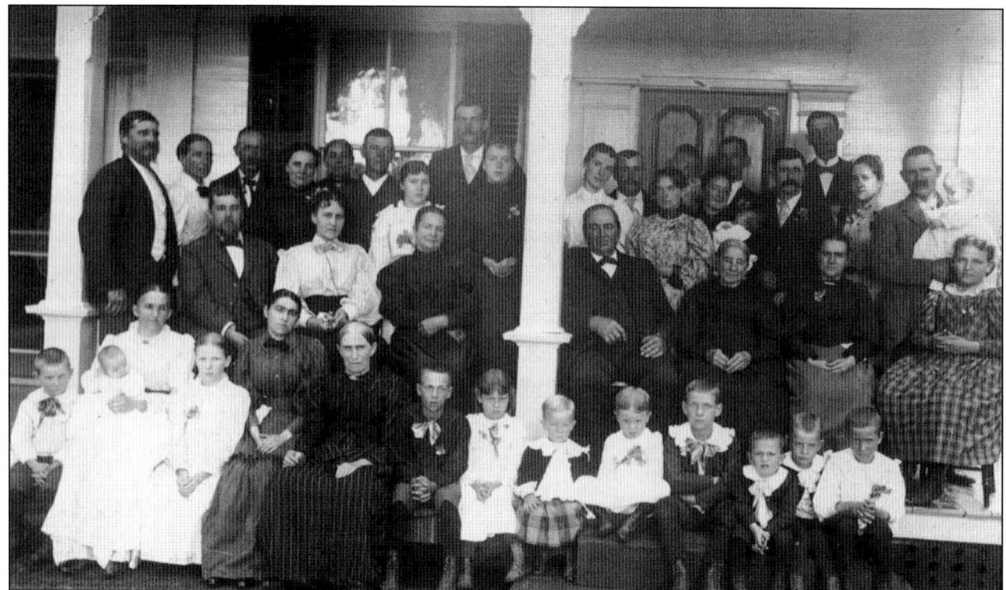

This image of the Harter family was taken at the Harter farm around 1895. Later, the farm was known as the Swain family farm. It was purchased by John and Forrest Swain, who married sisters Ede and Clara Harter. (Courtesy of Virginia Swain Knox.)

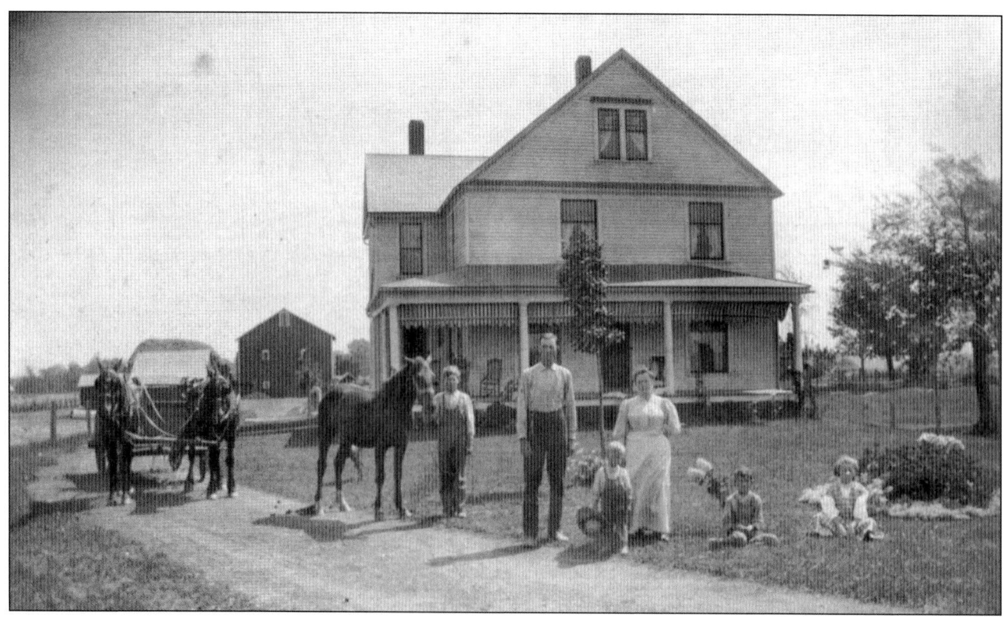

This image was taken at 4903 Hametown Road in the early 1900s and shows, from left to right, Paul (holding the horse), John M., Clifford (with the hat), Ede, Fred, and Ruth Swain. The house was built by John in 1885, but the barn and a log cabin were constructed on the property earlier. The 38-acre farm is still in use today and owned by Mike Quinn. The barn succumbed to a devastating fire in 2007 and was a total loss. (Courtesy of Mike Quinn.)

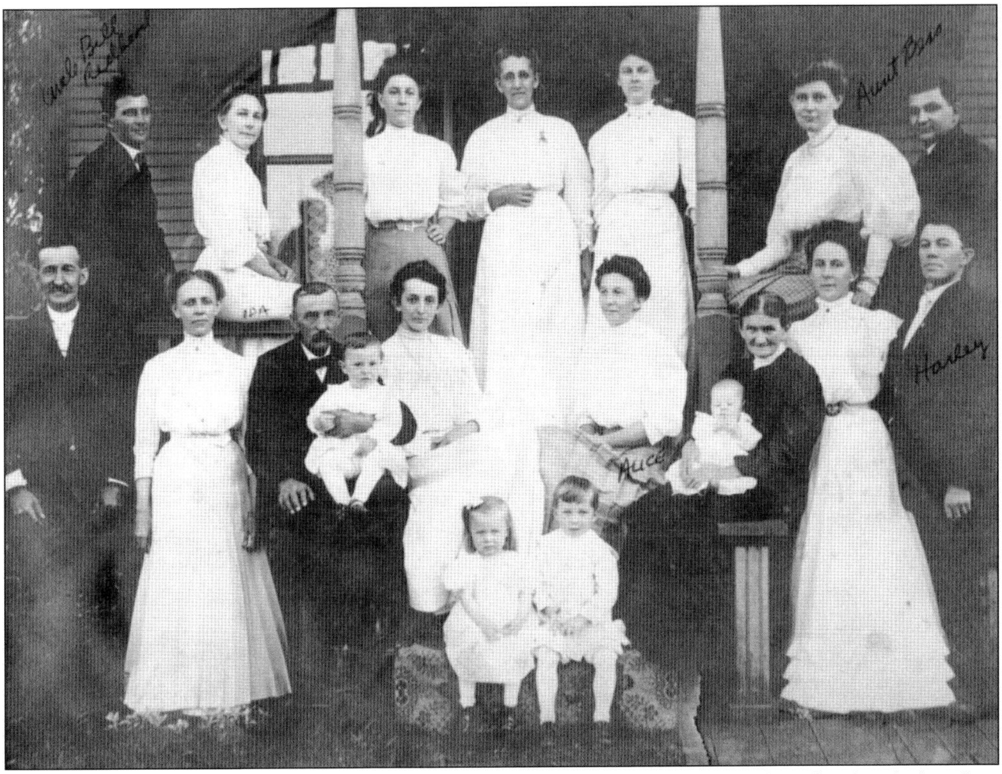

Pictured here on an unknown date is the John and Jennie Knecht family. The family lived in Loyal Oak on Cleveland Massillon Road and owned the cider mill across the street. (Courtesy of Kaye Redhead.)

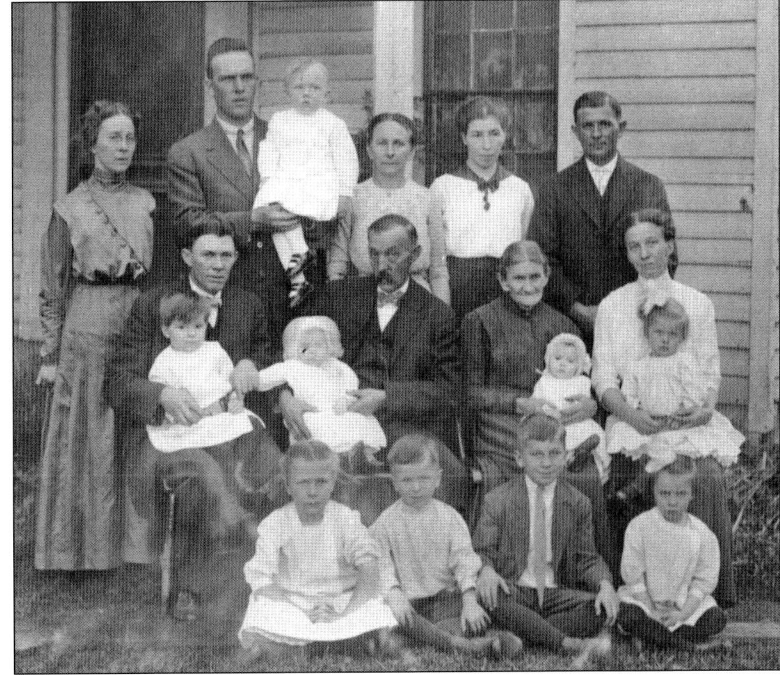

Featured in this undated photograph is the Redhead family of Loyal Oak. (Courtesy of Kaye Redhead.)

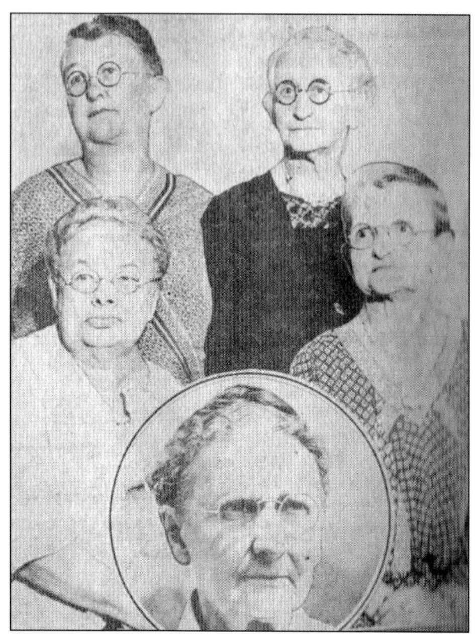

Pictured here in 1934 are, from left to right, (inset) Ella Menzer; (first row) Alice Miller and Rosie Harris; (second row) Cora Erich and Mary S. Harter. These women were members of the oldest sewing club in the community at the time, the Ladies Aid Society, which began with 25 members in 1887. Meetings were held in homes of the members and once a week at Grace Evangelical and Reformed Church in Loyal Oak.

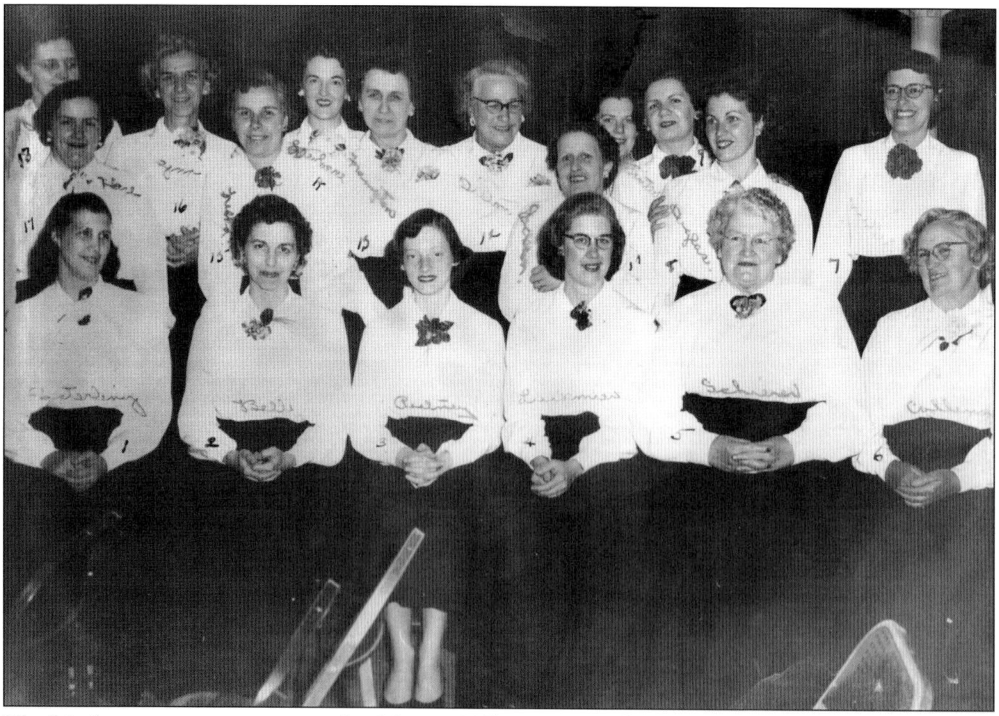

The Mothersingers were organized in Norton Village on March 3, 1953, and the group was directed by Mildred Luckmeier, accompanied on piano by Mary Ruth Hare. The women sang for various clubs, groups, and churches in the area. From left to right are (first row) Elouise Easterling, Billie Bell, Alberta Putney, Mildred Luckmeier, Mary Schierer, and Wilma Collins; (second row) Mary Ruth Hare, June Frecka, Vera Frampton, Bessie Jackson, Phyllis Douglas, and Camilla Miller; (third row) Tillie Seiberling, Rose Zinn, Amy Lawhorn, Rosella Dillon, Mary Lu Piersol, and Kathryn Pinter.

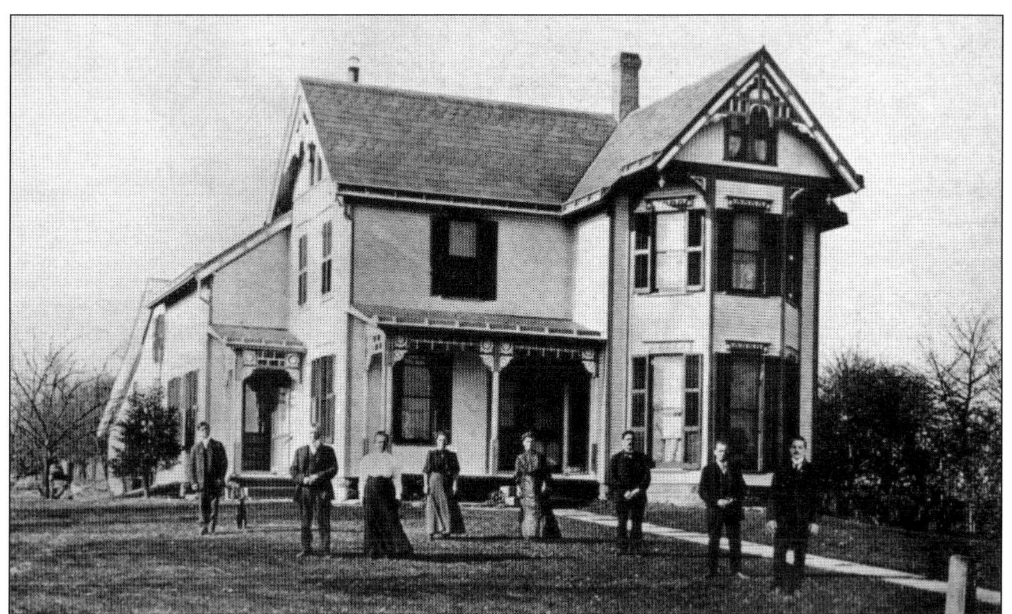

The homestead of John Jacob Breitenstine included 378 acres of land on Kungle Road. After working on his father's farm until he was 24, John married Lydia Keller. He then worked six years as a coal miner, and his earnings enabled him to purchase a 24-acre farm. John amassed considerable wealth, which included five farms and a productive coal mine, and he and Lydia had eight children. Memories of the original Breitenstine home have been carefully archived, and they include making applesauce, cider, and horseradish, picking edible mushrooms and gathering nuts, roasting homegrown peanuts, and making maple syrup and homemade butter. The farm was near a railroad track, and hobos rode the rails, marking the places where they could get a good meal. The Breitenstines were one of them. Gypsies were said to come in bands, and John Jr. carried a big black whip just in case.

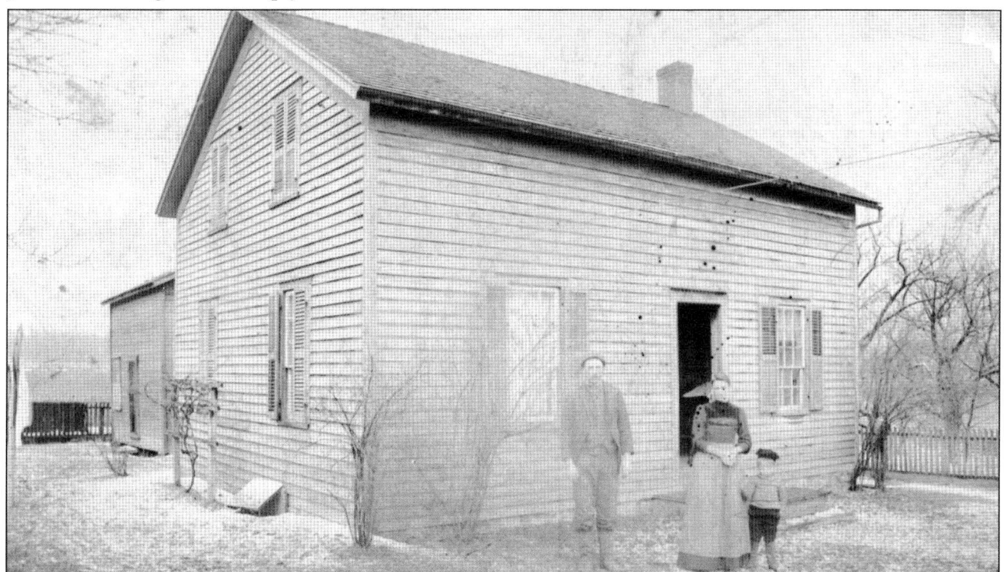

Just south of Loyal Oak was the Boerstler homestead. Shown here on March 4, 1895, from left to right, are Milt, Katie, and Russell Boerstler.

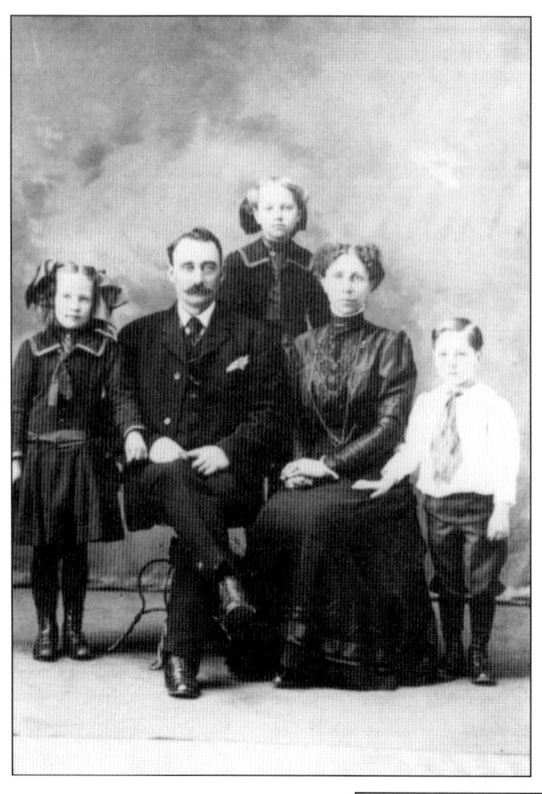

Pictured here in 1910 are, from left to right, Alice Snyder Pressler, Arthur Daniel Snyder, Mabel Snyder Pressler, Katie Snyder, and Arthur Christian Snyder. The Snyder family resided at 3013 Akron-Wadsworth Road, the farm that was originally owned by the Hoertz family. The Snyder and Pressler family names were common along a long stretch of Akron-Wadsworth Road from Loyal Oak toward the east. (Courtesy of Wayne Pressler.)

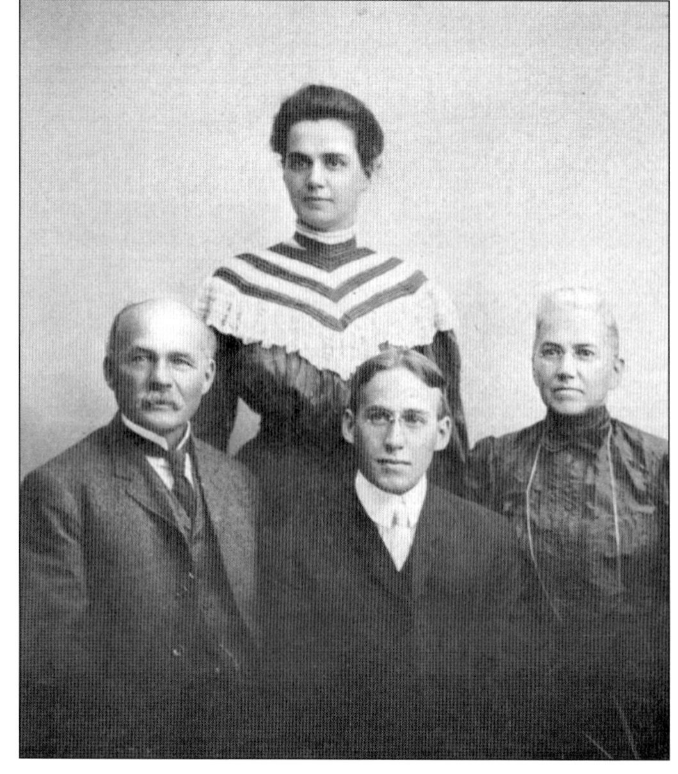

John M. Hoertz was born on October 22, 1852, and he lost both of his parents before the age of 10. He purchased a home in Norton on Akron-Wadsworth Road in 1882 and grew fruits and vegetables, which he transported in wagonloads to Barberton and Akron to sell. John married Mary L. Harris in 1875, and they had two children: Ada Alberta and Harry Ernest. Ada graduated from Norton High School and taught school for two years, and Harry graduated from Norton High School and worked for Goodrich Rubber Company in Akron. (Courtesy of *Centennial History of Summit County, Ohio and Representative Citizens.*)

During World War II, the Redhead family in Loyal Oak received this vague Western Union telegram. Donald Redhead, who enlisted in the Marines right out of Norton High School, was wounded when a Japanese man exploded a grenade by him and one of his friends. Donald, a corporal and radio operator in the 2nd Marine Division who saw intense action in Tarawa and Saipan, was the only one to survive this attack. He was held in reserve in Tinian, preparing to go to Iwo Jima and Okinawa, and part of the occupational forces that went into Hiroshima after the dreaded atomic bomb was unleashed. Redhead died in 2011 at the age of 88. (Both, courtesy of Kaye Redhead.)

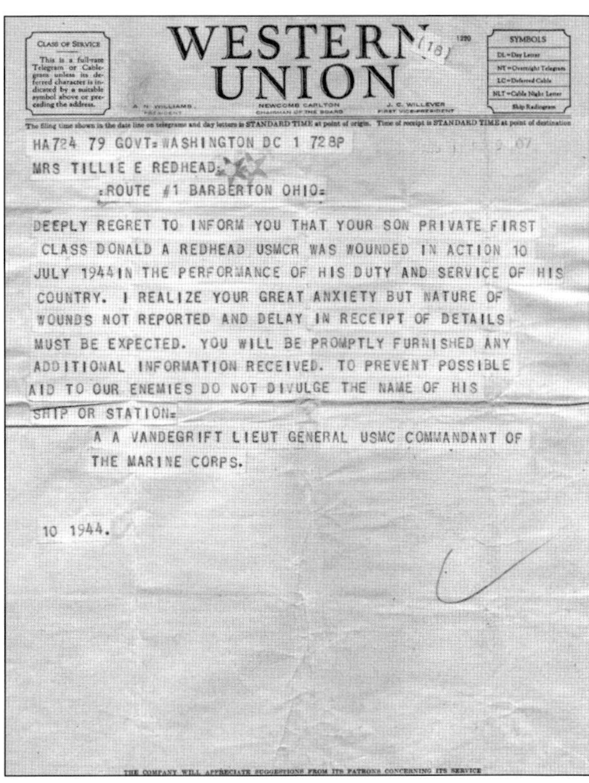

CLASS OF SERVICE

This is a full-rate Telegram or Cablegram unless its deferred character is indicated by a suitable symbol above or preceding the address.

WESTERN UNION

(18) 1220

A. N. WILLIAMS, PRESIDENT — NEWCOMB CARLTON, CHAIRMAN OF THE BOARD — J. C. WILLEVER, FIRST VICE-PRESIDENT

SYMBOLS

DL=Day Letter
NT=Overnight Telegram
LC=Deferred Cable
NLT=Cable Night Letter
Ship Radiogram

The filing time shown in the date line on telegrams and day letters is STANDARD TIME at point of origin. Time of receipt is STANDARD TIME at point of destination

HA724 79 GOVT=WASHINGTON DC 1 728P

MRS TILLIE E REDHEAD=

=ROUTE #1 BARBERTON OHIO=

DEEPLY REGRET TO INFORM YOU THAT YOUR SON PRIVATE FIRST CLASS DONALD A REDHEAD USMCR WAS WOUNDED IN ACTION 10 JULY 1944 IN THE PERFORMANCE OF HIS DUTY AND SERVICE OF HIS COUNTRY. I REALIZE YOUR GREAT ANXIETY BUT NATURE OF WOUNDS NOT REPORTED AND DELAY IN RECEIPT OF DETAILS MUST BE EXPECTED. YOU WILL BE PROMPTLY FURNISHED ANY ADDITIONAL INFORMATION RECEIVED. TO PREVENT POSSIBLE AID TO OUR ENEMIES DO NOT DIVULGE THE NAME OF HIS SHIP OR STATION=

A A VANDEGRIFT LIEUT GENERAL USMC COMMANDANT OF THE MARINE CORPS.

10 1944.

THE COMPANY WILL APPRECIATE SUGGESTIONS FROM ITS PATRONS CONCERNING ITS SERVICE

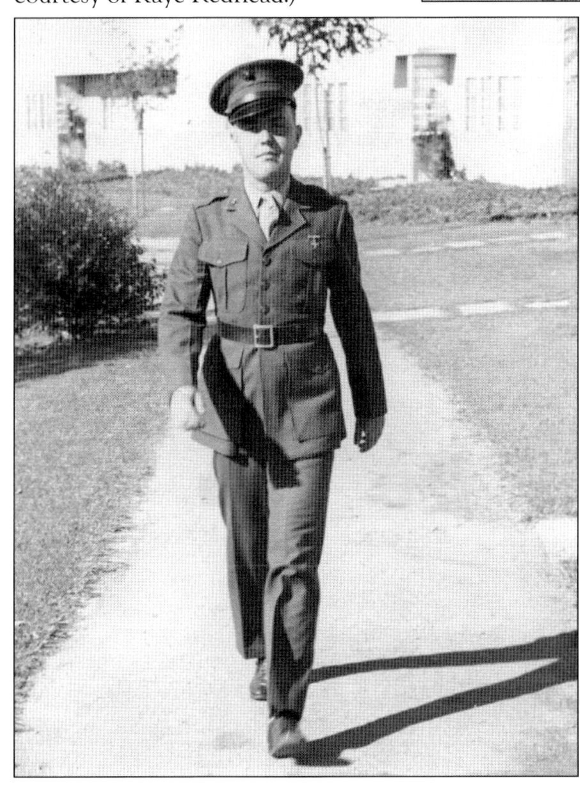

ARMY
SEPARATION QUALIFICATION RECORD

LAST NAME – FIRST NAME – MIDDLE INITIAL	ARMY SERIAL NUMBER	GRADE	DATE OF ENTRY INTO ACTIVE SERVICE	SEX	DATE OF BIRTH
Englehart Anna	A-507 845	Pvt	8 May 44	M	31 May 22

PERMANENT ADDRESS FOR MAILING PURPOSES (Street and Number – City – County – State)
398 Margaret St., Akron 6, Ohio

CIVILIAN EDUCATION

HIGHEST GRADE COMPLETED	LAST YEAR OF ATTENDANCE	HIGHEST DEGREE RECEIVED	MAJOR COURSE OF STUDY	NAME AND ADDRESS OF LAST SCHOOL ATTENDED
9	1940	None	Commercial	Garfield High School Akron, Ohio

OTHER TRAINING OR SCHOOLING
None

SERVICE EDUCATION

SERVICE SCHOOL: None
ARMY SPECIALIZED TRAINING PROGRAM: None

CIVILIAN OCCUPATIONS

MAIN OCCUPATION (TITLE): Riveter, Pneumatic
SECONDARY OCCUPATION (TITLE): None

JOB SUMMARY
Used air gun to do riveting on fin and wing assembly of airplane. Spread the rivet shank and shapped the lead with a pneumatic hammer. Reamed and bucked rivet holes with electrically driven reaming tool.

NO. OF YEARS	LAST DATE OF EMPLOYMENT	NAME AND ADDRESS OF EMPLOYER
2	20 Apr 44	Goodyear Aircraft Corp. Akron, Ohio

MILITARY SPECIALTIES

YEARS	MONTHS	GRADE	PRINCIPAL DUTY	ARMY CODE NO.
	1½	Pvt	Basic Training	
	7½	Pvt	Cook	060

SUMMARY OF MILITARY OCCUPATION AND CIVILIAN CONVERSIONS (Shown by title)
Plans to return to previous civilian job in essential war industry.

SUMMARY OF MILITARY OCCUPATION AND CIVILIAN CONVERSIONS (Shown by title)
None

* THIS INFORMATION BASED ON SOLDIER'S STATEMENT. (Indicate by * any items not supported by military records)

DATE OF SEPARATION	SIGNATURE OF SOLDIER	SIGNATURE OF SEPARATION CLASSIFICATION OFFICER
27 Jan 45	Anna Englehart	James Bond JAMES BOND CAPT AGD

W.D., A.G.O. FORM NO. 100 15 July 1944

Anna Englehart Redhead (shown below left with a friend) enlisted in the Army Air Corps on April 13, 1944. An original Rosie the Riveter, she used an air gun to rivet the fins and wing assemblies of airplanes at the Goodyear Aircraft Corporation in Akron, Ohio, and also worked as a cook. In 1946, Anna married Donald Redhead, a US Marine, and they had three children. (Both, courtesy of Kaye Redhead.)

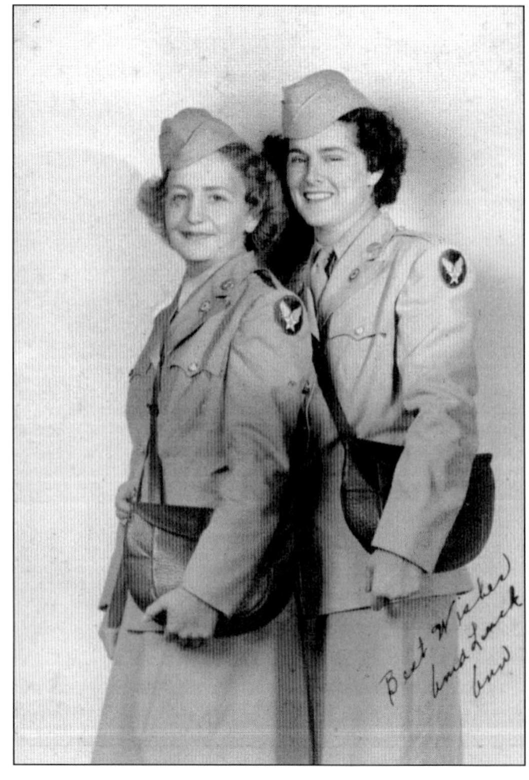

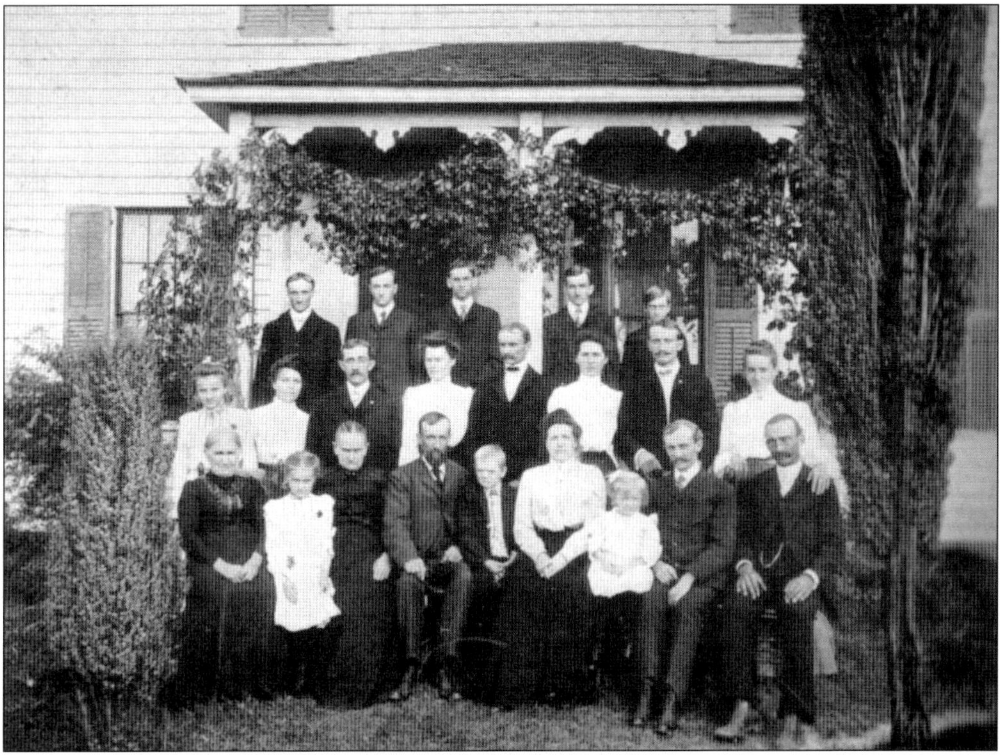

It was about 1908 when the Augustus Oleander Oplinger family posed for this photograph. At an early age, Oplinger moved to different farms in Norton with his mother and father. He was a resident of Norton and made farming and dairying his main interests. From the age of 22 to 25, he also worked at the carpenter's trade. Oplinger served on the Norton School Board and married Isabella Houser on November 23, 1869. They had a total of 14 children: 10 boys and 4 girls. (Courtesy of *Centennial History of Summit County, Ohio and Representative Citizens.*)

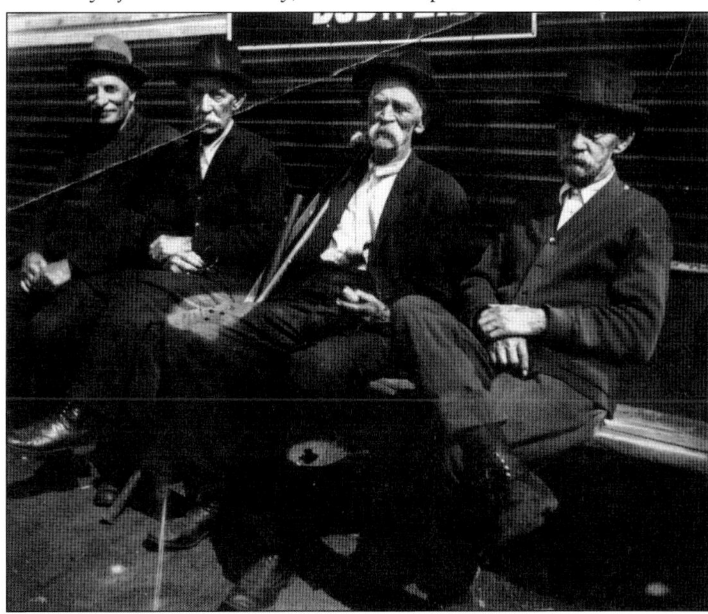

Four gentlemen are sitting outside of a business in Loyal Oak in this undated photograph. From left to right are Jake Bower, Al Knecht, Jake Werntz, and John Knecht. (Courtesy of Kaye Redhead.)

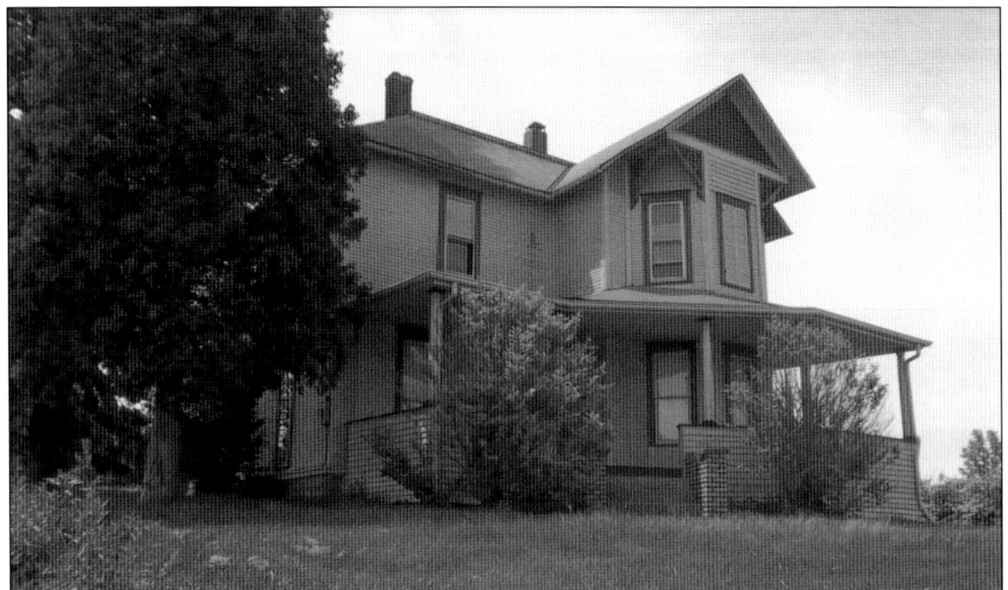

John and Mary Esch Boerstler came to Ohio in 1846 and had five children. They eventually bought land south of Loyal Oak in Norton Township and named their property Brentwood Farm. William Diehm and his wife, Cora Miller Diehm, bought Brentwood Farm from the Boerstlers in 1909. William also worked on the canal at that time. The farm was sold to the Stiles Development Company, which turned it into a residential community. The farmhouse still stands today on Cleveland-Massillon Road at the entrance of Brentwood Estates. (Author's collection.)

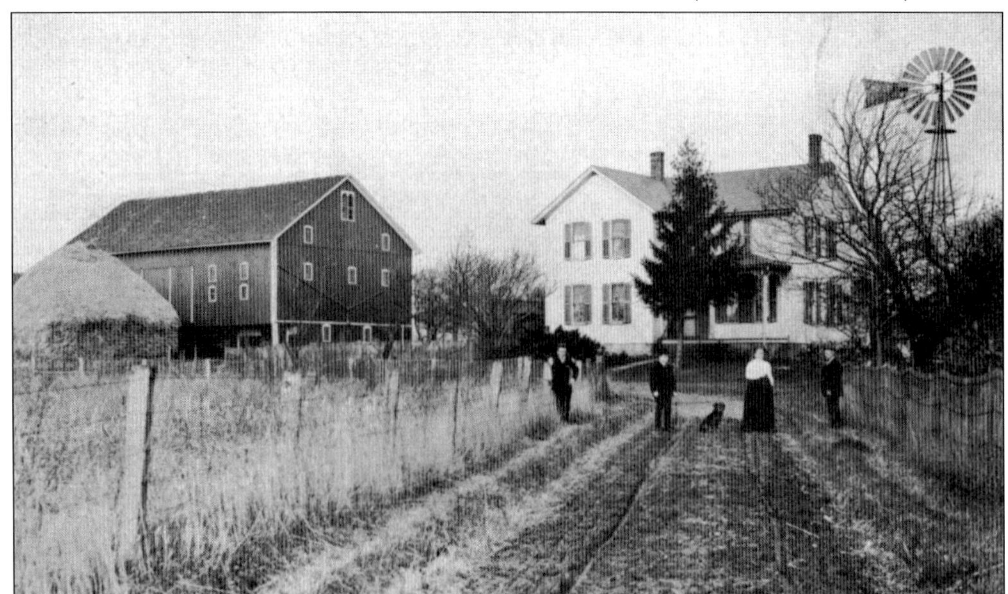

Reuben B. Baughman was a leading farmer of Norton Township who worked 99 acres of land one mile south and west of Johnson's Corners. Reuben was born in the hamlet of Hametown, Ohio, on July 12, 1850, and he learned the carpenter trade and became a well-known contractor, running a large wholesale lumber interest. He later acquired 308 acres of farmland and owned a store property at Hametown. In September 1898, Reuben died, leaving a widow, two sons, and three daughters.

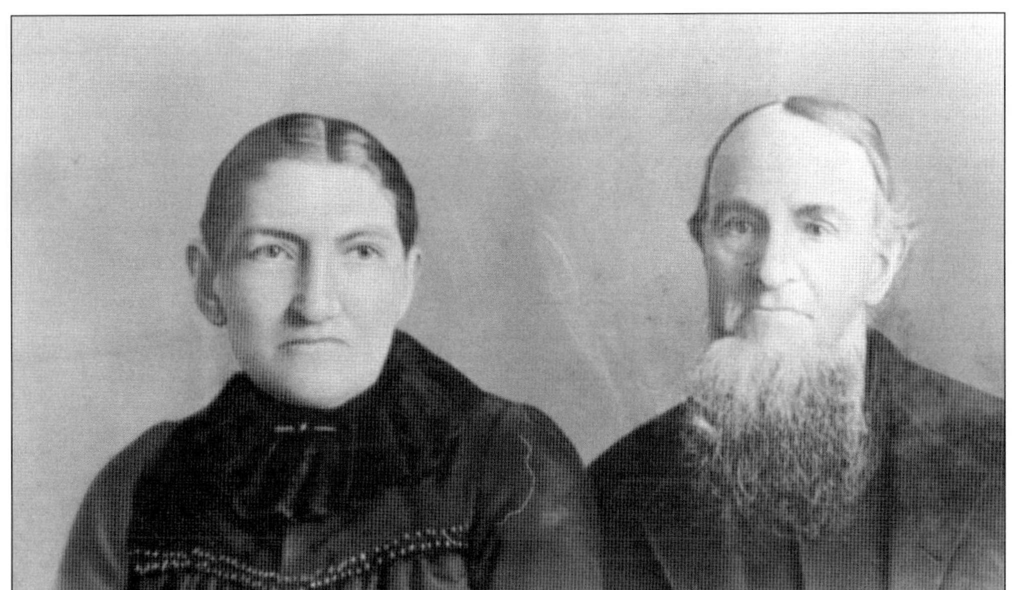

Augusta Young was born on July 30, 1840, to Rowena French Young and Thomas Young. Prior to meeting her husband, William George, she was an elementary school teacher. William was a farmer from Pennsylvania whose first wife had died, and around the time of the Civil War, he came to Ohio, where he met and married Augusta. They had a farm at 1085 Norton Avenue, on which they raised their six children. Augusta died in 1902, and William followed in 1904. (Courtesy of Betty Bodo.)

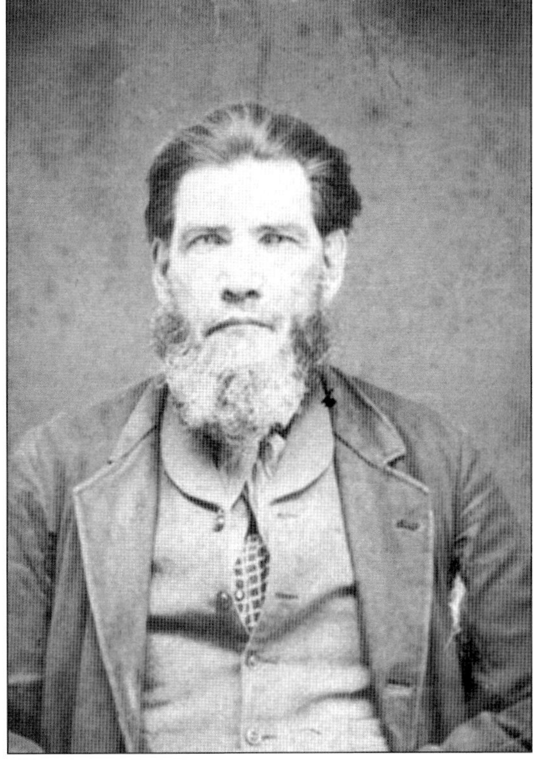

Thomas Gilman Young, a Civil War veteran, was a shoemaker, postmaster, and grocery store owner. In a letter, one of Young's daughters wrote, "Father is doing well selling whiskey and tobacco to the Irish. He sells if for $1.75 a gallon. These Irish are so afraid of him that they never make any of a disturbance there. He has got an old pistol and he makes them believe he would as soon shoot one of them as not."

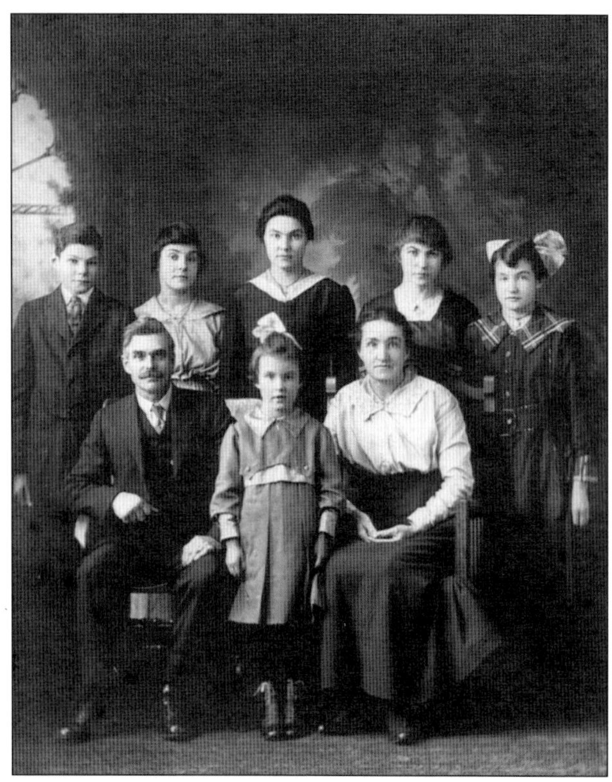

William and Elva Minnich are pictured here with their six children about 1916. From left to right are (first row) William, Pauline, and Elva; (second row) Harold, Aura, Ruth, Maude, and Lucille. William was said to be handsome and jovial and took his responsibilities as the head of a household seriously, often taking on additional jobs to provide for his family. Elva loved making pies and cookies and baking bread twice a week. She preserved fruit from the orchards, was an accomplished tailor, and sewed clothes for many people in her family. (Courtesy of Betty Bodo.)

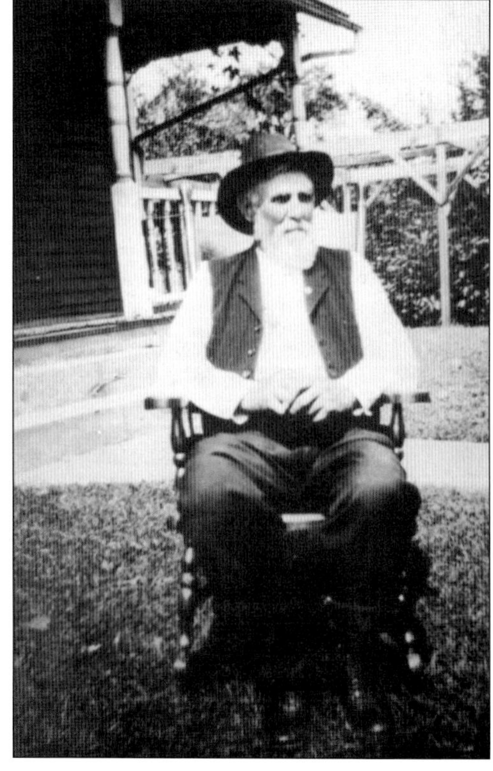

Joseph Minnich, who was born April 4, 1846, came from a German-speaking family that lived farther south in Ohio. He came to be the owner of a farm on Norton Avenue and married his first wife, Elizabeth Enfield, and had five children. Joseph served in the Civil War, and his second wife, Phoebe, received his pension. Joseph died in 1908, and he and Elizabeth are buried side by side in Loyal Oak Cemetery. (Courtesy of Betty Bodo.)

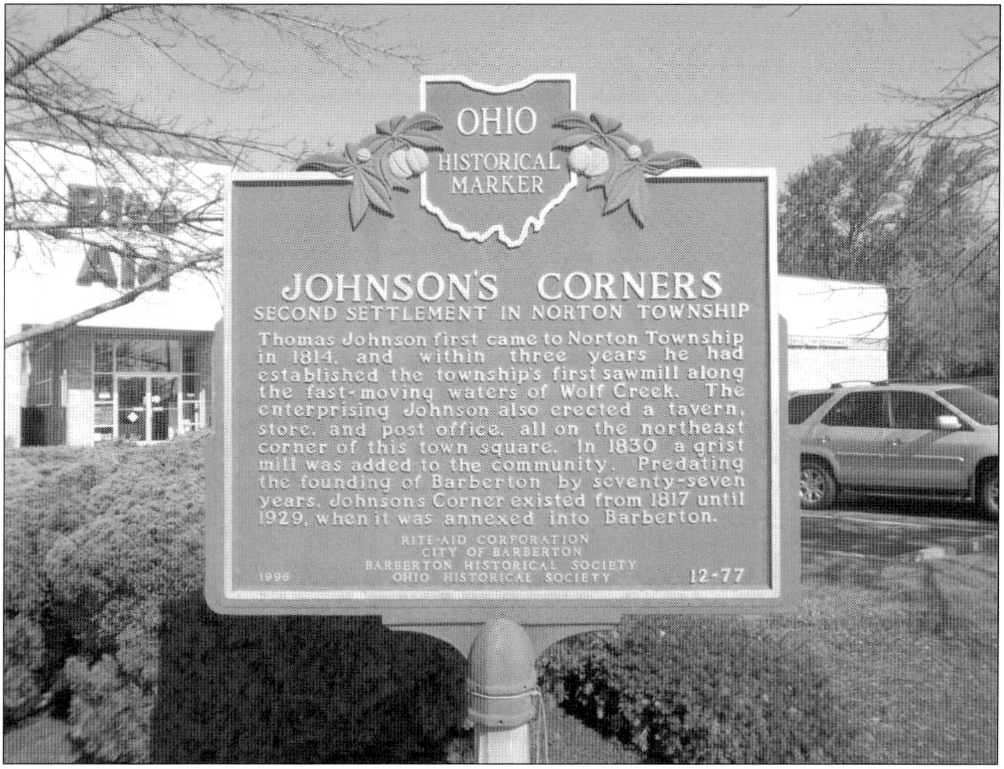

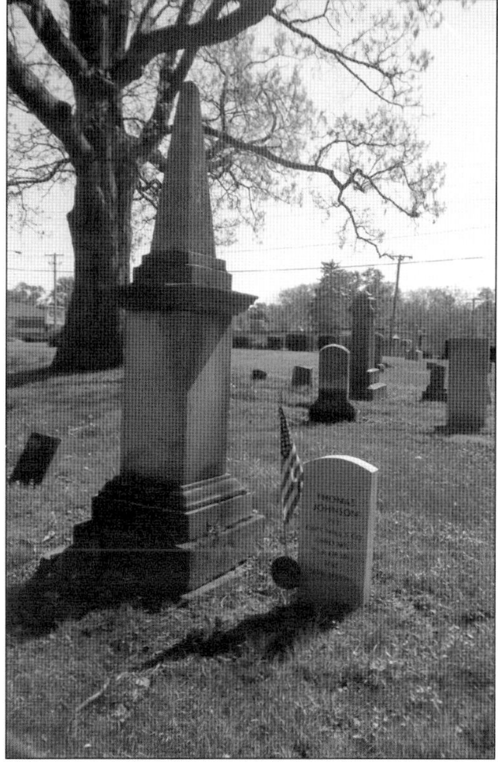

Thomas Johnson, a native of Ireland, came to America in 1797, and he was said to have been involved with counterfeiters in the Cuyahoga Valley. Johnson's Corners became the hangout for the gathering of the brotherhood headed by Jim Brown and his brother Dan. Ultimately, the shady practice caught up with Johnson, and in the fall of 1833, he got himself into financial trouble in Portage County and was bound over to the court. After remaining in hiding, Charles Miller, a prominent citizen, came forward and talked Johnson into releasing valuable information about the brotherhood to the authorities in exchange for dropping the charges against him. Johnson, despite his association with the counterfeiters, had a reputation of the strictest integrity in all of his dealings. He led a strictly upright life until his death in 1836, was married to Elizabeth Johnson, and also fought in the War of 1812. Thomas has a large monument at his grave in Norton Center Cemetery, along with a newer 1812 marker recently installed. (Both, author's collection.)

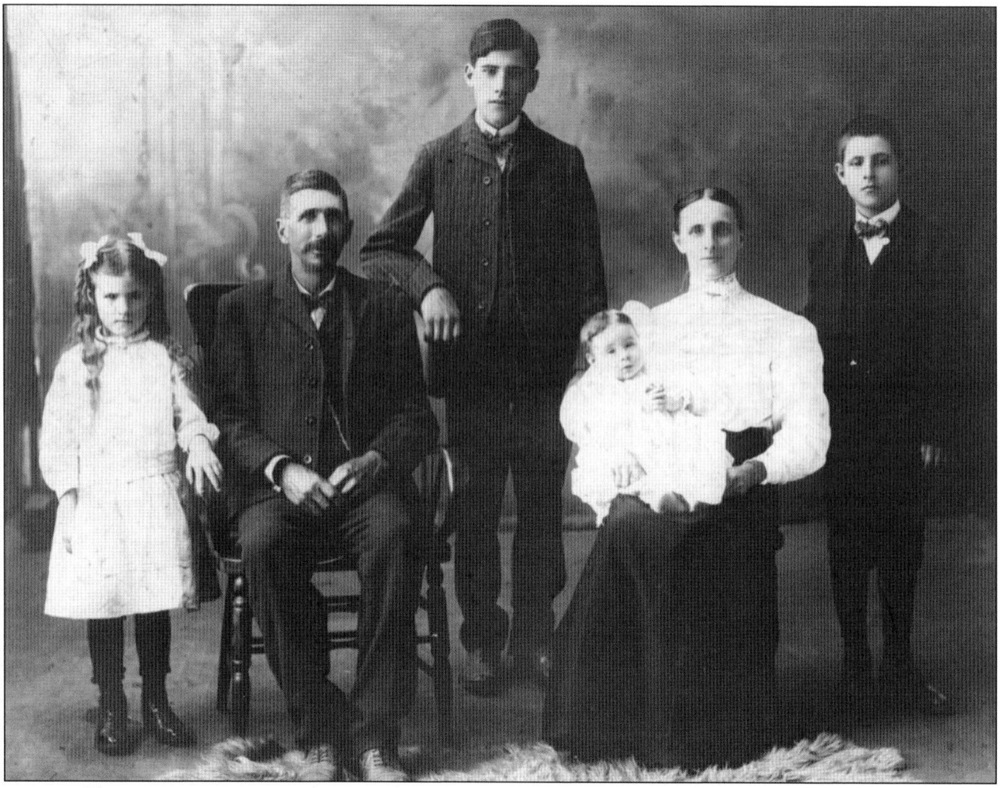

Pictured here in 1907 are members of the Waltenberger family; from left to right are Letha, Frank, Charles, baby Esther, Mary (Harter), and Clarence. The family resided in a beautiful Victorian farmhouse at 3973 Akron-Wadsworth Road, and their farm consisted of 160 acres, on which they raised beef cattle, hogs, chickens, wheat, oats, and corn. They also had an extensive apple orchard. From the historical record, there was a circle of trees on the property that Frank never cultivated, as it was apparent it was an Indian burial ground. Large mounds were quite visible Almost every summer, a band of gypsies would camp at the crossroads below the house, and Frank usually gave them hay and oats. The farmhouse was destroyed by fire in the mid-1980s. The Seabeck family, living there at the time, lost everything, but they rebuilt a brick home on the same site.

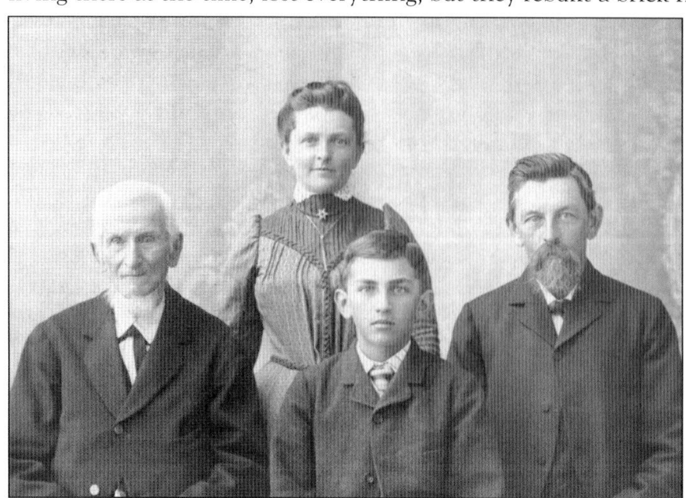

The Wertman homestead was located at 3459 Cleveland-Massillon Road, and today, the home is occupied today by Tom Dayton of Dayton Nurseries. From left to right are Joseff, Melissa, Fred, and John Wertman.

Two

Reading, Writing, Arithmetic, and Places of Worship

Norton Township's earliest schools were one-room buildings. The 10 original schoolhouses were Skunks Misery, Hametown, Snyders Corners, Seiberling, Bartges, Canada, Western Star, Sherman, Loyal Oak, and Johnson's Corners. Children were not to walk more than two miles to attend school because Norton was founded as a farming community, and children were needed for work at home.

First through eighth graders attended the schoolhouse at the corner of Hametown and Akron-Wadsworth Roads. Inside, benches lined each wall of the space, and there were three rows of desks. A teacher's desk was upon a raised platform in the front, and a pot-bellied stove sat in the center of the room. During a student holiday program in the mid-1920s, the classroom's kerosene lights failed, and Model T automobiles had to shine headlights into the windows so that the evening's production could continue.

The first public high school was erected at Norton Center and served the community from 1839 to 1869. In 1915, a brick structure was erected, and the two schools stood side by side until the first school was torn down. In 1928, a brick four-room building was erected in Loyal Oak, and a six-room structure was built at Sherman for the purpose of eliminating the one-room schools.

Norton's churches include Baptists, Methodists, Orthodox, Nazarene, Lutheran, Catholic, Charismatic, Full Gospel, Restorationist, Assemblies of God, Apostolic, Mennonite, Church of Christ, Brethren, the United Church of Christ, and at one time, a Mormon congregation. Religious worship in Loyal Oak was inaugurated four times by various religious bodies between 1816 and in 1845, when a Lutheran and Reformed Society was organized. A Methodist society was succeeded by a Baptist group, then followed by the Disciples who built a house of worship on the northeast corner of Loyal Oak. This group disbanded, and the Congregational church moved in; however, the congregation vacated the property after a few years.

In 1847, a church called Union Church, as it was shared by both the Lutheran and Reformed, was built in Loyal Oak. In 1885, the decision was made to dissolve and establish separate churches. The stone church was torn down, and a new church was built, which still stands today, known as the Trinity Lutheran Church. The Reformed were offered land to build, and their church was erected and dedicated in 1886. In 1878, the United Brethren erected a church in Western Star on land deeded by Nathan Starr. Several Methodist congregations also came together in New Portage and Johnson's Corners in the mid-19th century.

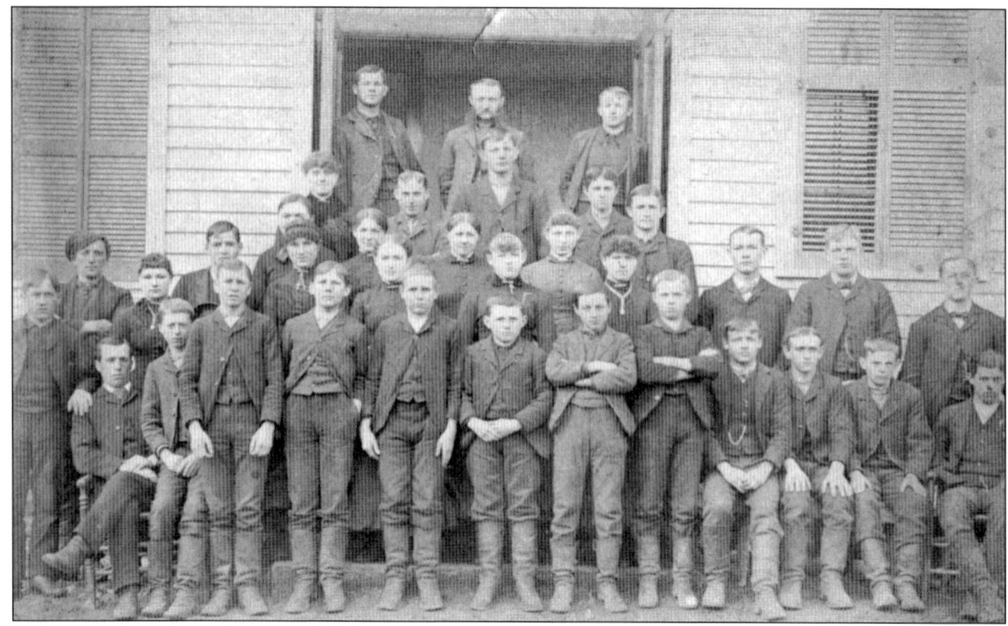

In 1885, the students of Norton High School pose in front of the white wooden schoolhouse on Greenwich and Cleveland-Massillon Roads. The original wooden Norton High School was erected at Norton's geographical center in 1892, pictured below in 1904. The first class of three females graduated in 1895, and they all became teachers.

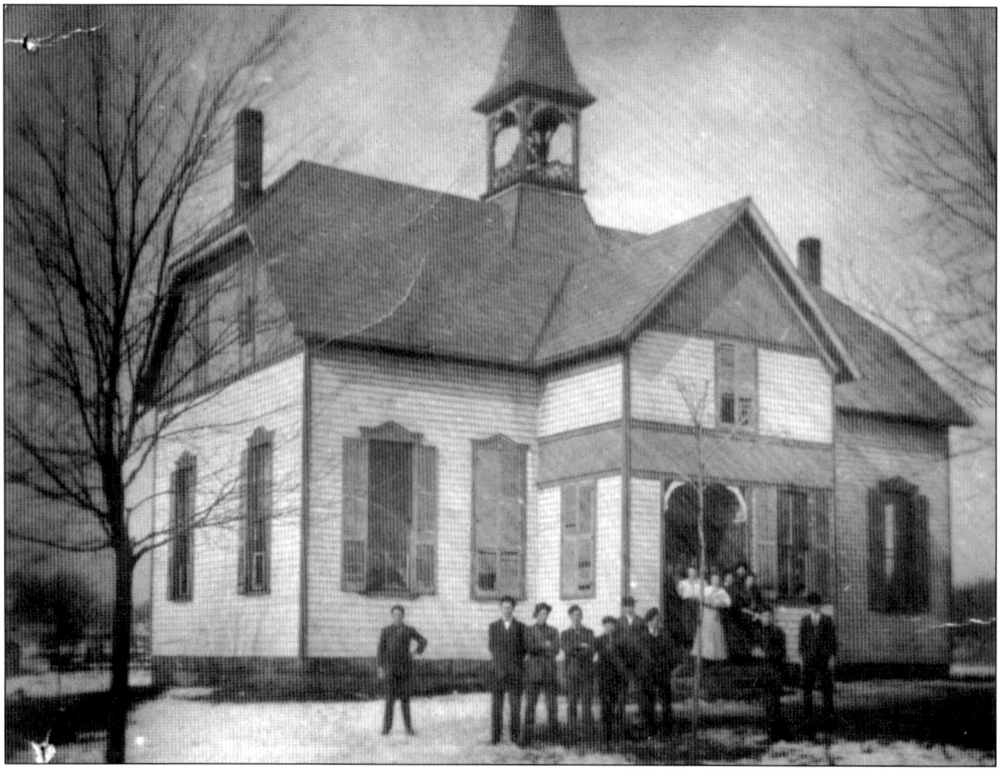

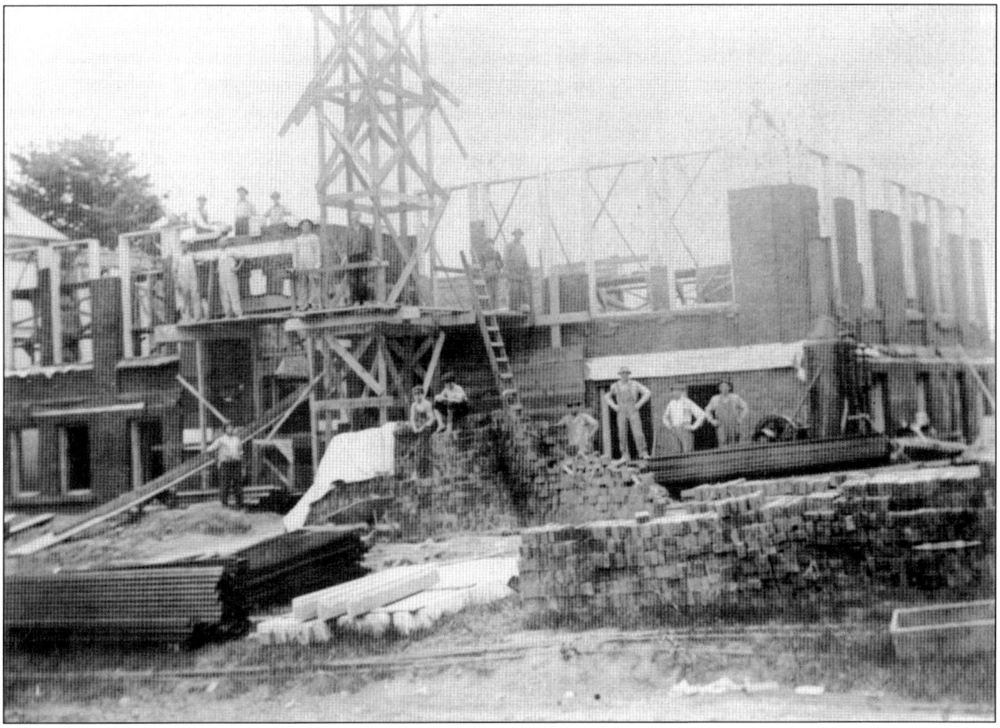

In 1912–1915, a brick structure was erected next to the wooden school and held as many as 500 students in four classrooms used for the high school and two elementary grades. For a time, both schools stood side by side until the brick school was completed. Above, workers pose for one of the only known images during the building of this structure. Two young boys are seen playing on the mound of bricks in the center. The wooden structure was demolished, and the materials were repurposed into a home now occupied by the Miller family at 1096 Norton Avenue. An addition was added to the brick school in 1936, pictured below around 1938. Currently, it is known as the Cornerstone School and slated to be demolished for the widening of Cleveland-Massillon Road.

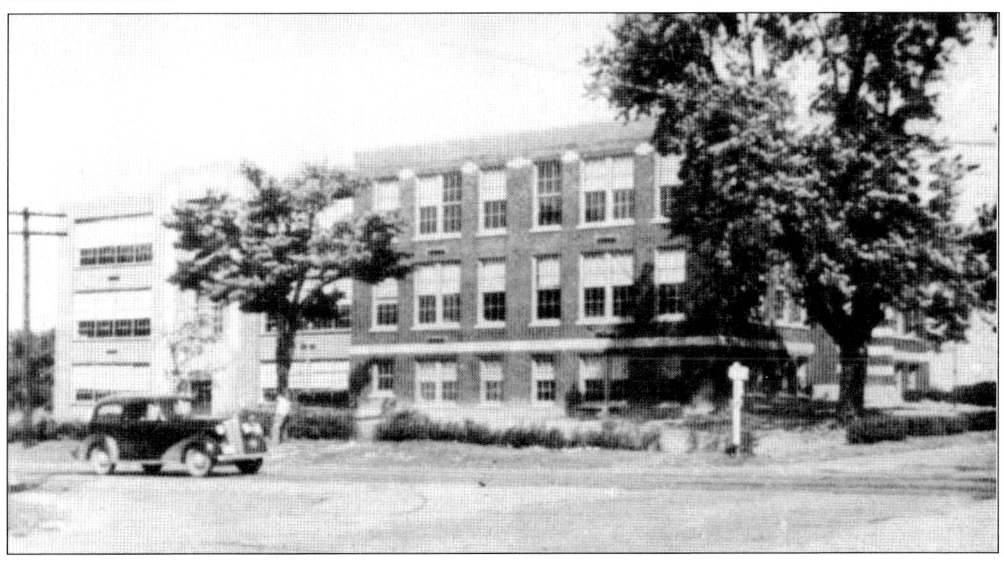

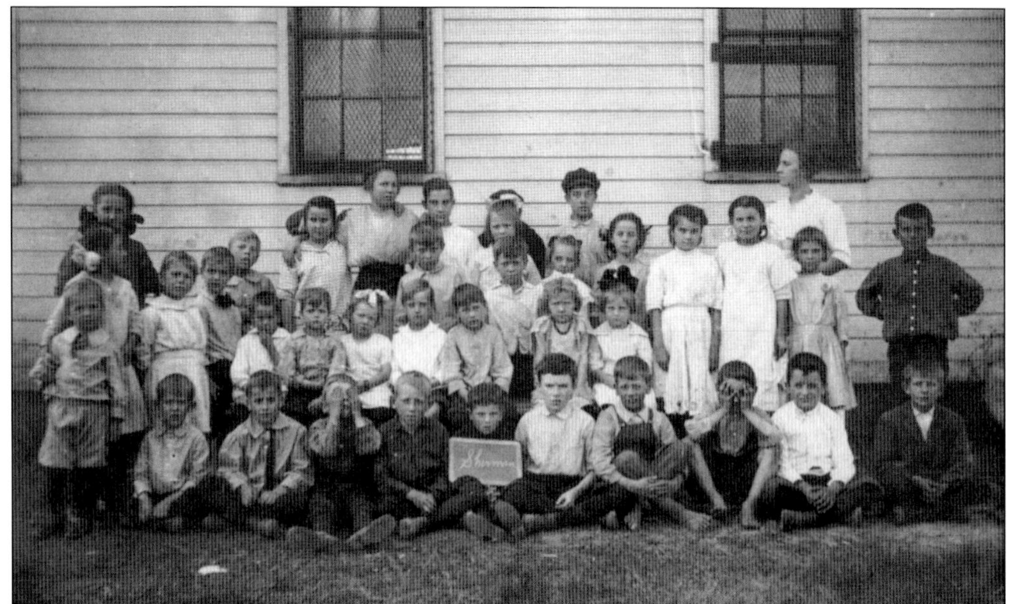

This undated photograph was taken at the one-room schoolhouse in the hamlet of Sherman. Seated in front are two boys who both decided to hide their faces.

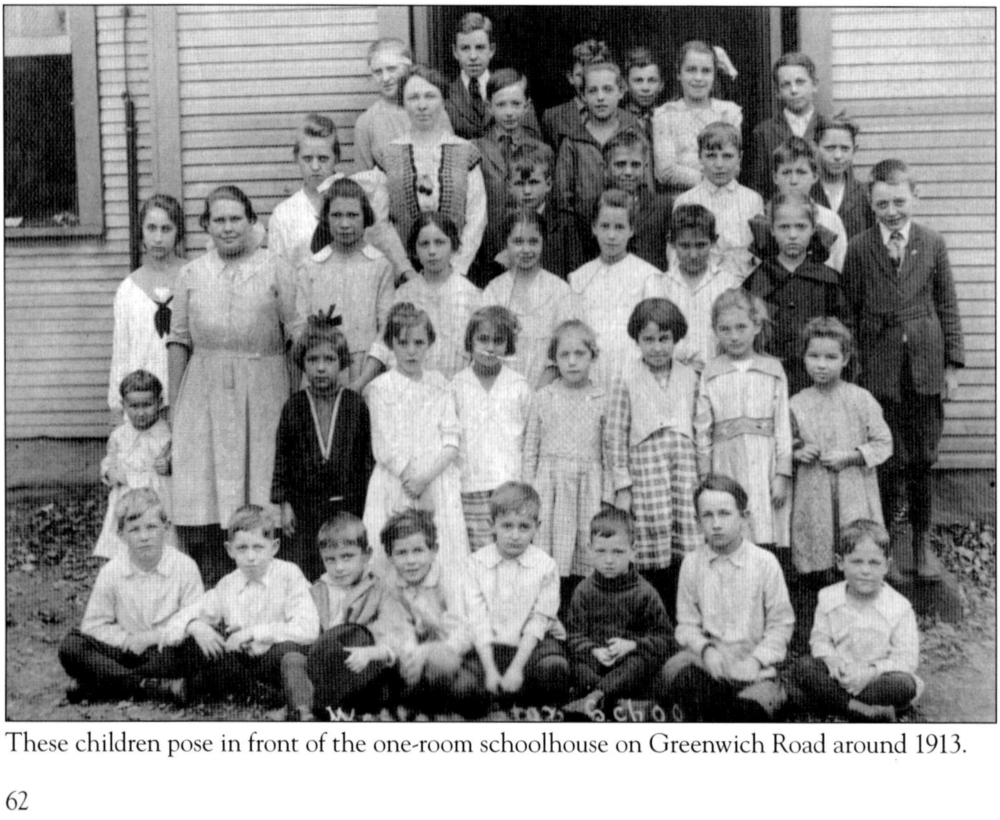

These children pose in front of the one-room schoolhouse on Greenwich Road around 1913.

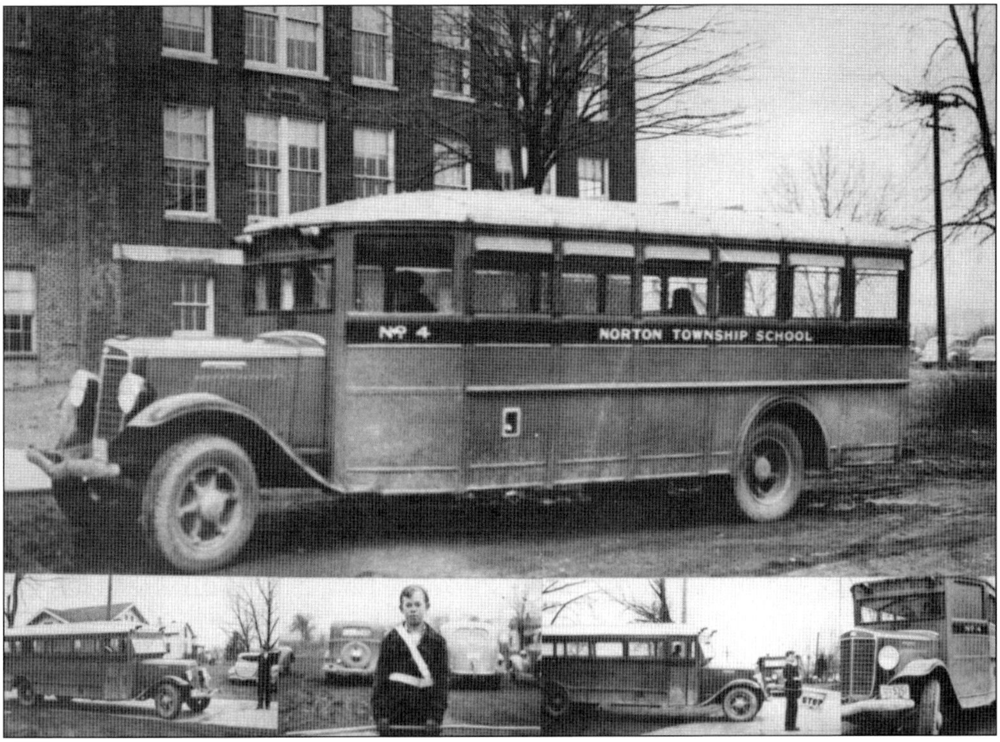

It was not until 1933 that children began to be transported to local schools in Norton. Harry Mong drove a blue school bus equipped with side seats running the length of the bus, and the first yellow bus was driven by John Riley "Pop" Snader. Today, there are 22 bus stalls, a repair area, storage, and administration offices all housed in an expanded garage building. Norton maintains a fleet of 32 buses with 44 drivers and aides, two mechanics, and a helper; approximately 1,900 of 2,500 total students are transported daily.

The school paper was the best medium for acquainting the public with the activities and interests of the high school. The first issue of the *Torch* appeared at Norton High School on March 4, 1926. It had instant appeal to the student body as a means of expression and a chance to try out their talents in journalism. The *Torch* was printed on a mimeograph machine and included news articles, editorials, original stories, jokes, advertising, and cartoons. The *Nohiscan* was the first yearbook, created in 1928. The word "Nohiscan" is comprised of the first two letters of the words "Norton High School annual." The name was dropped after the 1930s.

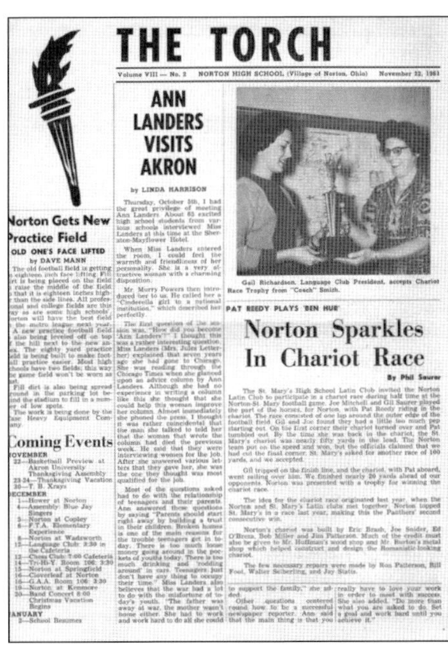

THE TORCH

Volume VIII — No. 2 NORTON HIGH SCHOOL (Village of Norton, Ohio) November 22, 1961

Norton Gets New Practice Field

OLD ONE'S FACE LIFTED

by DAVE MANN

The old football field is getting an eighteen inch face lifting. Fill dirt is being placed on the field to raise the middle of the field so that it is eighteen inches higher than the side lines. All professional and college fields are this way as are some high schools. Norton will have the best field in the metro league next year.

A new practice football field is also being leveled off on top of the hill next to the new annex. The eighty yard practice field is being built to make football practice easier. Most high schools have two fields; this way the game field won't be worn as fast.

Fill dirt is also being spread around in the parking lot behind the stadium to fill in a number of low spots.

The work is being done by the Case Heavy Equipment Company.

Coming Events

NOVEMBER
22—Basketball Preview at Akron University
Thanksgiving Assembly
23-24—Thanksgiving Vacation
30—T. B. Xrays

DECEMBER
1—Hower at Norton
4—Assembly: Blue Jay Singers
5—Norton at Copley
6—F.T.A. Elementary Experience
8—Norton at Wadsworth
12—Language Club: 3:30 in the Cafeteria
12—Chess Club: 7:00 Cafeteria
14—Tri-Hi-Y. Room 106: 3:30
15—Norton at Springfield
16—Cloverleaf at Norton
18—G.A.A. Room 106: 3:30
19—Norton at Kenmore
20—Band Concert 8:00
Christmas Vacation Begins

JANUARY
2—School Resumes

ANN LANDERS VISITS AKRON

by LINDA HARRISON

Thursday, October 5th, I had the great privilege of meeting Ann Landers. About 65 excited high school students from various schools interviewed Miss Landers at this time at the Sheraton-Mayflower Hotel.

When Miss Landers entered the room, I could feel the warmth and friendliness of her personality. She is a very attractive woman with a charming disposition.

Mr. Murry Powers then introduced her to us. He called her a "Cinderella girl to a national institution," which described her perfectly.

The first question of the session was, "How did you become 'Ann Landers'?" I thought this was a rather interesting question. Miss Landers (Mrs. Jules Letterher) explained that seven years ago she had gone to Chicago. She was reading through the Chicago Times when she glanced upon an advice column by Ann Landers. Although she had no experience in writing a column like this she thought that she could help this woman improve her column. Almost immediately she phoned the press. I thought it was rather coincidental that the man she talked to told her that the woman that wrote the column had died the previous week. He said that they were interviewing women for the job. After she answered various letters that they gave her, she was the one they thought was most qualified for the job.

Most of the questions asked had to do with the relationship of teenagers and their parents. Ann answered these questions by saying "Parents should start right away by building a trust in their children. Broken homes is one of the main reasons for the trouble teenagers get in today. There is too much loose money going around in the pockets of youths today. There is too much drinking and 'rodding around' in cars. Teenagers just don't have any thing to occupy their time." Miss Landers also believes that the war had a lot to do with the misfortune of today's youth. "The father was away at war, the mother wasn't home either. She had to work and work hard to do all she could to support the family," she added.

Other questions centered round how to be a successful newspaper reporter. Ann said that the main thing is that you really have to love your work in order to meet with success. She also added, "Do more than what you are asked to do. Set a goal and work hard until you achieve it."

Gail Richardson, Language Club President, accepts Chariot Race Trophy from "Coach" Smith.

PAT REEDY PLAYS 'BEN HUR'

Norton Sparkles In Chariot Race

By Phil Saurer

The St. Mary's High School Latin Club invited the Norton Latin Club to participate in a chariot race during half time at the Norton-St. Mary football game. Joe Mitchell and Gil Saurer played the part of the horses, for Norton, with Pat Reedy riding in the chariot. The race consisted of one lap around the outer edge of the football field. Gil and Joe found they had a little too much pep starting out. On the first corner their chariot turned over and Pat tumbled out. By the time she was back in the chariot, the St. Mary's chariot was nearly fifty yards in the lead. The Norton team put on the speed and won, but the officials claimed that we had cut the final corner. St. Mary's asked for another race of 100 yards, and we accepted.

Gil tripped on the finish line, and the chariot, with Pat aboard, went sailing over him. We finished nearly 20 yards ahead of our opponents. Norton was presented with a trophy for winning the chariot race.

The idea for the chariot race originated last year, when the Norton and St. Mary's Latin clubs met together. Norton topped St. Mary's in a race last year, making this the Panthers' second consecutive win.

Norton's chariot was built by Eric Brash, Joe Snider, Ed O'Brien, Bob Miller and Jim Patterson. Much of the credit must also be given to Mr. Huffman's wood shop and Mr. Burton's metal shop which helped construct and design the Romanistic-looking chariot.

The few necessary repairs were made by Ron Patterson, Bill Foot, Walter Seiberling, and Jay Statis.

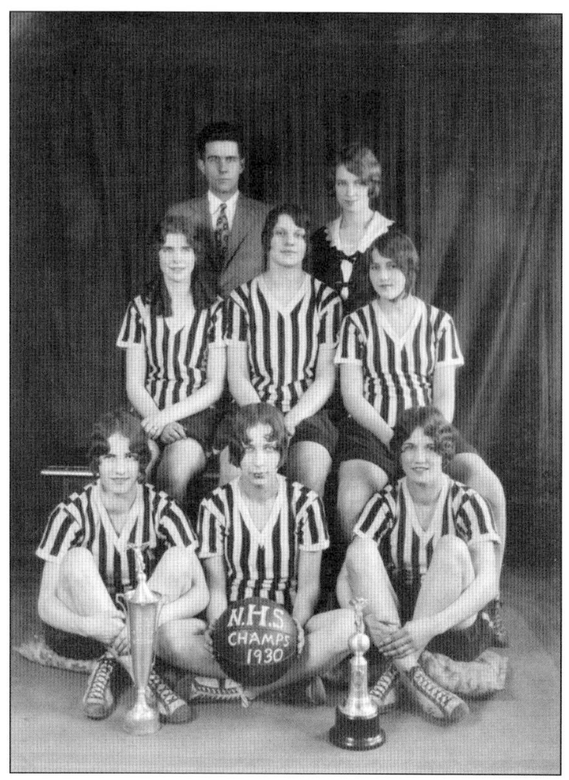

The championship girls' basketball team at Norton High School is shown here during their 1930–1931 season. Lead by coach J.F. Moore and Lucille Shatzer, the girls played not only for sport, but also for the honor and glory they could bring to their school. They went through a successful season to the highest goal attainable by participating in tournaments and county league championships, winning 25 consecutive games with a total of 463 points to their opponents' 208. At the time, Norton had no gym of its own and had to rely on the YMCA in Barberton for all practices and games.

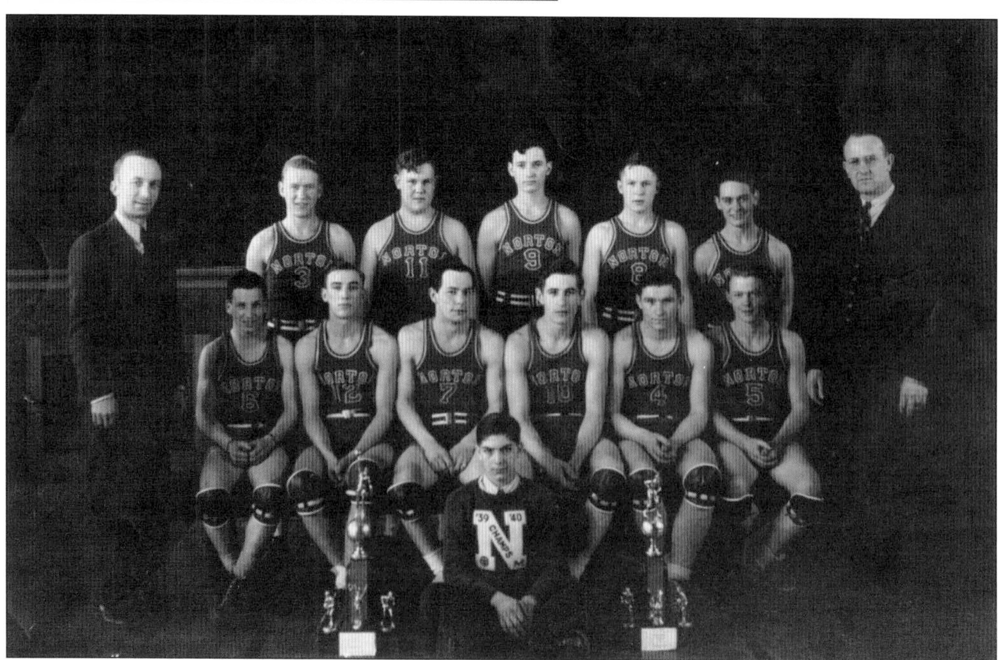

These are the 1939–1940 champion boys' basketball players. From left to right are (first row) Wesley Terrion; (second row) Bob Fritz, Bill Lepley, Jack Crow, George Borsos, Ben Rojniak, and Forest Rodabaugh; (third row) coach Harlin Fry, Dick Dockery, Dick Romig, Tony Mihelic, Bob Ramsthaler, Burril Larimore, and assistant coach H.J. Williamson.

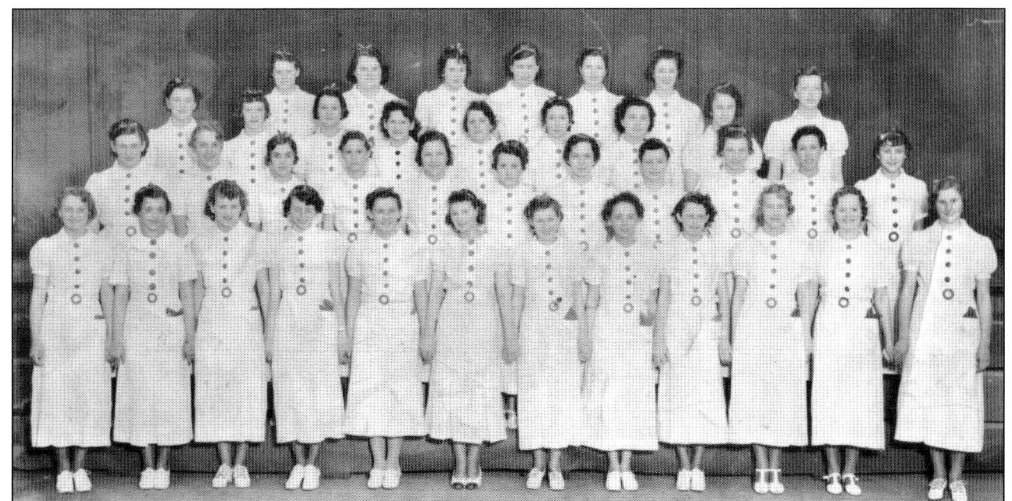

The Norton Girls Glee Club is pictured here in 1935. They sponsored musical comedies, took part in music festivals, and sent delegations to the state chorus in Columbus. From left to right are (first row) Beatrice Thompson, Sara Haupt, Blanche Grant, Jean Pressler, Martha Swain, Tresa Yurkoshek, Marie Swinehart, Lauretta Warner, Camilla Pressler, Eileen Harter, Beverly Larimore, and Donna Zeizig; (second row) Elsie Werner, Margaret Mong, Pearl Harris, June Steiner, Mae Breitenstine, Lois Bauer, Jennie Gerberich, Evelyn Roy, Evelyn Dunak, Jean Wells, and Fern Heller; (third row) Florence Watkins, Betty Jane Clapper, Ada Shaw, Alyce Basler, Mildred Neitz, Arlene Coulter, Eleanor Cunningham, and Mary Porter; (fourth row) Maxine Seiberling, Mardell Hefflefinger, Helen Ferguson, Cecilia Ondrik, Joan ?, and Evelyn ?.

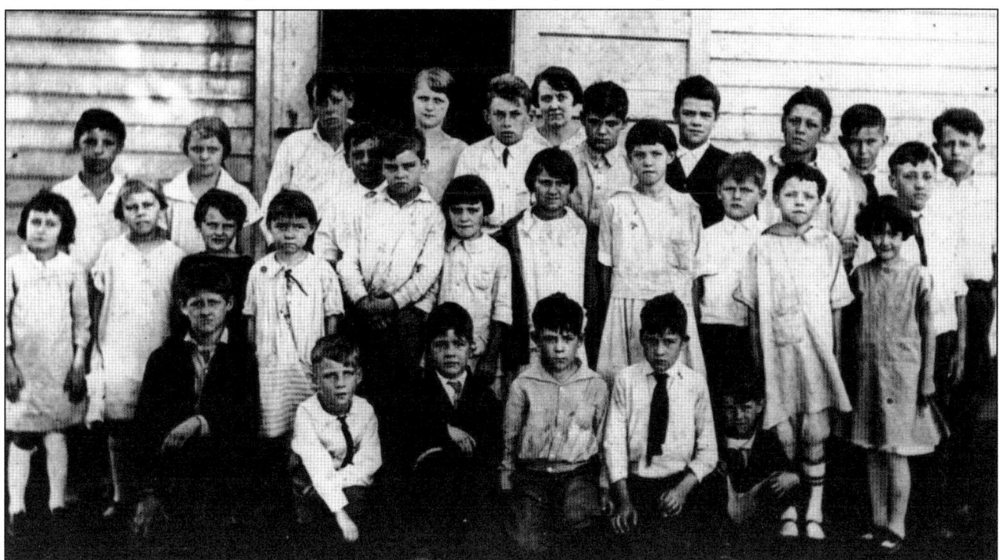

Pictured here in 1926–1927, at the one-room schoolhouse at the crossroads of Hometown and Akron-Wadsworth Roads, are, from left to right, (first row) unidentified, Earl McFarren, Wilfred Steiner, Fred Mitchell, Bernard Steiner, and Myron Kauffman; (second row) Marie Swinehart, Evelyn Grosjean, Ruth Jolly, Dorothy Scanlon, Armer Campbell, Freda Campbell, Irma Snyder, Ruth Scanlon, Gaylord Frase, Mildred Scanlon, and Gladys Flickinger; (third row) Helen Scanlon, Marian Miller, Richard Snyder, Max Buehler, and Norman Snyder; (fourth row) Dorathea Miller, Mrs. Miller (teacher), two unidentified students, Gerald McFadden, and Richard Grosjean.

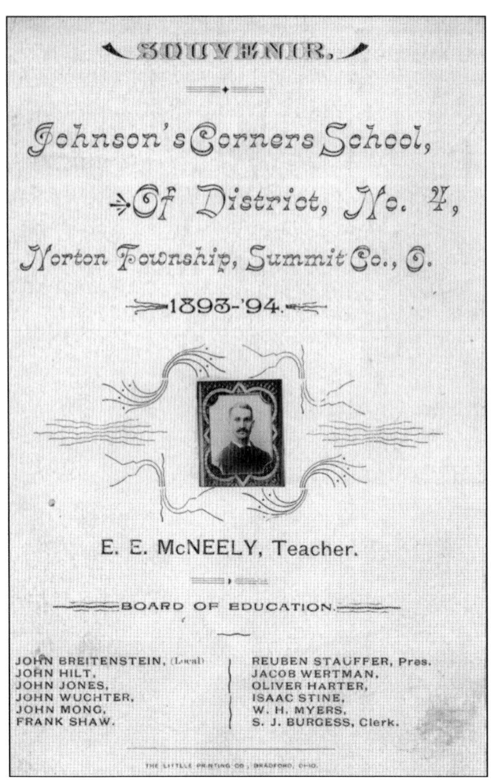

SOUVENIR.

Johnson's Corners School,

Of District, No. 4,

Norton Township, Summit Co., O.

1893-'94.

E. E. McNEELY, Teacher.

BOARD OF EDUCATION.

JOHN BREITENSTEIN, (Local)	REUBEN STAUFFER, Pres.
JOHN HILT,	JACOB WERTMAN,
JOHN JONES,	OLIVER HARTER,
JOHN WUCHTER,	ISAAC STINE,
JOHN MONG,	W. H. MYERS,
FRANK SHAW.	S. J. BURGESS, Clerk.

THE LITTLE PRINTING CO., BRADFORD, OHIO.

Before students attended larger schools in the area, they attended one of about 12 one-room schoolhouses scattered throughout Norton. Johnson's Corners School was the first one-room schoolhouse in Norton Township. This souvenir card shows teacher E.E. McNeely and lists his students. The boys were, Elmer, Wallace, Howard, Charles, Eddie, and Clarence Boden; Milton and Newton Breitenstine; John and Eddie Butzer; Earnest and Elvin Harter; George Hout; Clever, and Jessie Lantz; Roy and Leonard Marshall; William Miller; and Ira, George, Eddie, Robert, and Jonnie Whitehead. The girls listed were Mattie Breitenstine, Mary Butzer, Maudie Cranford, Alma and Effie Harter, Maggie Hout, Myrtle Lantz, and Nellie Marshall.

WESTERN STAR ACADEMY.

Report of [illegible] Scholarship

For the Month Ending [illegible], 1884.

Number times tardy	3	Political Geography		Algebra		Written examinations	5
Number min's tardy	20	Physical Geography	96	Composition		Average scholarship	2
Number days pres't	26	Mental Arithmetic	80	Declamation	85	Punctuality	85
Reading	83	Practical Arithmetic	70	Book Keeping		Attendance	
Spelling	80	Grammar		Writing	80	No. pupils in school	42
Defining	90	History		Deportment	75		
		Language	75			General Average	$1 4/10

Explanation of Marks —100 denotes a perfect examination; others are proportional. 60 is the lowest standard allowed for advancement. Parents will please examine and sign this report.

Parent's Name, Levi Nash

H. C. MILLER, TEACHER

A one-room schoolhouse on the south side of Greenwich Road in Western Star was used for grades one through eight. Next to the school was a church called United Brethren and an academy. All three buildings are still standing today and used as housing. The 1884 report card shown here was from the Western Star Academy for a student with the last name of Nash and signed by parent Levi Nash.

Custodians of the Norton High School are shown here in the boiler room in 1948. Formerly called janitors, Howard Scheck and Cecil McEndrie were in charge of cleaning, stocking, mopping, sweeping, polishing floors, locking and unlocking the school, picking up litter, and setting up rooms. They were also in charge of keeping the coal-fired burner working to heat the school.

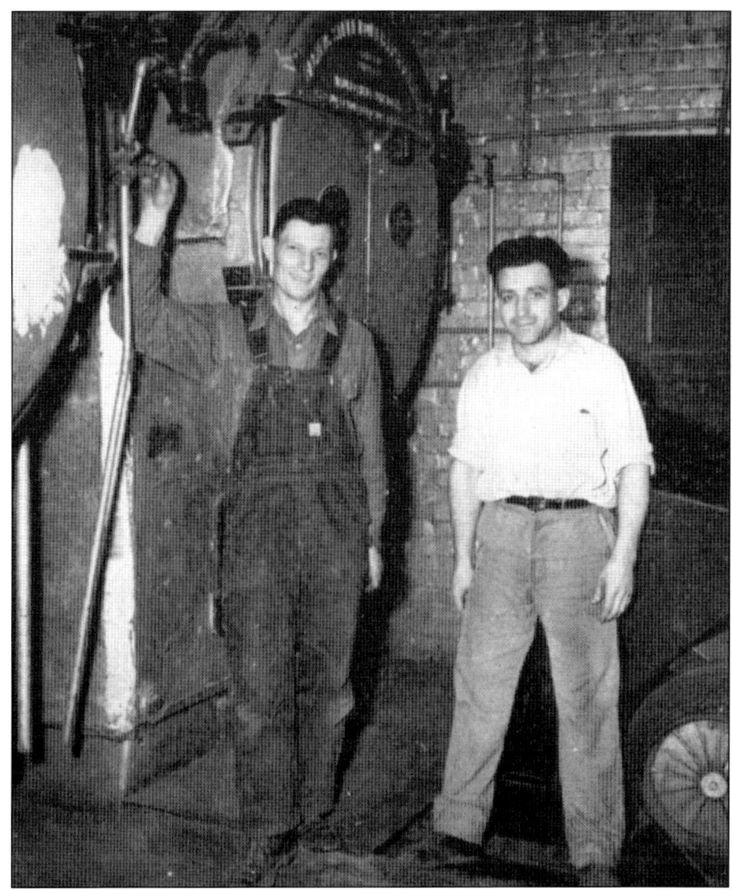

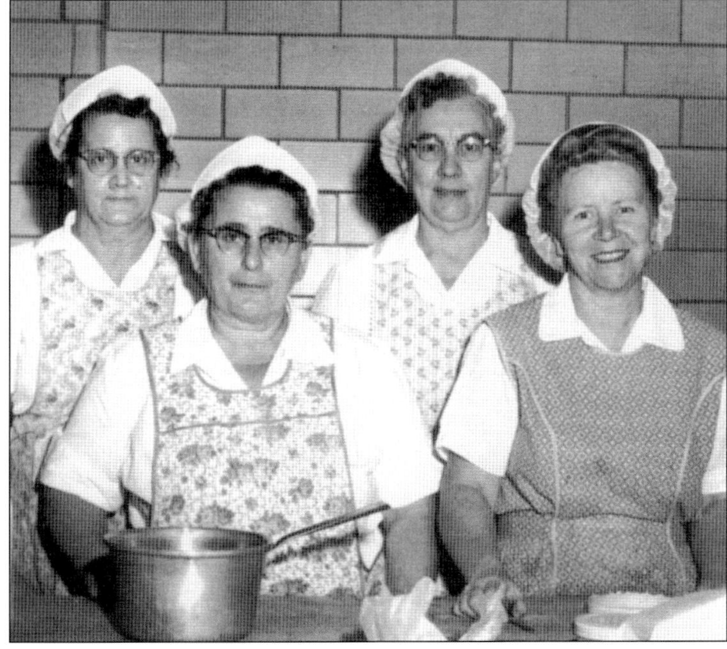

The Norton High School cooks pictured here in 1963 are, from left to right, Mrs. Roberts, Mary Danko, Hilda Butler, and Nancy McCommons.

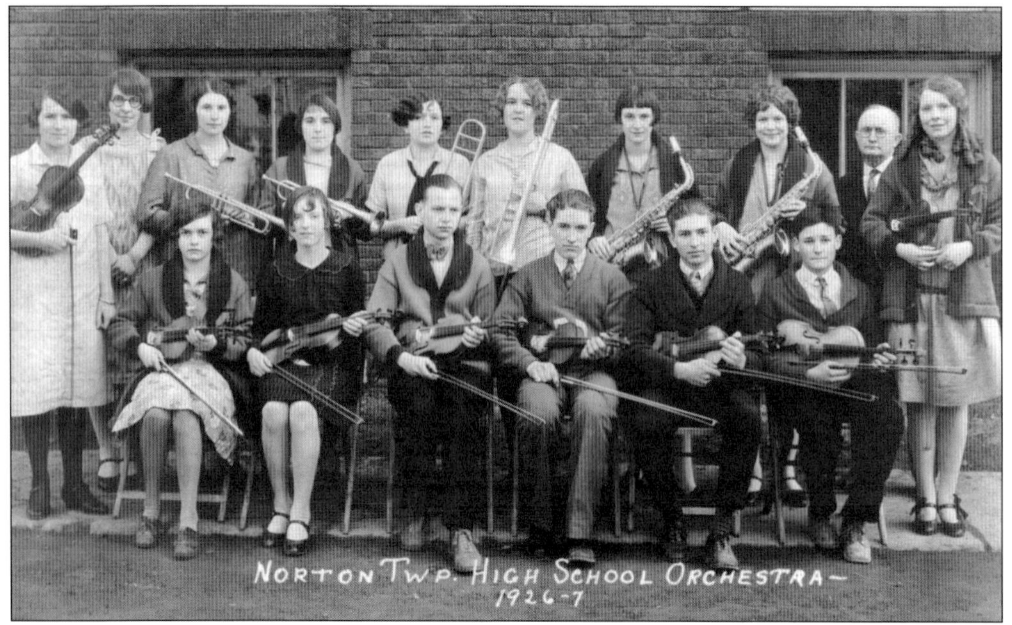

Norton's orchestra was held in high esteem in the county for years, due to the untiring efforts of Mr. Evans, who was under the direction of Mr. Boden. They entertained the teachers at the Music Institute, performed for the Copley Farmer's Institute, and later played for the Richfield Alumni Banquet. The orchestra also played for spring music festivals. The orchestra also played for spring music festivals and surrounding communities.

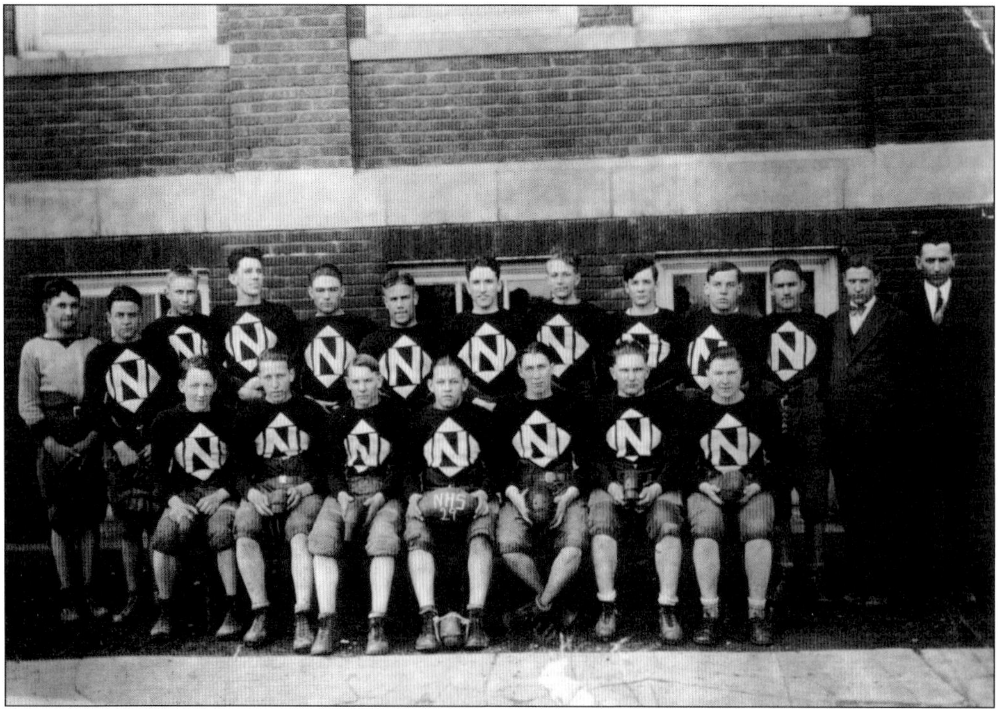

The football team of 1929 was undefeated. They played against Springfield, Peninsula, Twinsburg, Coventry, Tallmadge, Mogadore, and Greensburg.

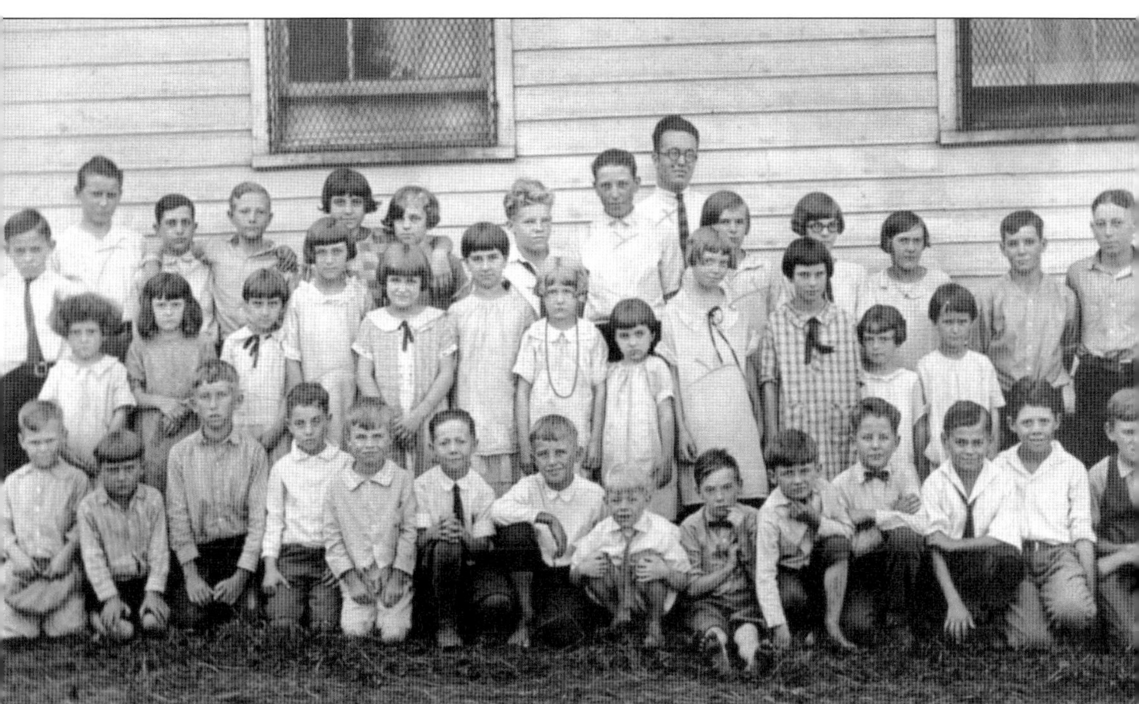

The only intact one-room schoolhouse in the area can be found in Loyal Oak. The building was home to many businesses over the years, including a doctor's office run by Dr. Bugay. The building also housed Toland Dolls and was most recently a motorcycle shop. The building stands vacant, and discussion has been circulating about restoring it to its original state. Included in this photograph taken in 1927 are, from left to right, (first row) Glen Blackburn, Mike Ellebrook, Norman Ellebrook, Kenneth Harris, Howard Stump, Marion Blackburn, Martin Ellebrook, Eugene Clapper, Paul White, Caroll Funk, Eugene Hardesty, Richard Clapper, Frank Young, and Andy Ellebrook; (second row) Bauer, Eva Pinter, Mildred Harris, Charlene Bowers, Fern Young, Eileen Harter, Pearl Harris, Louise Young, Margaret Stump, Jean Pressler, and Cora Young; (third row) Harry Clapper, John Pinter, Herbert Victor, Wayne Harter, teacher Mr. Hunt, Elsie Victor, Dorothy Wheeler, Glenn Clapper, Warren Nice, Harriet Bowers, Lillian Harris, Erma Bauer, George Smith, and Roy Snyder.

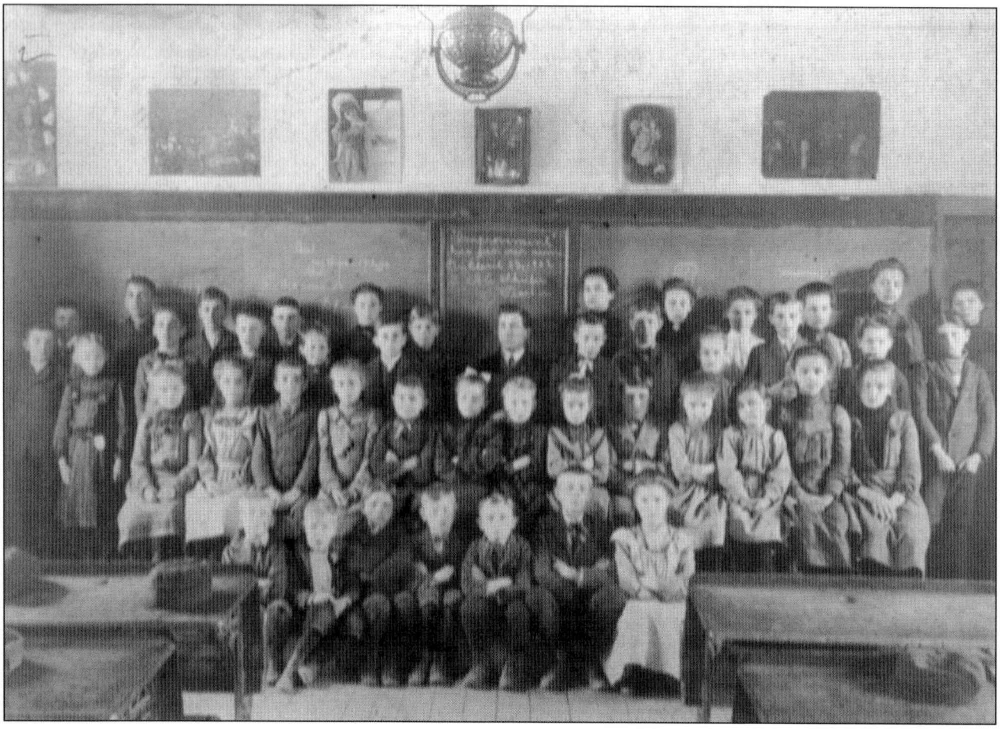

Most of the photographs of children in one-room schoolhouses were taken outside of the school or in other locations. This image is one of the only known looks inside the Loyal Oak one-room schoolhouse. The phrase "Improvement has been our aim" can be seen on the center of the chalkboard in this image from April 23, 1903. B.A. Shriber was the teacher at the time.

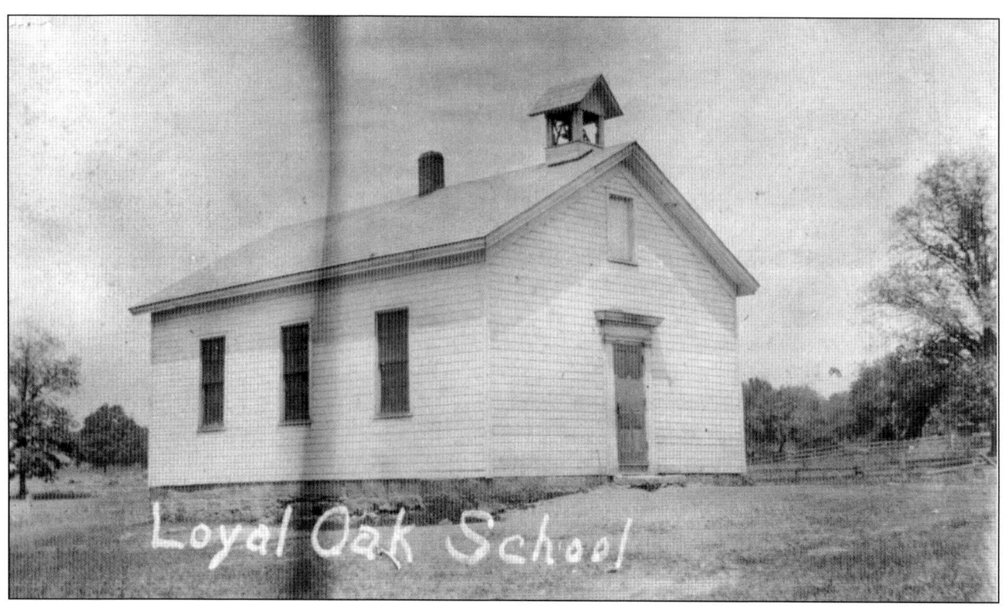

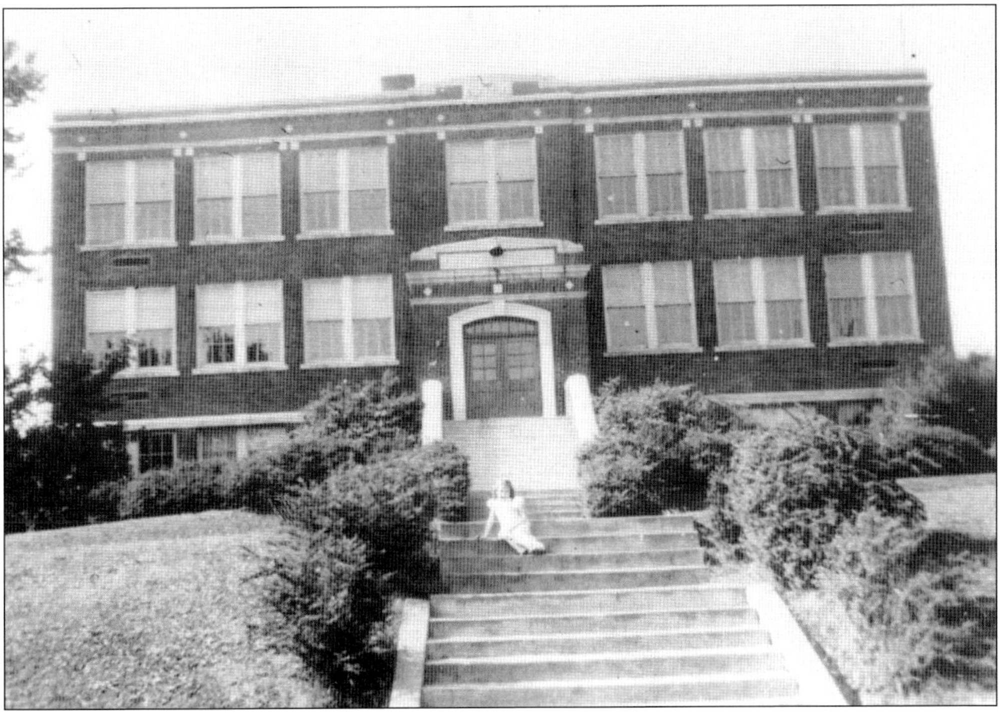

Sitting on the steps of the Loyal Oak School in 1946 is Carol Sue Butcher Jones, a 1958 graduate of Norton High School. The Loyal Oak School was built in 1928, only 13 years after the building of the Norton Center School, to help eliminate the need for one-room schoolhouses. This was a brick four-room building. The school was closed in 1986 and demolished in 2007.

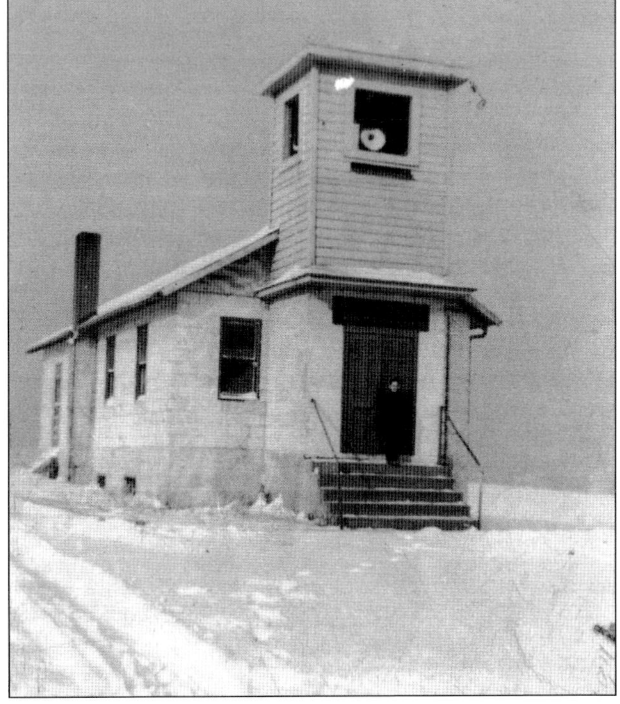

Standing in front of the Bible Holiness Church in 1946, located at 4112 Summit Street, is Pastor Jake Goff. The parishioners of the church did not make friends with all of the neighbors. A local farmer tired of the Sunday call to worship took a potshot at the bell and put a crack in it. In 1965, the church was rebuilt and came into the Nazarene denomination. Renamed Mount Summit Church of the Nazarene, Pastor Harold Buffman was at the helm. Today's pastor of the church is John Lee. Tragically, during the time this book was being written, the church burned to the ground. (Courtesy of Sandra Witchey Shockley.)

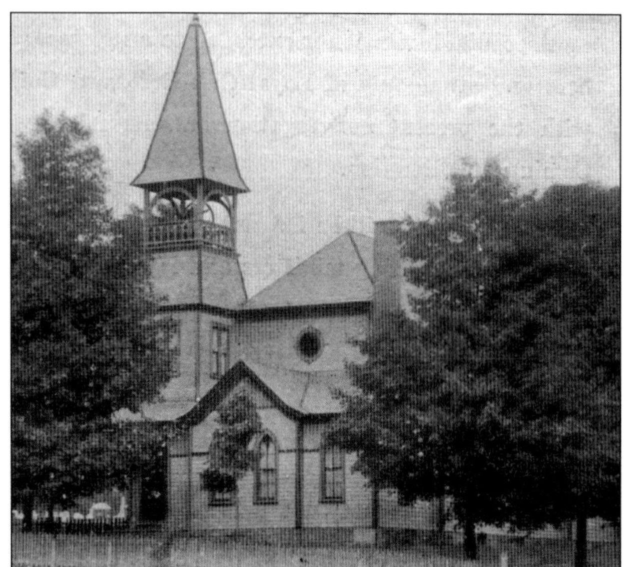

Grace United Church of Christ was originally founded in 1845 by a congregation of farmers who were part of the German and Reformed Church. The building was constructed in 1865, and the Prairie-style sanctuary is typical of the interiors of rural Reformed churches of the period. The architecture of the church is American Carpenter Gothic with an asymmetrical plan, front porch, belfry, and steeple. The church and the original bell are still in use today.

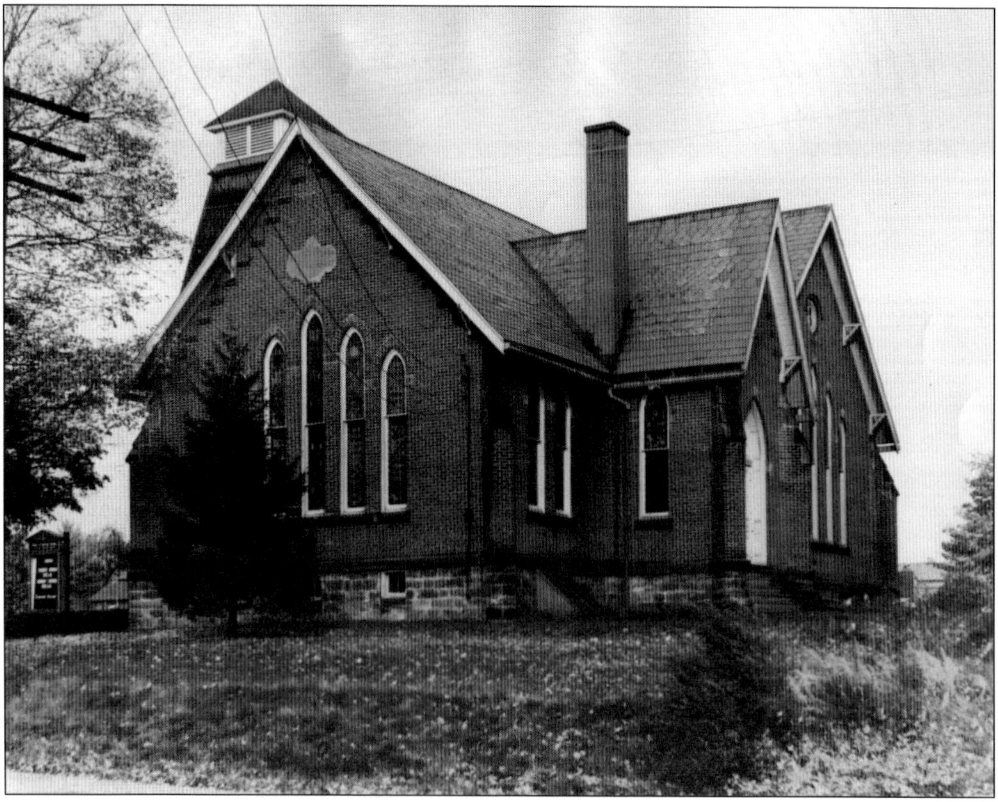

The Lutheran church was built in 1885, replacing a two-story stone structure that the congregation shared with the German Reformed Church since 1851. The congregations met on alternate Sundays. The Reformed congregation sold their interest to the Lutherans who dismantled the edifice and used the stones for the foundation of their brick building. The church boasts an antique organ, which is in use every Sunday. One of the oldest cemeteries, the Loyal Oak Cemetery, is behind the church.

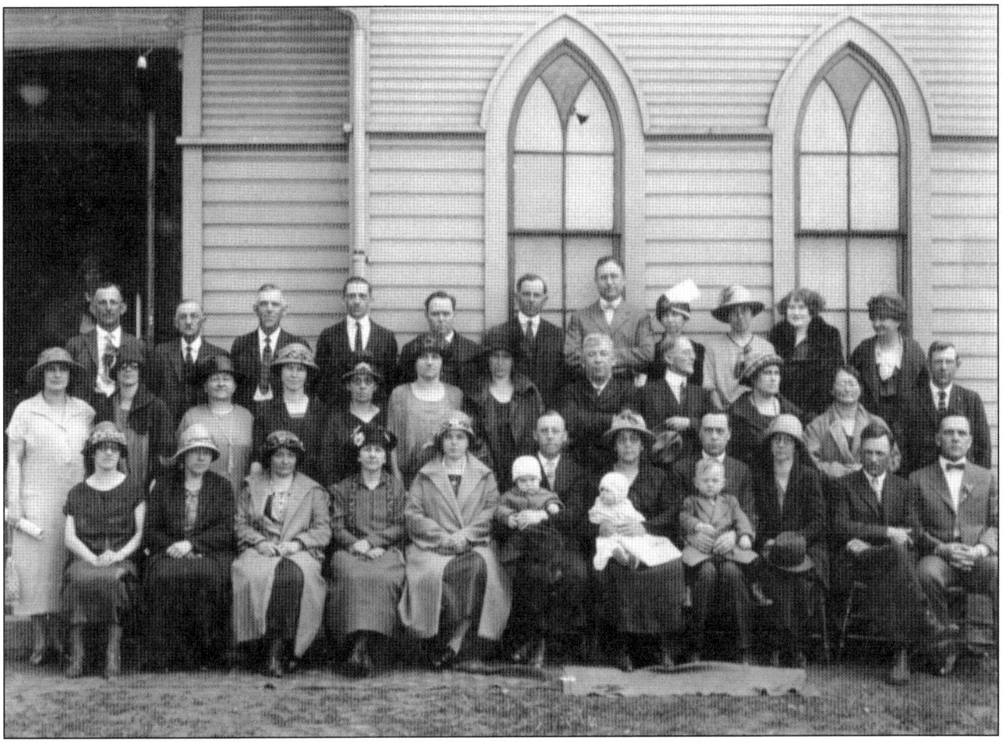

In February 1925, folks lined up on the front yard of the Loyal Oak Reformed Church. Pictured here are, from left to right, (first row) Mable Ehrich, Mrs. Harry Wetsel, Mrs. William Smith, Ida Redhead, Maude Harris, Chester Blackburn, holding Carl, Angeline Blackburn (holding Ethel), Amos Redhead holding Donald, Lilly Redhead, Fred Harris, and William Redhead; (second row) Mildred and Hazel Bowers, Cora Ehrich, Anna Knecht, Mary Ehrich, Beulah Sweet, Edith Bowers, William Smith, Mr. Evans, Mrs. Whitehead, Clara McCamon, and unidentified; (third row) Addie Ehrich (doorway), John Knecht, Elmer McCamon, Harry Wetsel, Joe Sweet, Robert Stump, unidentified, Bert and Blanch Schriber, Edith McQuiston, Mrs. Simpson, and Mrs. Evans.

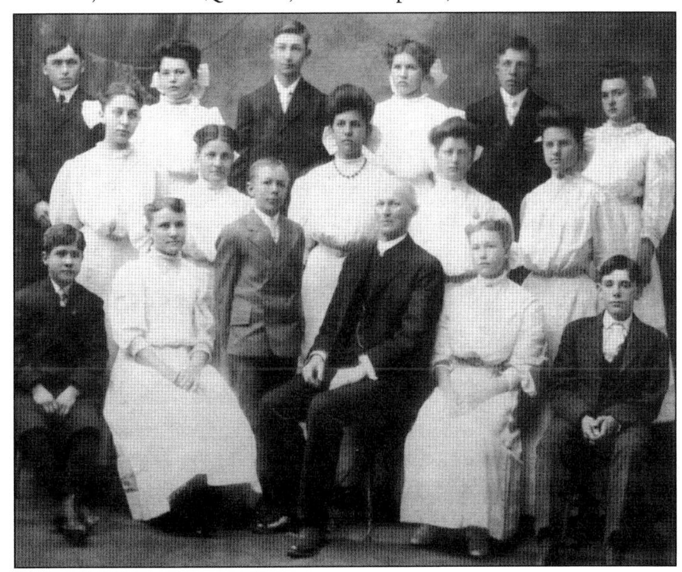

In 1907, this class was confirmed at the Loyal Oak Trinity Lutheran Church. Pictured from left to right are (first row) Raymond Lahr, Chloe Myers, George Harter, Pastor Engers, Carrie Harter, and Lloyd Hoch; (second row) Ruth Boerstler, Faith Shellhart, Hilda Moser, Effie Dutt, and Verna Myers; (third row) Homer and Hanah Miller, Grant Riggle, Florence Frase, and Earl and Grace Miller.

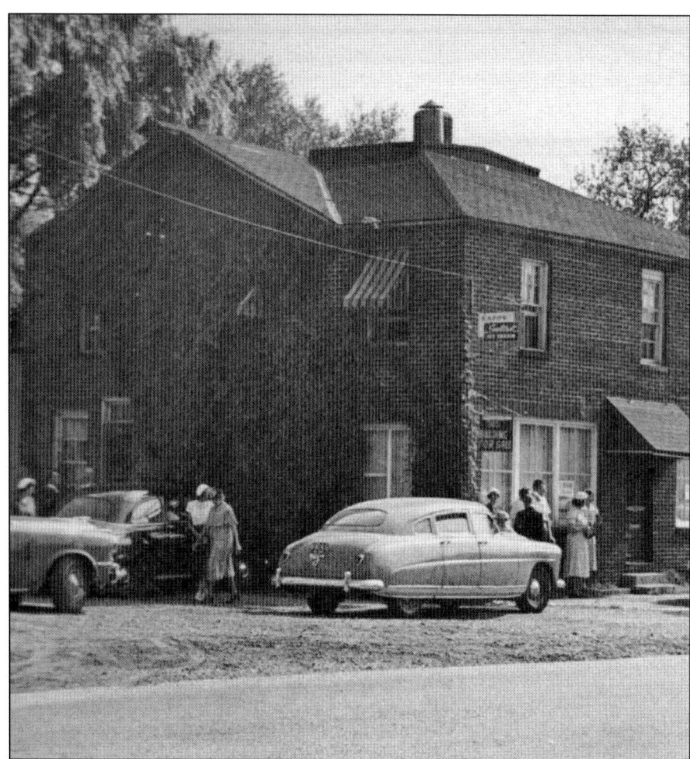

St. Andrew the Apostle Church was established on May 11, 1951, with the first Sunday masses being held in the hamlet of Western Star. The first Sunday collection netted $38.20, and Fr. Stephen J. Blasko was the founding pastor. (Courtesy of St. Andrews Church.)

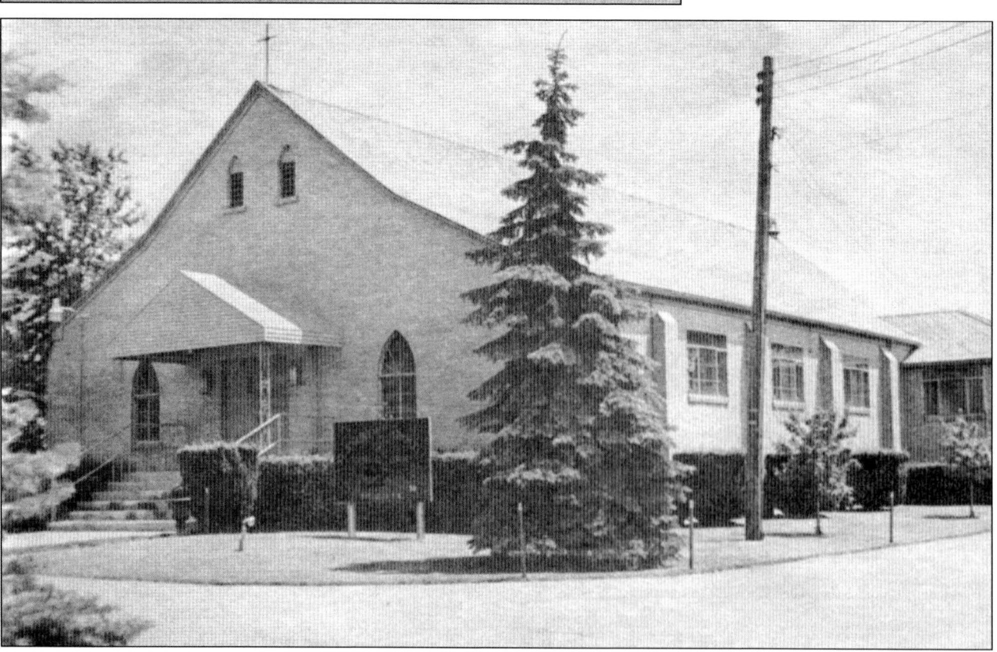

In August 1951, three acres were purchased in Sherman at 4022 Johnson Road, and a new church was built by its members. The first mass in their new home was celebrated on May 11, 1952. St. Andrew the Apostle Roman Catholic Church today is a parish of the Roman Catholic Diocese of Cleveland Ohio, and its current pastor is the Reverend James G. Maloney. (Courtesy of St. Andrews Church.)

The congregation of St. Matthew Evangelical Lutheran Church was organized on March 16, 1910, in Barberton, Ohio. The first resident pastor was the Reverend Andrew Rolik. After having worshiped in their church in Barberton for a number of years, the congregation decided to build a new facility. Architect David Wycoff and contractor William Bird from Norton designed the new church at 5451 Cleveland-Massillon Road. On March 14, 2010, the congregation celebrated their 100th anniversary, lead by Pastor John Mashek. (Courtesy of St. Matthew Church.)

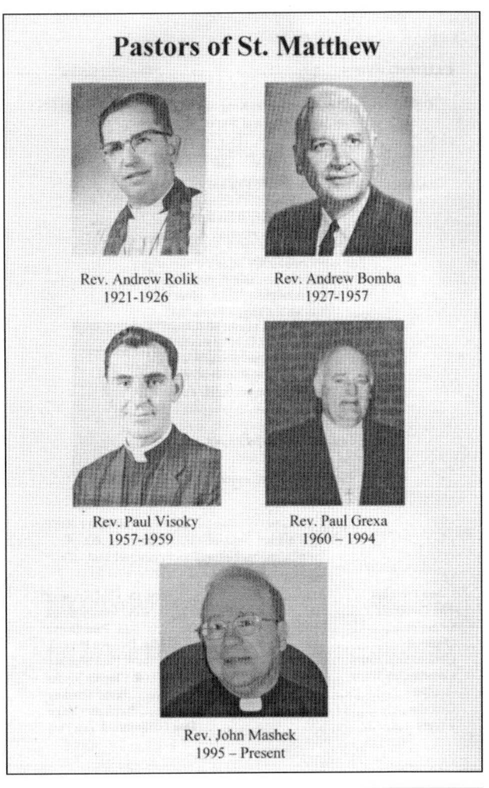

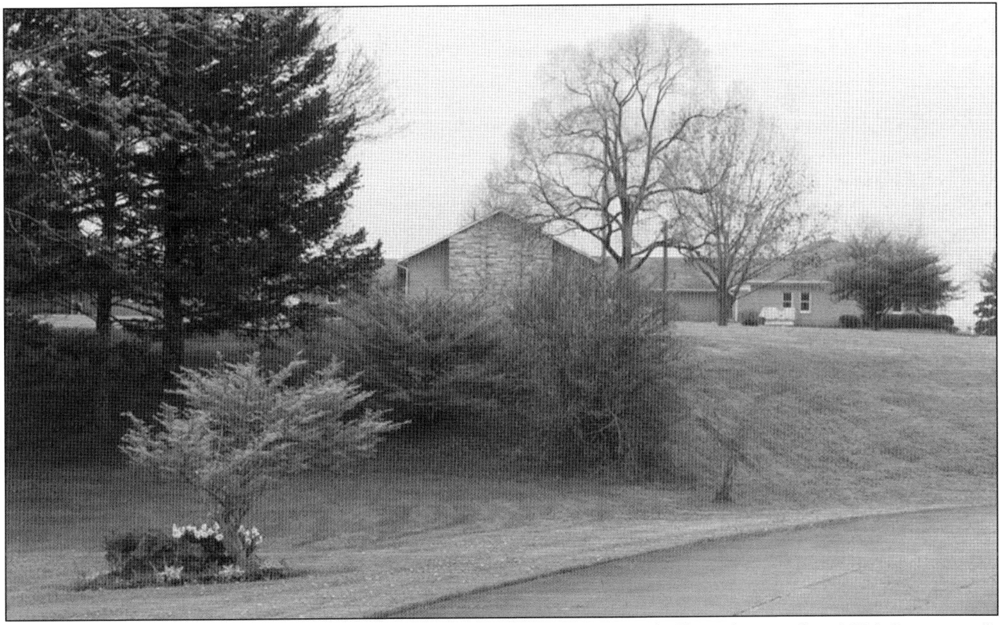

The Apostolic Church of Norton, known as the "church on the hill," is located at 3816 Greenwich Road. The church's roots started with the 1830s Anabaptist movement in Switzerland, led by Samuel Froehlich. The Apostolic name was chosen because the church wanted to follow the teachings of the apostles and Christ. The church property, formerly a farm, was purchased from Walter Seiberling. (Courtesy of Annette Simon.)

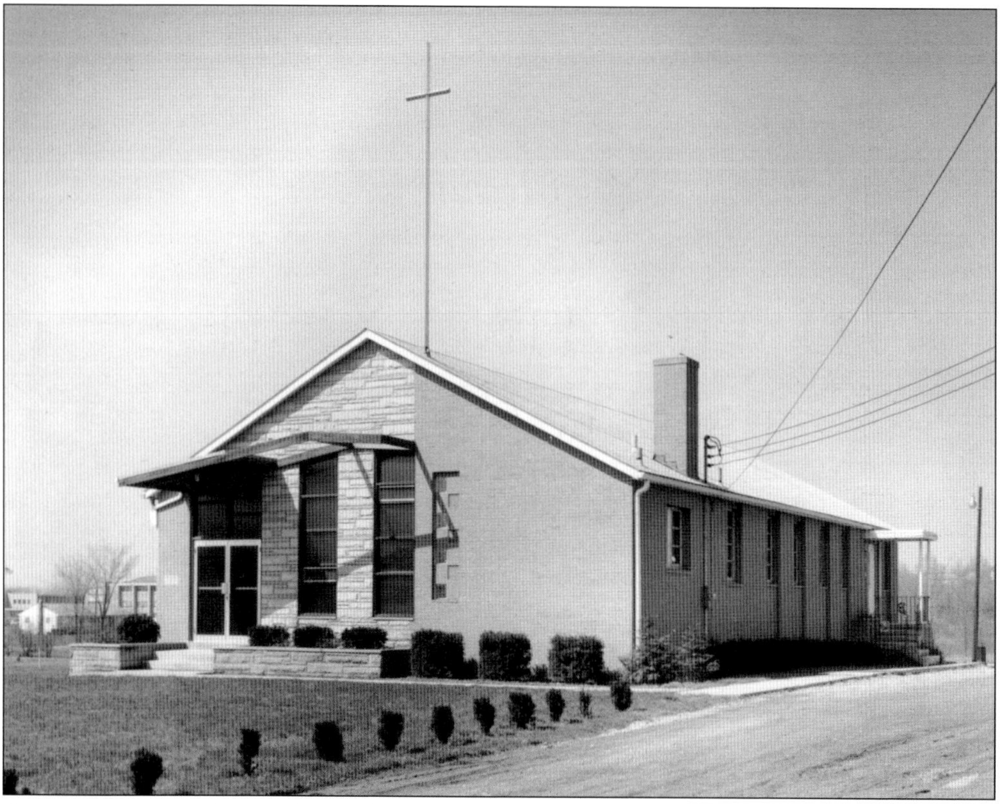

Years were met with financial struggle, moving locations, many pastors, and changing philosophy. This is a view of the original First Brethren Church. Joseph Fraterolli, a local, agreed to sell the land at 3970 Cleveland-Massillon Road for $15,000, and the dedication of the new building was in October 1960. Through many growing pains, the church has been added on to, and the name was changed to Grace Brethren Church. In 1995, Judgment House was created as an alternative to Halloween haunted houses and to give the community a clear gospel message. (Courtesy of Grace Brethren Church.)

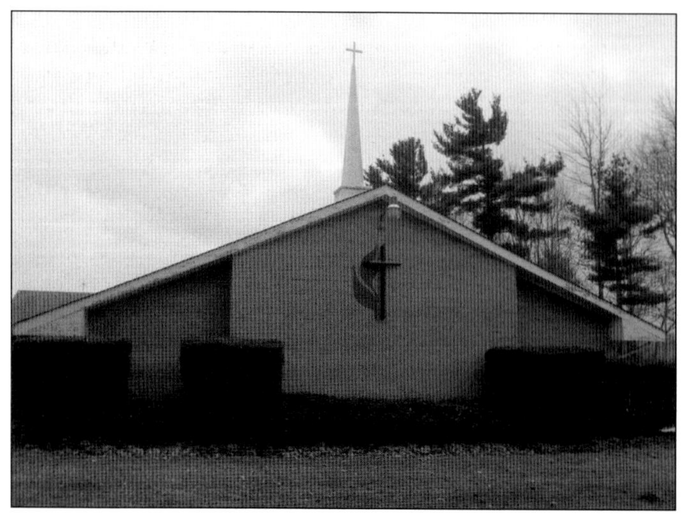

The dedication of a handful of individuals in 1971 created the vision of a new Methodist church in Norton. Initially meeting at the Loyal Oak Lake Park in a conference room, the members held their first Sunday service in the park building on March 5, 1972, with an attendance of about 50. A new church at 3406 Hametown Road was dedicated and named the Living Hope United Methodist Church in 1977. (Author's collection.)

Three

Interesting Sights and Sites, Then and Now

Norton offers something for just about everyone to enjoy—indoors and outdoors. For years, Norton has had garden clubs, Girl and Boy Scouts, various sports teams, and groups such as the Kiwanis, Women's Club, and Lions Club. In late September, the city hosts a cider festival, with games, food, and fun for all, organized by a private committee and sponsored by the Lions Club. It began in 1988 and was originally held in Loyal Oak, but the event was moved to the Columbia Woods Park in 2008.

Silver Creek Park is within the Norton boundary and maintained by the Metro Parks Serving Summit County. Originally the Harter Dairy Farm, it is now an 895-acre park with a boathouse, swimming, bridle trails, fishing, and hiking. Under the park is a maze of tunnels and shafts left from 19th-century coal-mining operations. Many other smaller parks make up the landscape dotted around Norton.

The Winery at Wolf Creek opened in 1980 and offers much for the senses, including wine parings, music, and tours. The Wolf Creek Players started in 2009 out with just a few citizens who wanted to showcase their talent and has grown by leaps and bounds to benefit the arts, culture, and humanities. Dayton Nurseries, built in the 1990s, features 17,000 square feet of greenhouses and a full-service garden center highlighting 800 varieties of perennials. Built in 1912, the Biery House and Museum is home to the Norton Historical Society and houses Norton memorabilia, agricultural tools, military uniforms, alumni material, and multiple displays indoor and out. Loyal Oak Lake Park has been a staple for families in the summer to swim, play basketball, picnic, or camp. There are two well-known golf courses available where one can play a few holes or hang out in the clubhouse, and for those who like automobile races, Barberton Speedway has just the answer.

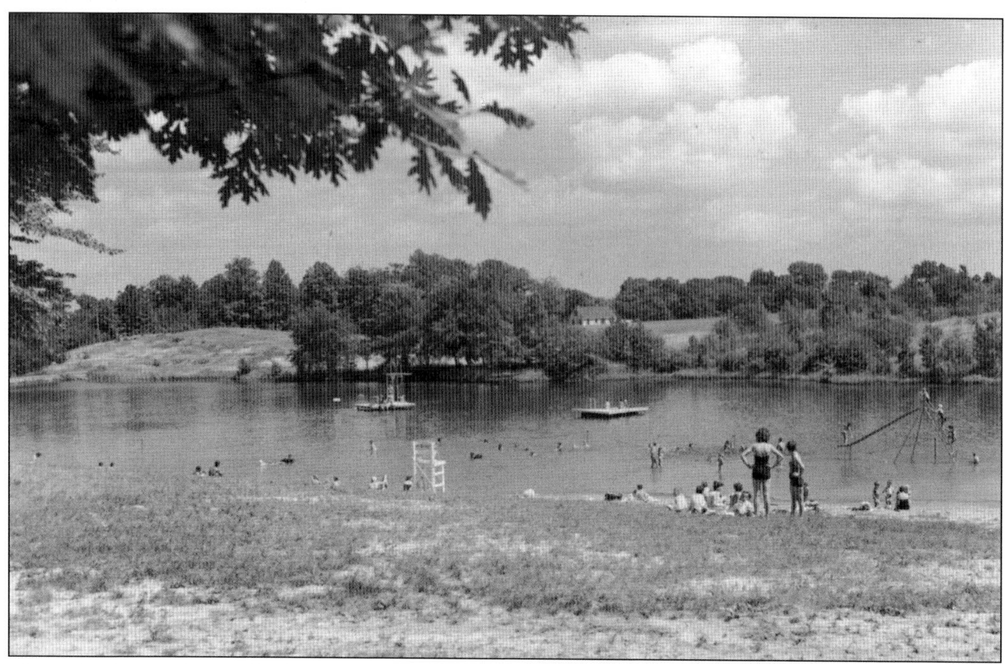

The lake located at 2678 Hametown Road, pictured here in the 1950s, was dug in the 1930s along with a dam to produce water on property owned by the Kalain family. Later opened as a swim club by the Brenner family, Bob Emery purchased the property in 1955. Emery transformed it into a recreational dream in 1957, operating the park until 1985. The park featured a six-acre lake with a 40-foot stainless-steel sliding board, two smaller slides, and three docks. There was a camping area, concession stand, shelters, swings, basketball courts, indoor games, a batting cage, golf range, tennis and horseshoe courts, and a softball diamond. In October 2013, the park was purchased by Kristopher and Amy Schmid and still exists today as the place to go for summer fun. (Courtesy of Denise Emery.)

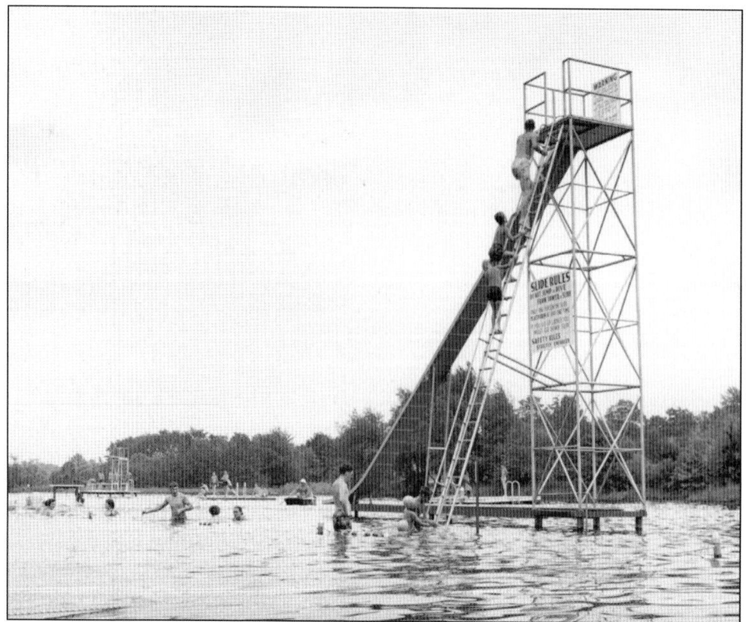

The 40-foot stainless-steel slide was a drawing card in its early years for adventuresome members. Going headfirst down the slide was against the rules, and observant lifeguards would note the offense with a whistle. (Courtesy of Denise Emery.)

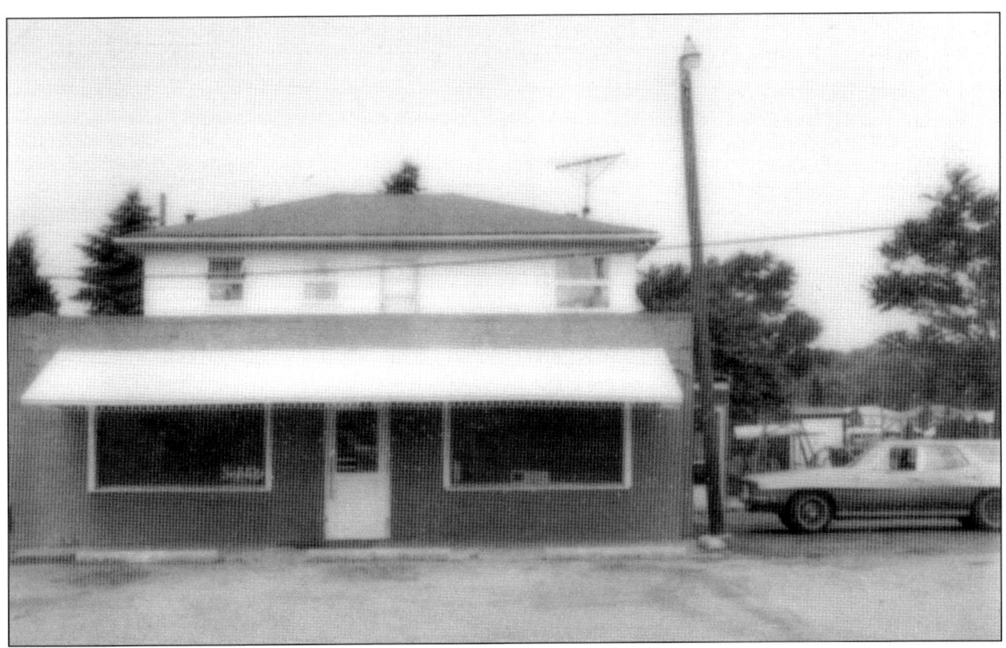

A 10-acre plot owned by Elmer (known as "Bill") and Mary Wenner, also known as Wenner's Allotment, located on Pleasant Drive, became the home of Wenner's Market in 1946. Bill, a meat cutter by trade, returned from serving in the US Navy as a machinist first class during World War II. In 1956, he and Mary opened the store for business. In 1966, the business changed to a tavern, and Mary took over as a barmaid and jack of all trades. Today, it is known as the Norton Pub. (Courtesy of Mary Wenner.)

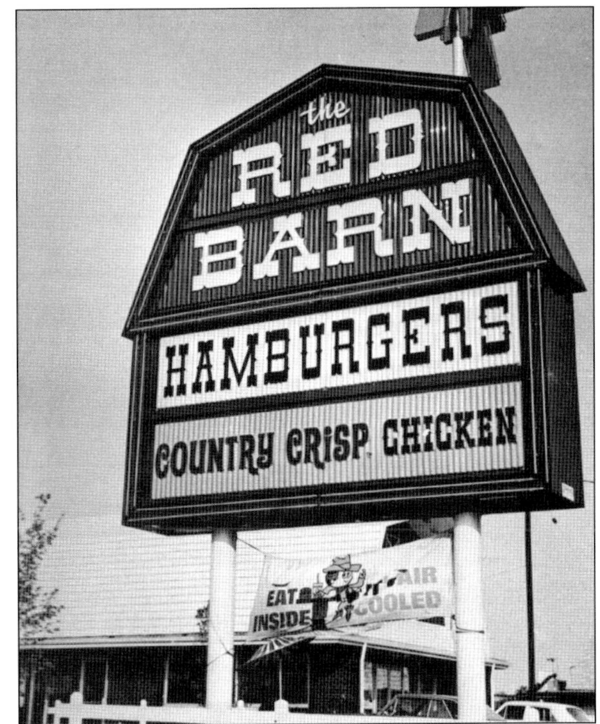

The Red Barn Restaurant, a fast-food chain founded in 1961, was located across from the Norton High School. This was the place to be after football and basketball games, to cruise, and just hang out. It was the first of its kind to offer a self-serve salad bar. Motel 6 bought it out in 1970, and with the owners ceasing to advertise and letting the leases expire, the last Red Barn closed in 1986. The Red Barn on Norton Avenue is presently the Norton Car Wash.

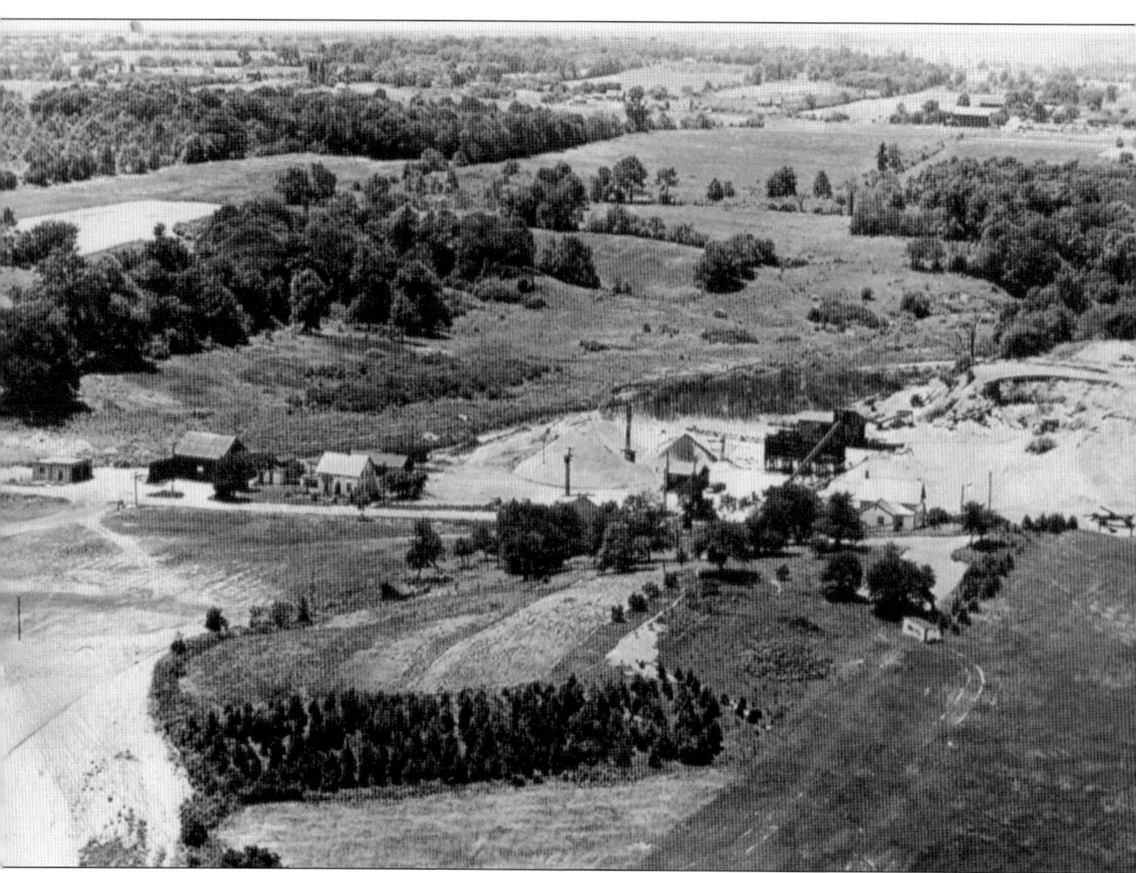

Pictured here in 1940 is Amlin Sand and Gravel, which was owned by Ed Amlin in the 1930s and located at 3322 Clark Mill Road. The business was a mining operation that ran raw material through the plant with different conveyors and screens to separate materials. Different types of sands, dirt, and sizes of gravel were sifted out through this process. Amlin sold the business to his two sons, Dick and Kenny, in the 1960s, and the business was renamed D & K. Harold Flesher eventually took over the operation while also running another similar business on McCoy Road, and the name was changed once again, this time to Fleshers Sand and Gravel. Harold's son Dallas bought the property on Clark Mill Road and ran both locations for several years. In 1991, James Fisher, Dallas's son-in-law, bought the business, and now it is owned by James Fisher Jr. The plant was eventually torn down and is now a supply yard. The family business is in its fourth generation. (Courtesy of Barbara Leksan.)

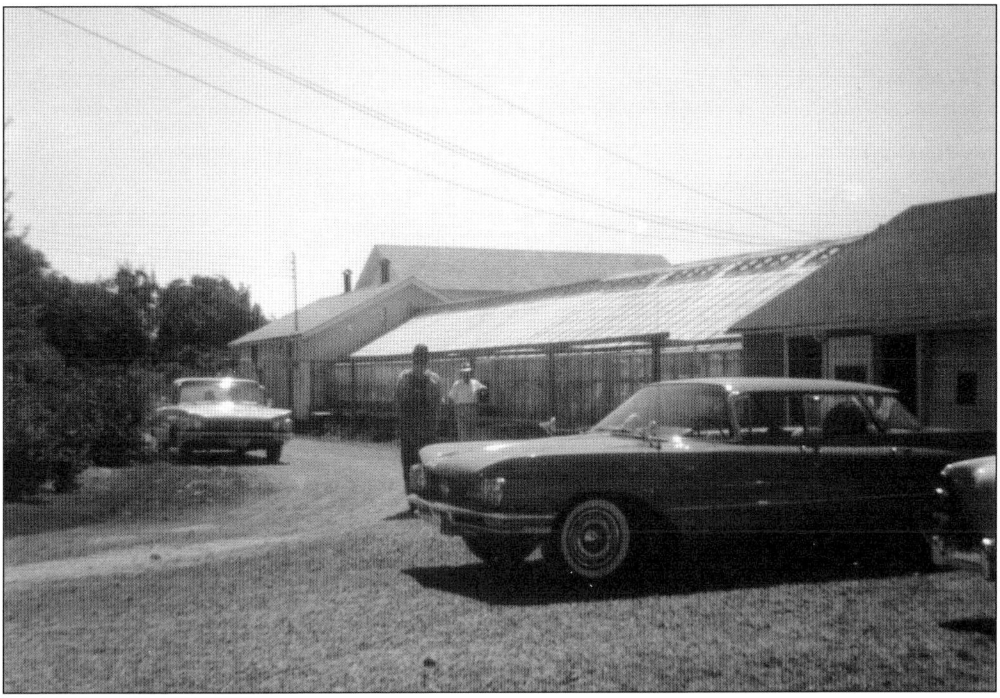

Pictured here in 1960 is a little-known nursery called White's Roses. Owned by James E. White and located at 3460 Cleveland-Massillon Road, the nursery specialized in roses, annuals, perennials, and trees and had a sales room and garden center. The nursery was demolished when Brentwood Estates was built. A field of roses in bloom is seen from the back side of the nursery. (Both, courtesy of Kaye Redhead.)

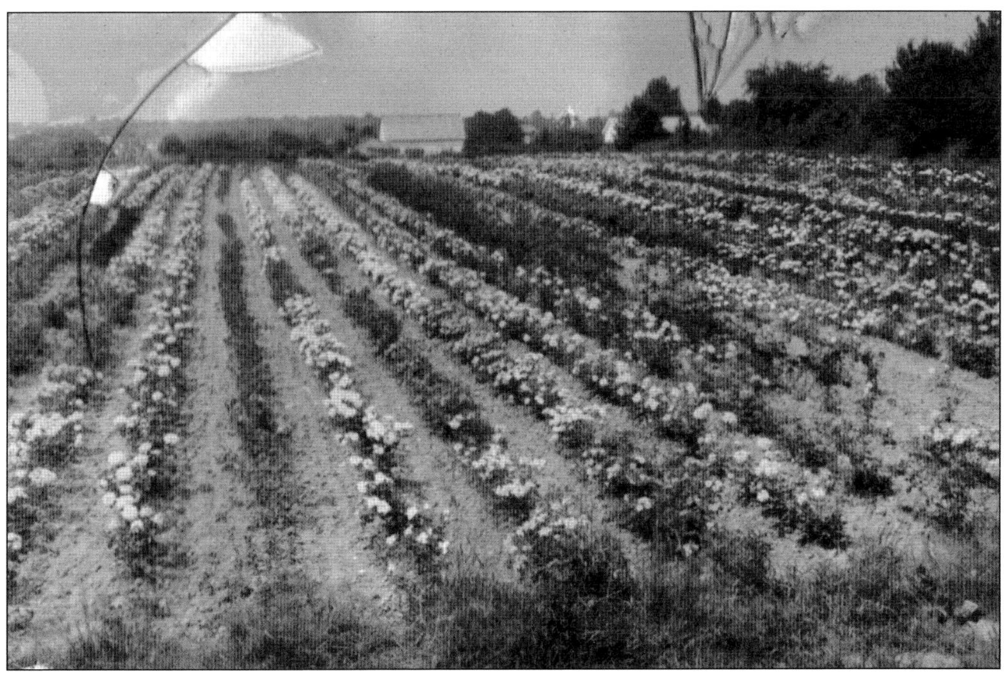

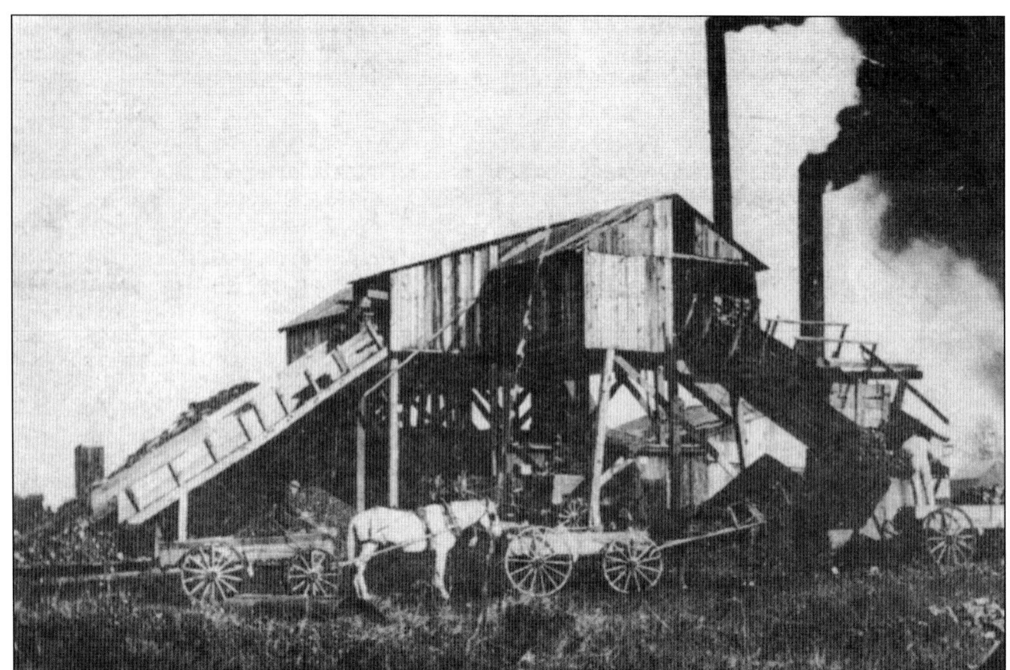

John D. Jones resided at the hamlet of Hametown and operated a thriving coal business. Jones was born in Glamorganshire, Wales, in 1851 and by the age of nine was working in the mines. At age 17, Jones came to America and joined his parents. A premature explosion of powder in one of the mines killed his father, David, in 1885. Jones married Elizabeth Boden, who was also born in Wales, and they had eight children. Their son Gomar became the president and secretary of the Hametown Coal Company. Like his father and grandfather, his whole life was identified with coal interests. In the photograph above is one of John Jones's original mines in the 1900s. Also shown here is a coal receipt from 1825. The coal was mined by hand, loaded on horse-drawn wagons, and delivered directly to the consumers in the Norton, Barberton, and Doylestown area. Geraldine Jones Wiese, granddaughter of John D. Jones, remembers riding the rickety old elevator into the shafts to collect drinking water in buckets.

Hametown, O., 5/2 1905

M

Bought Of **The Hametown Coal Co.,**

3980 Lump at $

1300 Nut at $

2680 Slack at $

The Hametown Coal Co.,

$14.74 Per

Paid

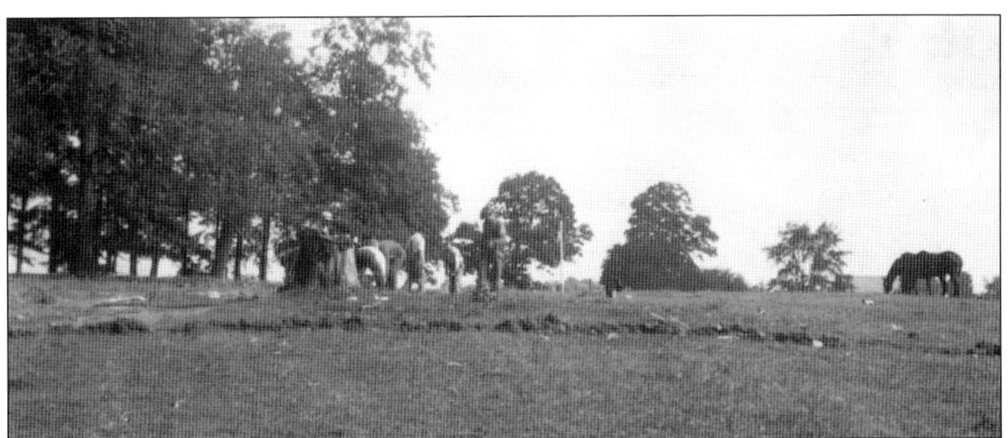

Brush-clearing crews were out on September, 12, 1921, taking out a stump on the soon to be ninth green of the Seiberling Country Club. The course was created for the employees of the Seiberling Tire and Rubber Company in Akron, but 35 years after the Seiberlings created it, the course was purchased by a group of men. The club was later owned by one of the sons of the group, James Petrou. In 1984, the course and clubhouse were purchased by Joseph "Joe" Flogge. The 140-acre property includes a clubhouse with a course of 18 holes on handsomely kept greens in a rolling landscape. A lovely banquet room and full bar is available year-round and seats 200 people. In 1926, luncheons were 75¢, dinners were $1, and a steak sold for only 50¢. A small store is attached, in which the public can purchase golfing equipment or sign up for lessons. In 2013, a devastating fire destroyed the 50-foot-by-200-foot pole building, which stored 52 golf carts and all of the mowing equipment. (Both, courtesy of Joseph Flogge.)

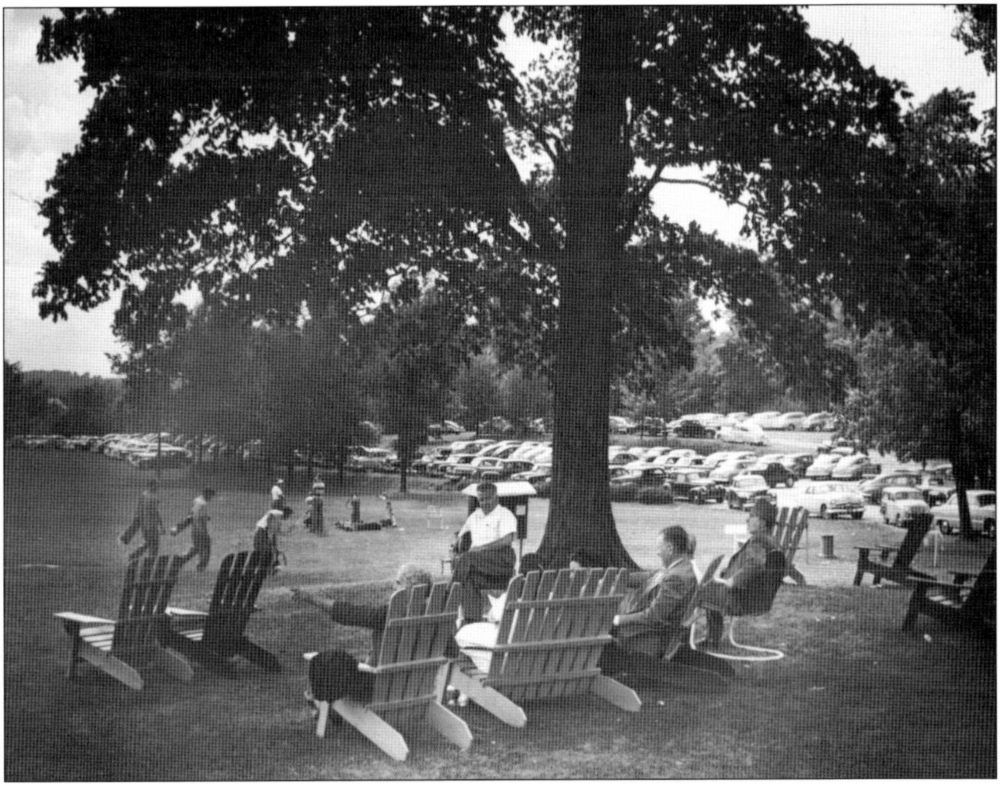

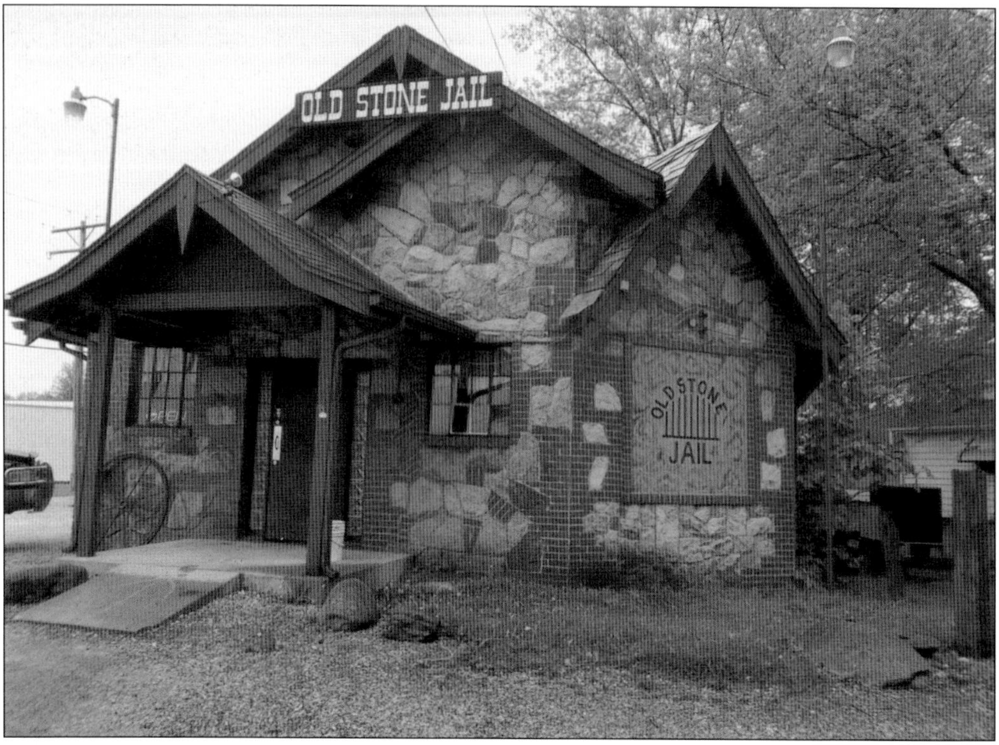

The Old Stone Jail at 5640 Wooster Road West is a bit of a misnomer in the community. The building was never used as a jail; it was a tavern for 78 years. Built as one of five known taverns, the Stone Jail was built in 1936 by the George J. Renner Brewing Company. The outside is a brick and sandstone patchwork and includes living quarters. George Jacom Renner was a native German, and he came to the United States in 1849. He partnered with and worked for brewing companies. With an interest in the production of ice, he later built an ice plant in Akron. Eventually, George's son William took over the business after the death of his father in 1921. The Stone Jail was built after Prohibition, and the brewery's products were then being distributed within a 200-mile radius from Akron. This portrait features George and what appears to be other company officers greeting visitors as they come in the door of the Stone Jail. (Both, author's collection.)

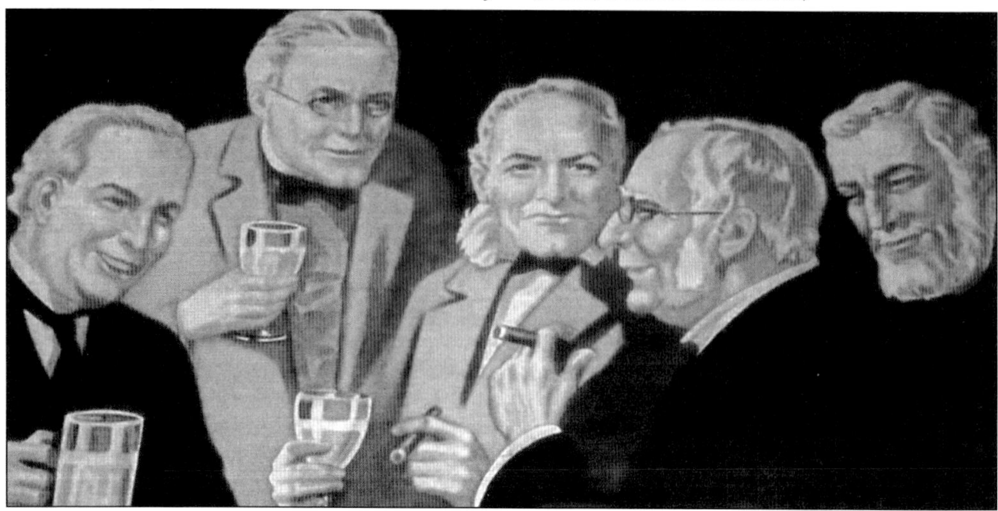

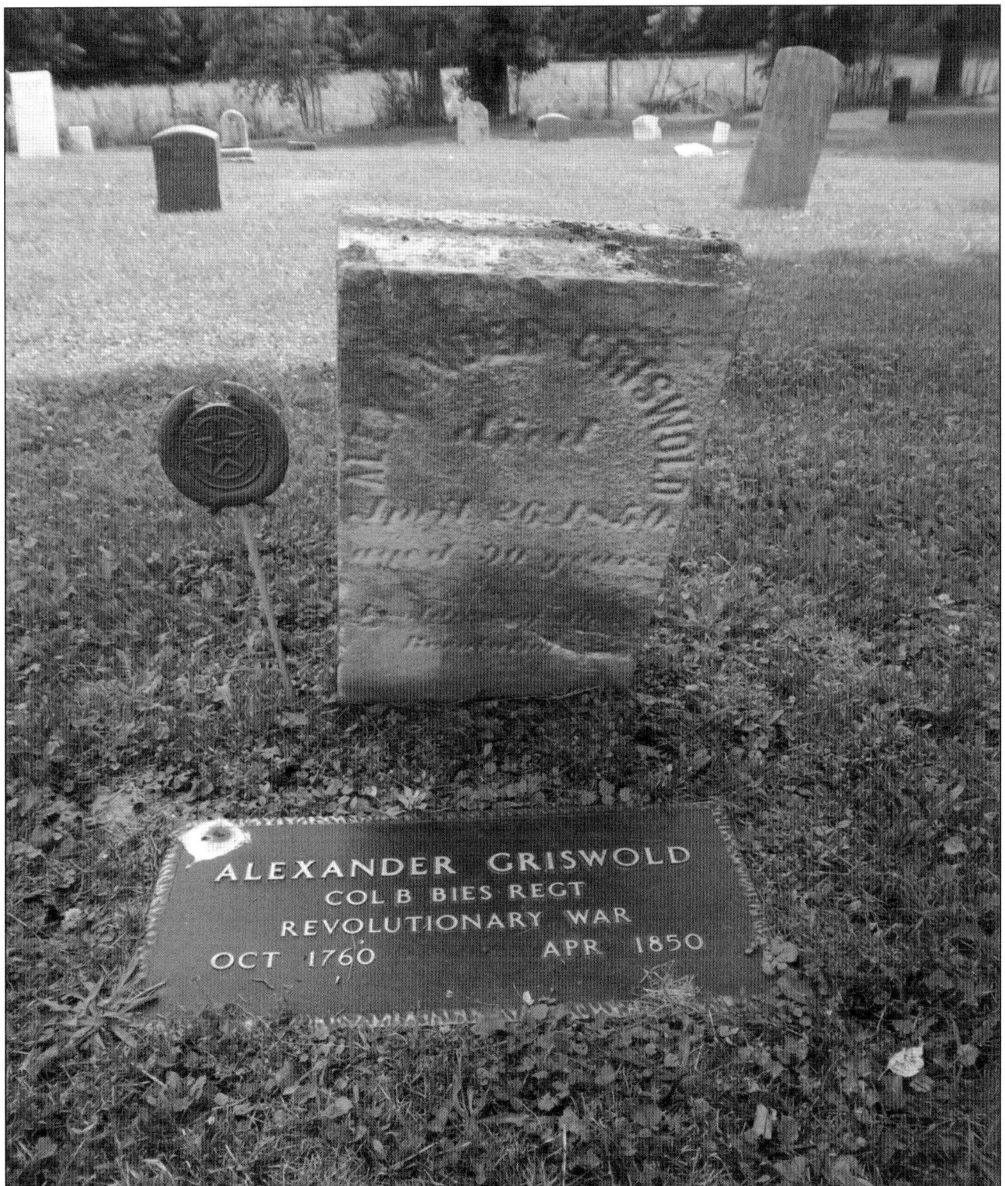

Alexander Griswold (1760–1850) rests beneath a gravestone in Western Star Cemetery. Griswold was a Revolutionary War veteran who served under Gen. George Washington. He was only 16 when he was captured by the British and confined on the prison ship *Jersey*, nicknamed "the Black Hole of Calcutta." For three months, Griswold survived on board the prison ship in a hold without air, exercise, or sufficient food, where filth, starvation, cruelty, and disease bore down on all of the captives. It is said that 13,000 men died on British prison ships by freezing, heat, infected water, putrid food, or a myriad of illnesses, including dysentery, typhoid, and smallpox. Being the youngest on board may be the reason that Griswold survived. After the war, he went back to live in Goshen, Connecticut, and became a wealthy farmer. Griswold married Lucy Humphrey, and they had eight children. With a dream of each child owning his or her own farm, the family packed their belongings on a wagon pulled by a team of oxen and made a dangerous six-week journey to settle in Norton. (Author's collection.)

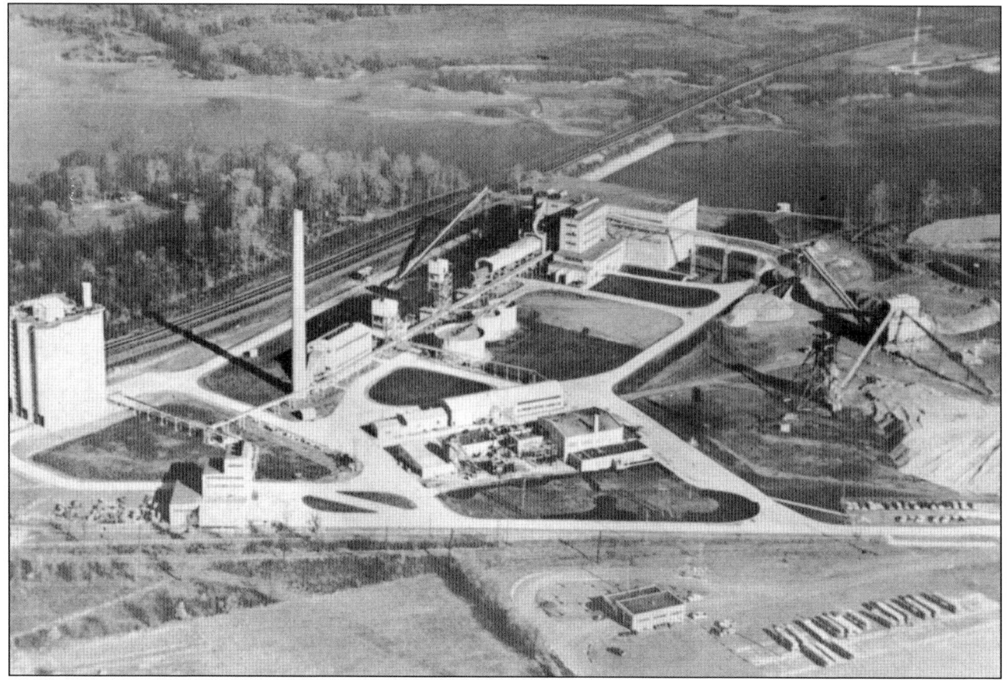

Pittsburgh Plate Glass Company, known as PPG, was built in 1899 in order to make soda ash for glassmaking. The PPG limestone mine is the world's deepest at 2,200 feet. The company also made chlorine, caustic soda, and calcium chloride. Their reclamation of former soda-ash waste-deposit sites, known as lime lakes, have won them recognition for environmental stewardship. (Courtesy of PPG Industries.)

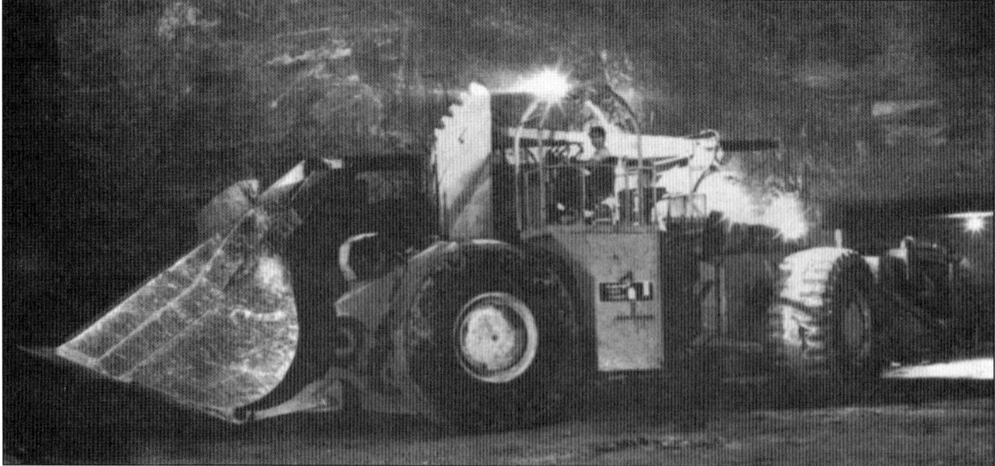

Giant front-end loaders, the world's largest measuring 20 cubic yards, were chewing up a million tons of limestone each year in the PPG mine. Keeping up with the mine's planned annual production of 1.17 million tons formerly required three shovels and seven 14-cubic-yard trucks. The loader manufactured by R.G. LeTourneau includes a bucket width of 14 feet, three inches and weight of nearly 30 tons. Its power comes from twin 465-horsepower GMC diesel engines, which drive four DC and one AC generator. These provide power for the unit's 200-horsepower electric wheels, controls, and lighting. The machines are fully articulated, and getting these giants below the surface required more than just a little ingenuity. (Courtesy of PPG Industries.)

Virtually nothing is known about the 1930s Red Lantern, which was at the junction of Route 17 and 21, now known as Norton Avenue and Cleveland-Massillon Roads. They offered Taystee toasted sandwiches, good music, and were open till 12:00 a.m. Ed McQuiston sold gasoline at the same location in the 1940s and 1950s. Today, the Holland Oil Company is on this site as a gas station and drive-thru beverage store.

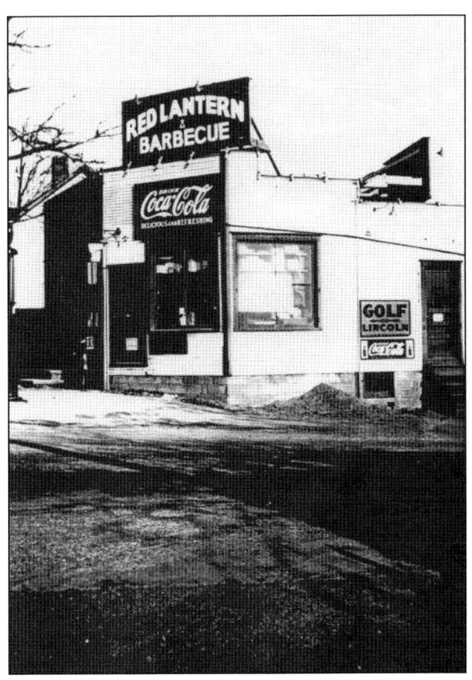

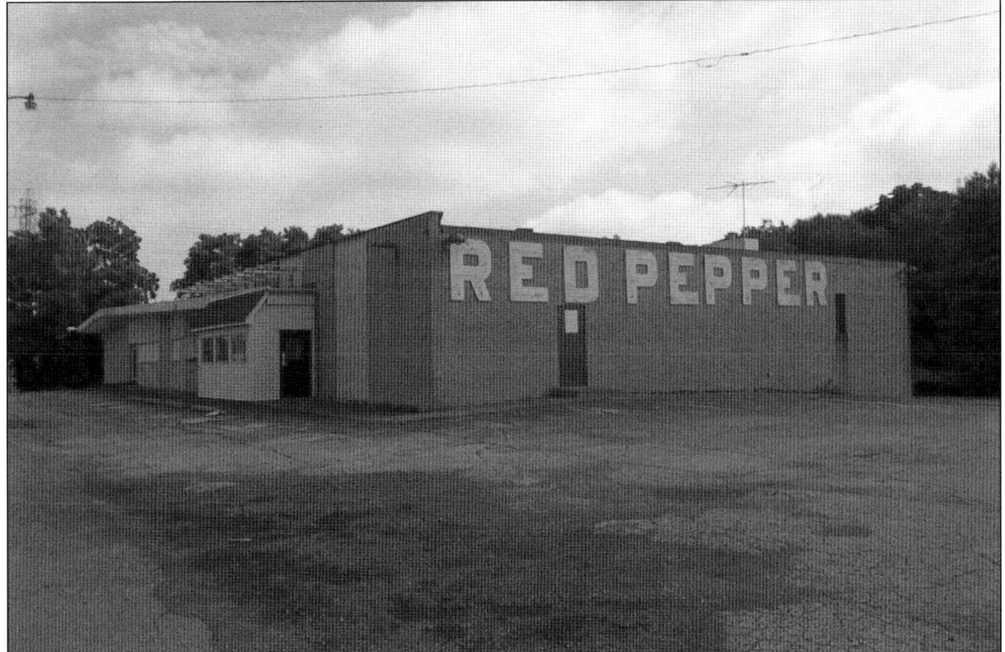

A baseball team called the Red Peppers were making a name for themselves in the 1930s, named after director Paul "Pepper" Sheeks and former University of Akron halfback Kenneth "Red" Cochrane. After World War II, former Akron Red Peppers player Louis "Bony" Juhasz opened the Red Pepper Steak House at 2661 Barber Road, featuring memorabilia from the 1930s team. In 1987, a restaurant review written by Jane Snow was published in the *Akron Beacon Journal*. The Red Pepper was referred to as "not your average restaurant" and described as a homey truck-stop kind of atmosphere with funky-utilitarian decor—Bony's football trophies are everywhere.

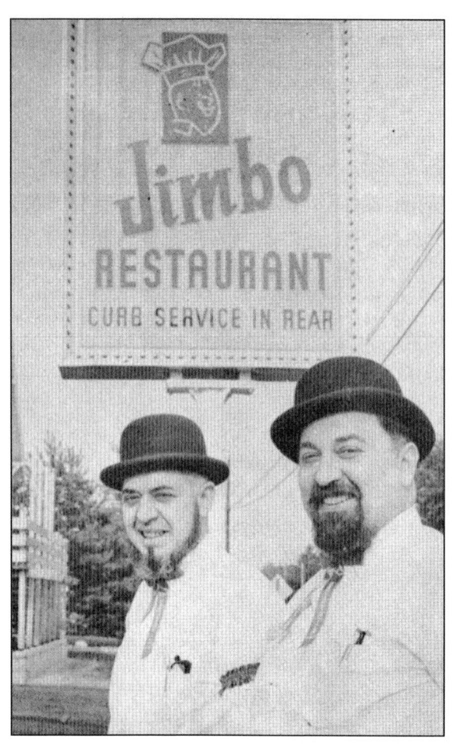

Jack (left) and James Georgiadis, pictured here, purchased DaVerns Restaurant in 1959 from Grant and Virginia Schlup, and the name was changed to Jimbo's Taystee Foods. Their motto was "For better eating without a fuss, always remember to eat with us." The last menu before they closed included the Super Jimbo Basket for $1.99, which included a Super Jimbo Burger, French fries, and coleslaw. A Jimbo's Hearty Breakfast was two eggs up, over, or scrambled, home fries, bacon or a sausage patty, and toast, all for $2.25. The restaurant closed in the 1990s. In 2001, the property was purchased by Barberton Citizen's Hospital, and the restaurant was removed.

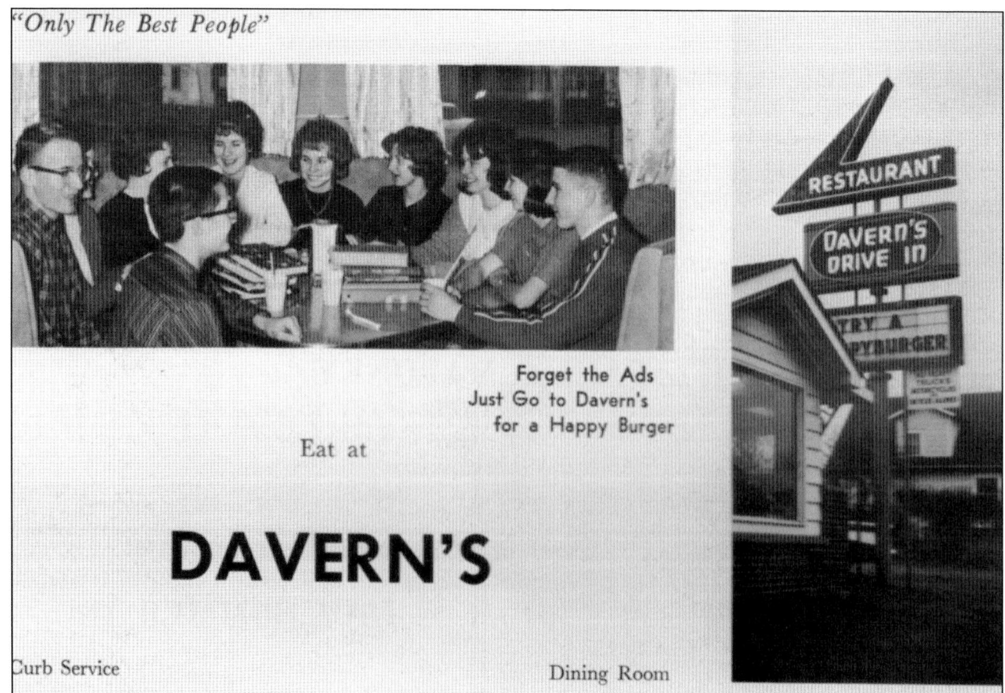

One of Ohio's first drive-in restaurants was opened in the 1930s by Dave McIntosh and Vern Slabaugh, hence the name DaVerns. It was the place to hang out for high school students, and for car hops, it provided the opportunity to accumulate savings for college tuition. Their Happy Burger was 55¢, the chicken basket was $1, and fountain specialties ranged from 20¢ to 55¢.

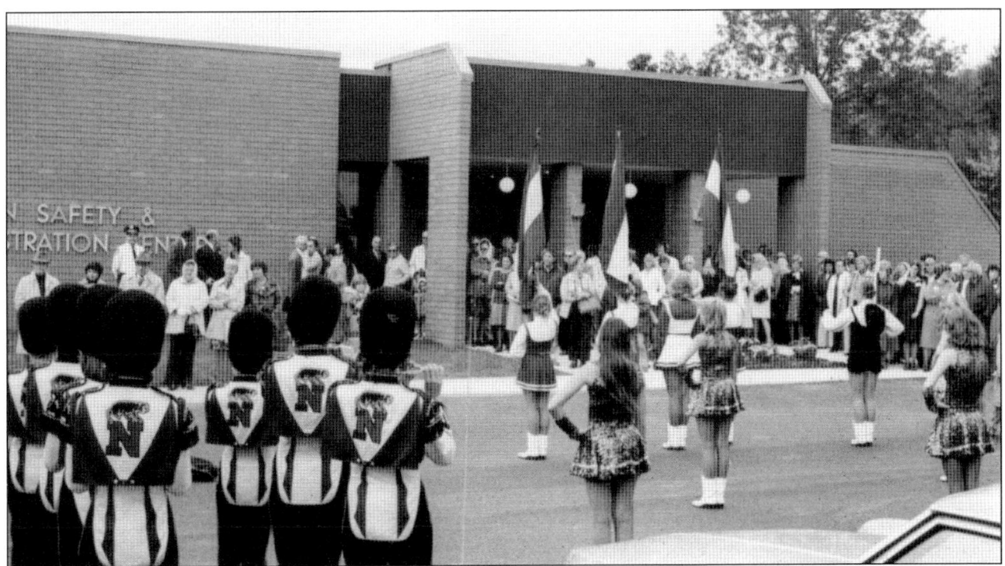

A new Norton Solar Safety Administration Center building was dedicated in 1978 as a prototype design for energy conservation as the first public building in Summit County to utilize solar heating. The building is still in use today, accommodating the departments of police, finance, city administrator, municipal engineer, zoning, clerk of courts, and the mayor. The Norton High School band, along with majorettes and the color guard, welcomed and celebrated the new building with Panther pride. Seen here are dignitaries, Norton officials, and Norton safety forces, as well as a large turnout of Norton citizens. (Courtesy of Frank Rooney.)

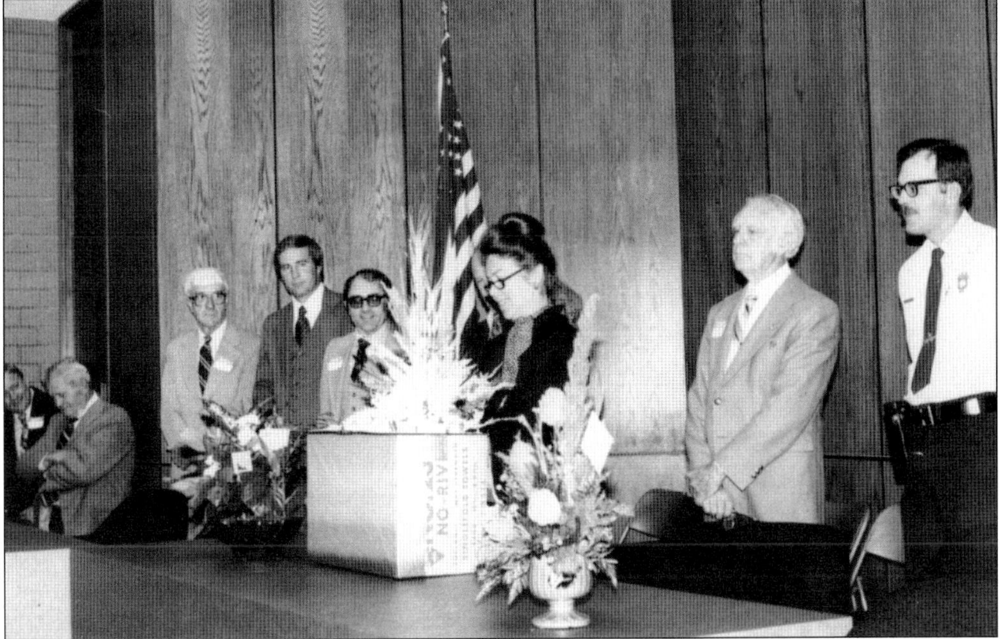

In 1978, shown here are, from left to right, Walter Peterman (vice president of city council), Ellis Seiberling, Ennis A. Morriss, John Sanders (administrative officer), Edwin Reid, Albert L. Wagner, Shirley McGuire (president of council), Mayor Edward Williams, and Fire Chief Michael Antoniotti. (Courtesy of Frank Rooney.)

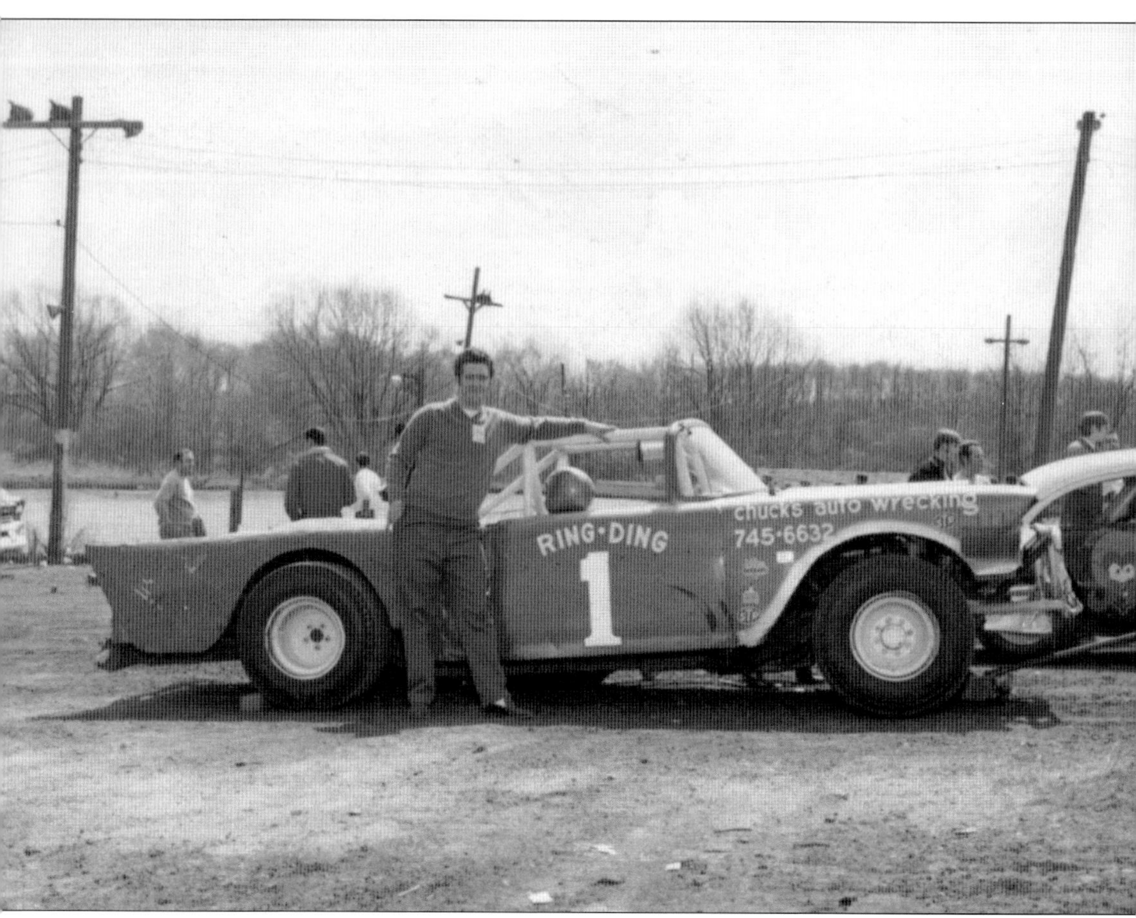

Opening in 1948, the Barberton Speedway, a quarter-mile asphalt oval located at 3389 Clark Mill Road, was owned by Russ Rubino and Vince Papps. Dale Weiderman was the track boss, and Jack Franklin was the pit boss. Most races were held on Saturday nights around 8:00 pm. Each race had 20 to 24 cars entered and included a helmet dash for number one and a heat race for the fastest 10 cars. They might have an Australian Pursuit Ace, which involved the fastest 10 cars racing with the fastest car placed in last position. There was no cost to enter the races, but there was an entry fee to get to the pits, $10 per person. To join the association it was $35 to $50 per year, and the entry to see the races was $6 per person. The only death attributed to the speedway was in 2001, when a racer lost control and died after crashing through billboards at the edge of the track and hitting trees. Pictured here is Larry "Ring Ding 1" Rininger and his 1957 Chevy convertible. (Courtesy of Larry Rininger.)

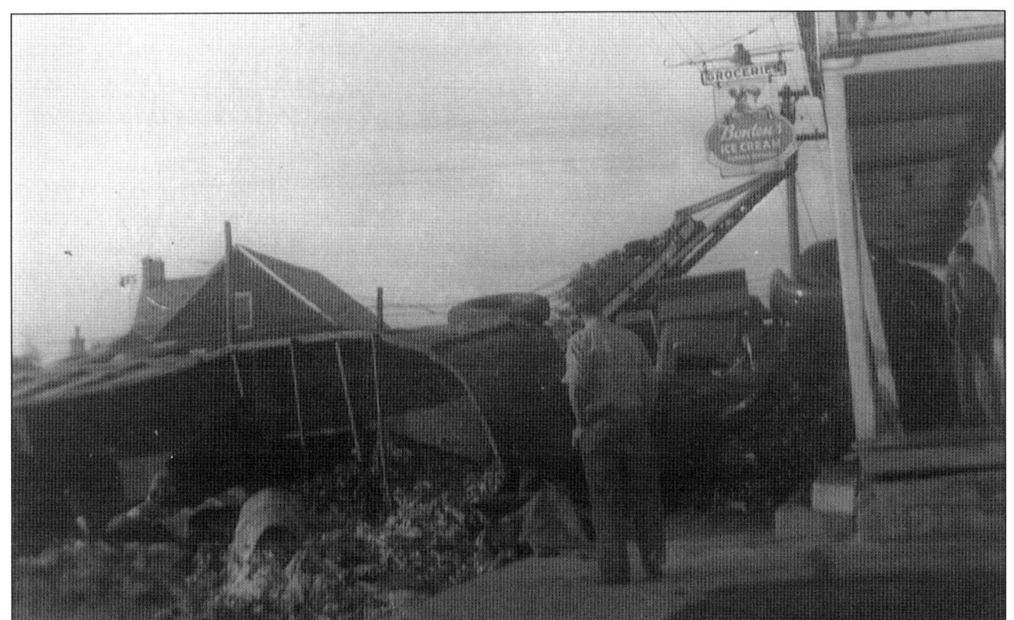

On a hot July morning in 1953, at the intersection of Cleveland Massillon and Akron-Wadsworth Roads, a truck heading north carrying slaughterhouse remnants in 55-gallon drums went through the light and struck a car carrying local people. Headed west from Akron after having visited a relative in an Akron hospital who had been hit by a car, everyone in the accident was killed. The truck ended up on the front porch of the Loyal Oak Country Store.

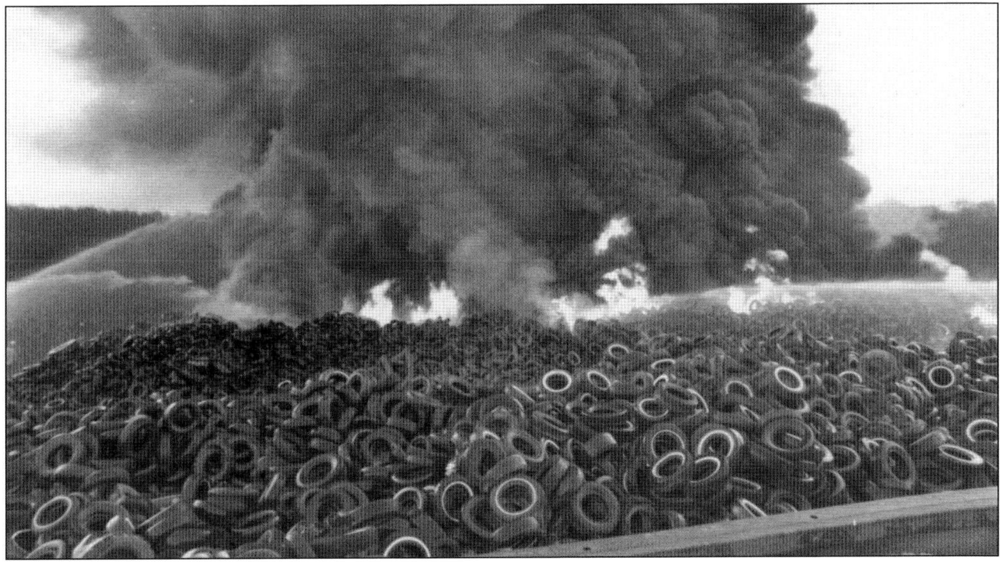

A prank that got out of hand cost $50,000 and caused multiple injuries to firefighters. A total of 20 area fire departments responded with 200 firefighters converged on Sid's Tire Service on Clark Mill Road in 1983. Sid Grebelsky, who bought the property in 1969, owned the land, which included 10 acres with tires piled as high as 20 feet, along with a 75-foot gully filled to the brim. 15 tankers had to be set up to shuttle water, and more than 2,800 feet of hose had to be laid. Sid's Tire Service was a scrap yard and sold tires for recapping. (Courtesy of the *Akron Beacon Journal.*)

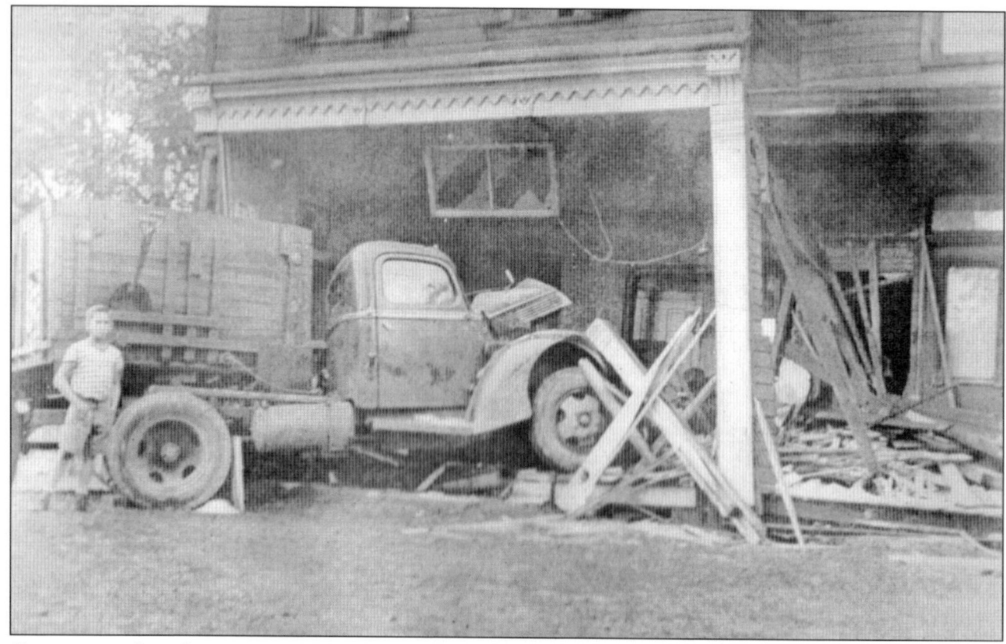

One warm October evening in 1941, an empty coal semi-truck approached the intersection of routes 21 and 261 from the north, struck a car, careened up a five-foot embankment, and smashed into Blackburn's Barber Shop. Three people inside were shaken, including a small boy in the barber chair and patron Wayne Ault, who was waiting his turn. This accident was the demise of the barbershop. At the time, owner Chester Blackburn was struggling to support his family, having tried his hand at selling automobiles, door-to-door sales, driving school buses, working as a custodian, then barbering. Originally the Whipple farmhouse, over time, the building held a post office and a dry goods store. As a barbershop, the price of a haircut was 25¢ for children, 35¢ for adults, and 15¢ for shaves. As for the fate of the crash victims, Elmer Morgan, 26 years old, and Mr. and Mrs. Frank Belden, ages 59 and 58, respectively, received minor injuries. The driver of the truck, 21-year old Joe Gumm of Cleveland, was held at the Barberton jail for reckless driving. (Both, courtesy of William Blackburn.)

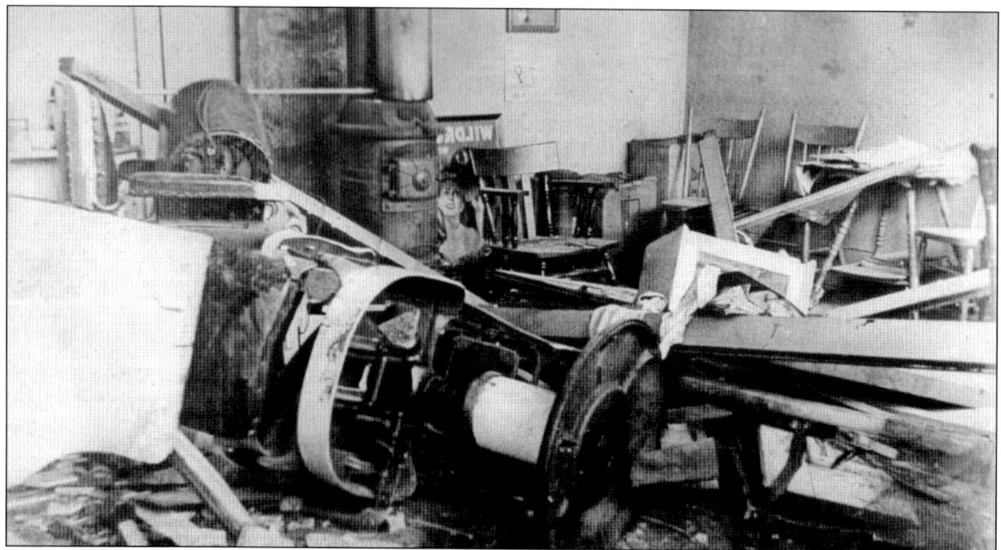

Norton celebrated its sesquicentennial in 1968, and during this festival, every man was required to grow a beard. Permits to grow beards were $1, and for those who preferred not to have a fuzzy face, it was $2. Whiskered fellows caught without their badges were hauled before a judge and jury appointed by the mayor. This photograph depicts the procession for the Burying of the Razor Ceremony. Ray Zor had his funeral, officiated by the Reverend Robert Gray, and was buried in the park at Norton Center.

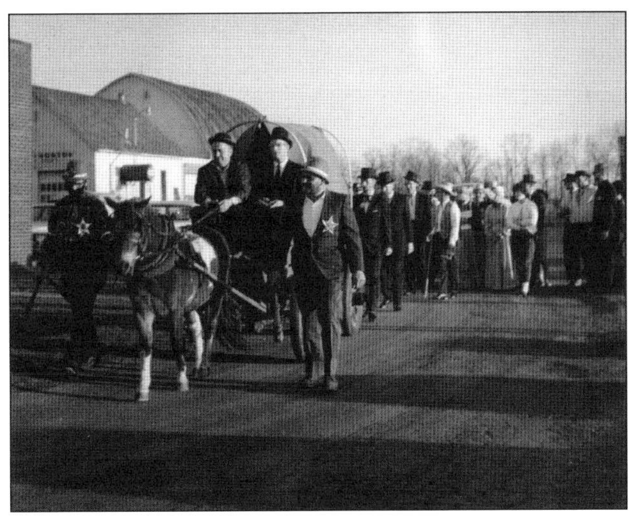

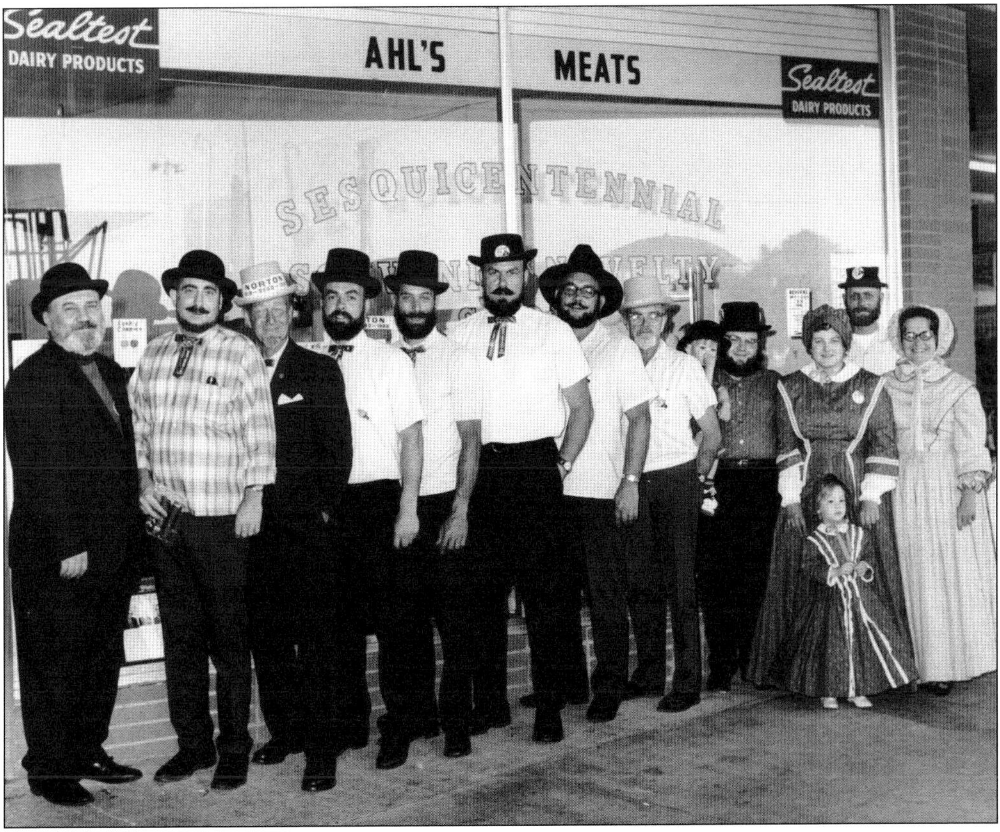

Many of the participants of the sesquicentennial pose in front of their headquarters in Norton Plaza Shopping Center. It took a village to create this week-long event, including Mayor John Henning, Ernest Seiberling and Denzil Leatherman (chairmen), Clarence Miller (treasurer), and Ann Readhead (secretary). There were 20 separate committees and participating organizations on hand to make this festival a genuine success.

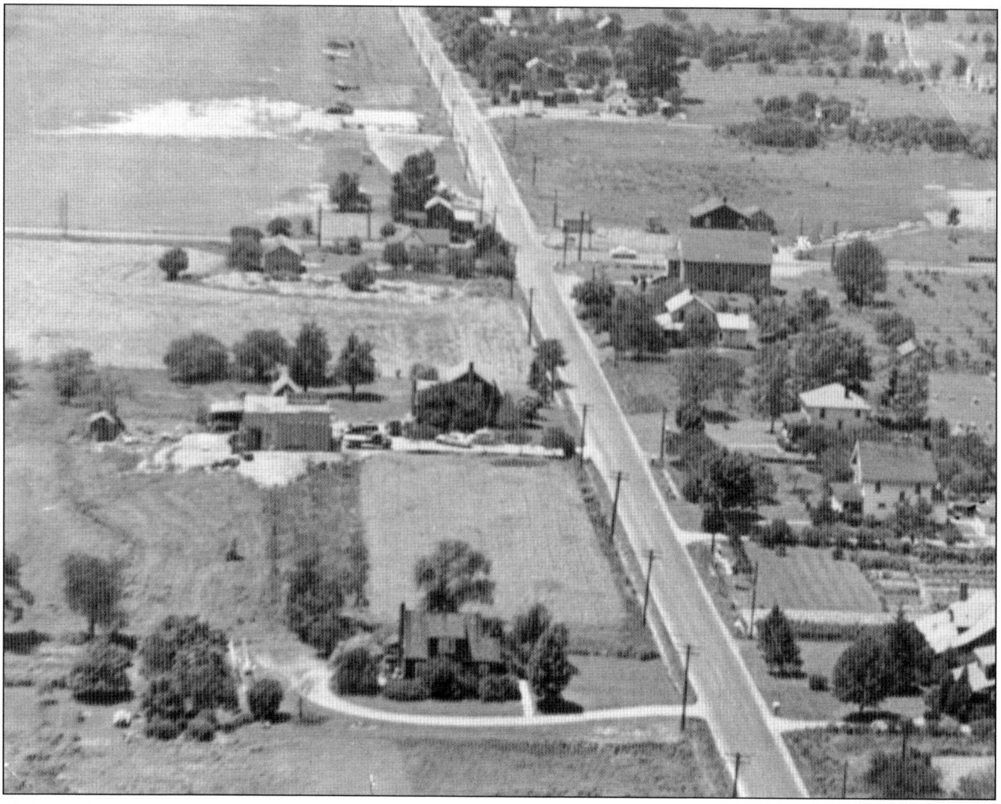

A little-known fact about Norton is that there was an airport at one time. The airport, known by Ling Field, Sherman Airport, or Barberton Airport, located in Sherman, opened on the farm of Jacob and Luella Ling in the 1920s. The field was on a small strip of land on Lot 82 on the southwest side heading south after the intersection of Hametown and Johnson Roads. Many young men learned to fly at Ling Field, with flying time kept at a makeshift office. There was a tower at the field and a small hamburger and pop stand. In 1938, the field was used to fly airmail; the first of which being flown under the authority of the Barberton Post Office. The plane was piloted by Frank Sick, a postal clerk with a pilot's license. On July 7, 1948, the hangar was destroyed by fire, and the field was closed. In this aerial photograph, one can see the planes shown on the field next to the hangar. Below, this sign, still in existence, was once used to direct individuals to the airfield. (Above, courtesy of Mauri O'Brodo; below, courtesy of Rodger Ramsthaler.)

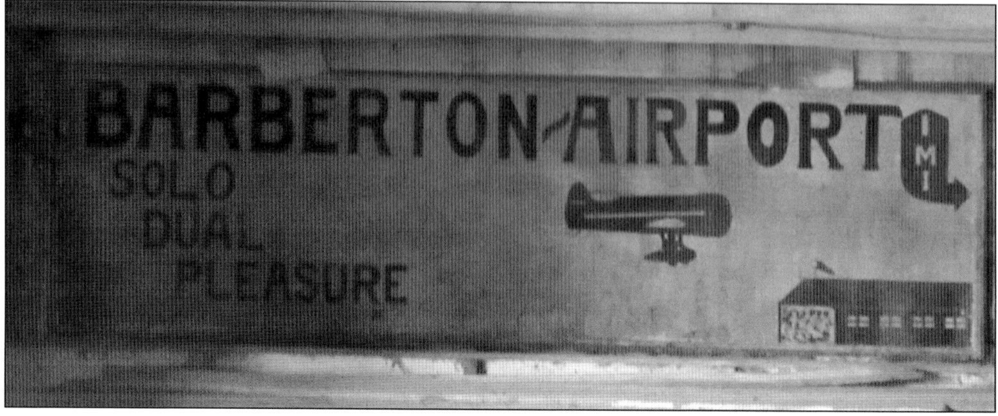

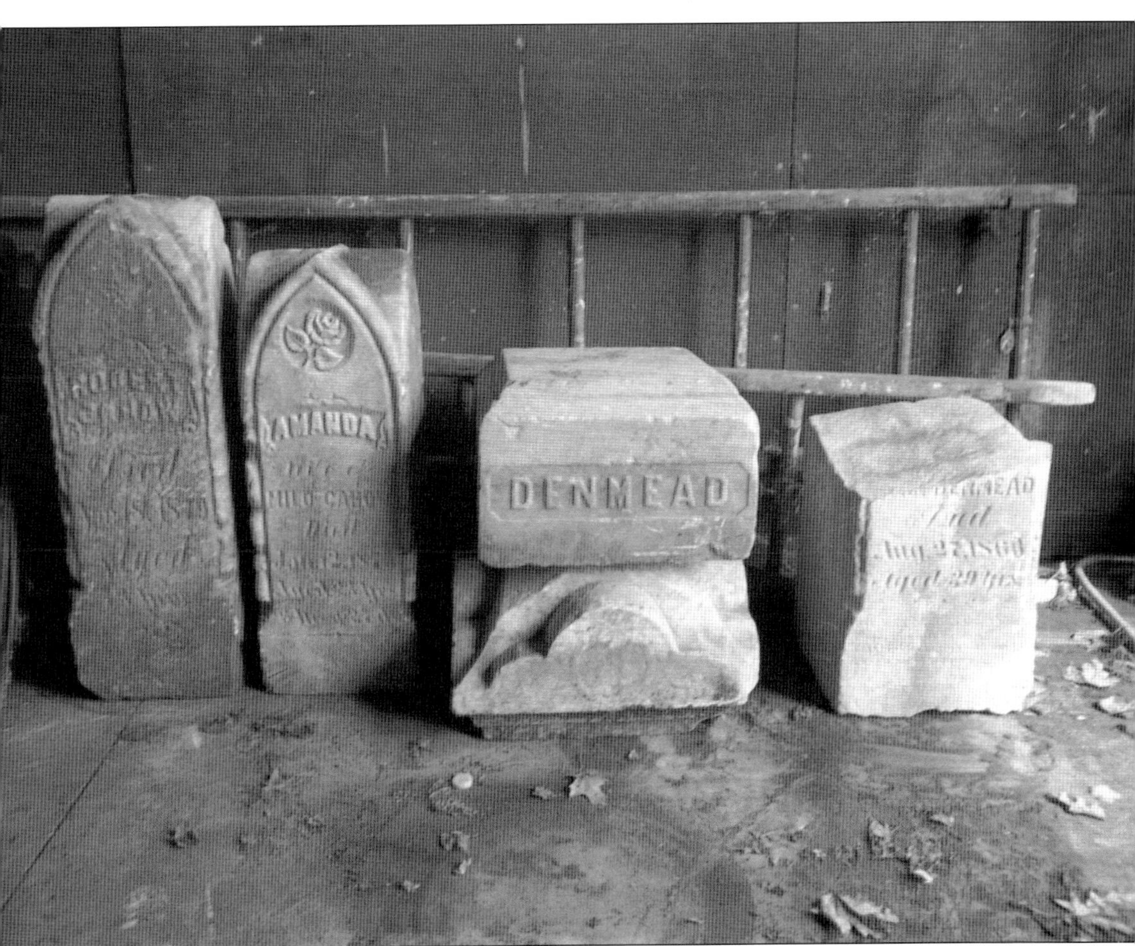

The history of Norton's churches would be incomplete without the mention of the great Mormon excitement between 1832 and 1838. There were said to be about 100 to 200 Mormons living in New Portage at that time. Joseph Smith settled at Kirtland, Ohio, to establish his earthly Zion along with elder Sidney Rigdon. Many Mormons left New Portage on the path to Zion. Elder Ambrose Palmer and his wife gave a piece of land to the Norton Township trustees to use as a cemetery. Eventually, this cemetery was cleared away for a playground, then a parking lot for a school. The stones were unceremoniously bulldozed over a hillside, but some were found and reset by Abraham Benavides in 1997. Seen here in this photograph are a few of the headstones that ended up in Copley Township on private property in a load of dirt in 1960. The president of the Norton Historical Society, Rodger Ramsthaler, and the author brought them to the Norton Historical Society Biery House and Museum for storage until they can be reset. (Author's collection.)

Western Star April 17 1829

We the Subscribers Promise to pay the Sum affixt to our respective Names to Norman Curtis & Mills Richards Committee for the Purpose of building a School House near the corner on the Town line Road to be Paid by the first of Oct. Next

	amount	
Mills Richards	$15.00	
Levi Clark	15.00	
Reuben Wheeler	5.00	
Henry Richards	15.00	
Ezekiel Richards	15.00	in good Whitewood Boards
Wm. D. Richards	15.00	materials or labor
Eben. [illegible]	1-00	
George McCarron	1-00	
Franklin E. Palmer	5.00	Two thousand of shingle in labour and the [illegible]
Milow Hayes	02.00	One thousand of shingle
William Bruner	03-00	In labour next fall
George Palmer	4 00	two hundred feet of clapboards to apply
[illegible] Palmer	3.00	[illegible] shingle
Norman Curtis	15.00	
Wm. C. Richards	15-00	
Clement C. Dickerman	4 00	
[illegible] Hoskinson		6 weeks board

One of the oldest existing original documents in Norton is the one shown here, dated April 17, 1829. It was an agreement between local families to subsidize and build a school that would also be used for religious purposes.

Western Star April 17 1829

Whereas we the Subscribers for the Purpose of a mutual understanding do agree to abide by the following Articles (Viz)

1st That we build a house 28 by 24. 10 ft. Posts in a good Substantial workman like manner and Paint the Same for the Purpose of holding Schools & religious Meetings

2nd That no Religious meeting Shall be appointed to obstruct or interfere with the Schools and their Shall be no Preferance given to any one denomination of Christians

4th That S^d house be built on the Town line Road North of the Bean Brook So called on the land owned by Mills Richards in Norton

5th That the building committee M. Richards & N. Curtis be requested to [illegible] from any one unless he or they Subscribe a Sum equal to their Property & other advantages to be left to the discretion of S^d Committee

Subscribers Names	Subscribers Names
Mills Richards	Norman Curtis
Levi Clark	Wm. C. Richards
Henry Richards	Clement C. Dickerman
Reuben Wheeler	
Ezekiel Richards	
Wm. D. Richards	
George McCarron	
Eben. [illegible]	
Franklin E. Palmer	
Milow Hayes	
William Bruner	

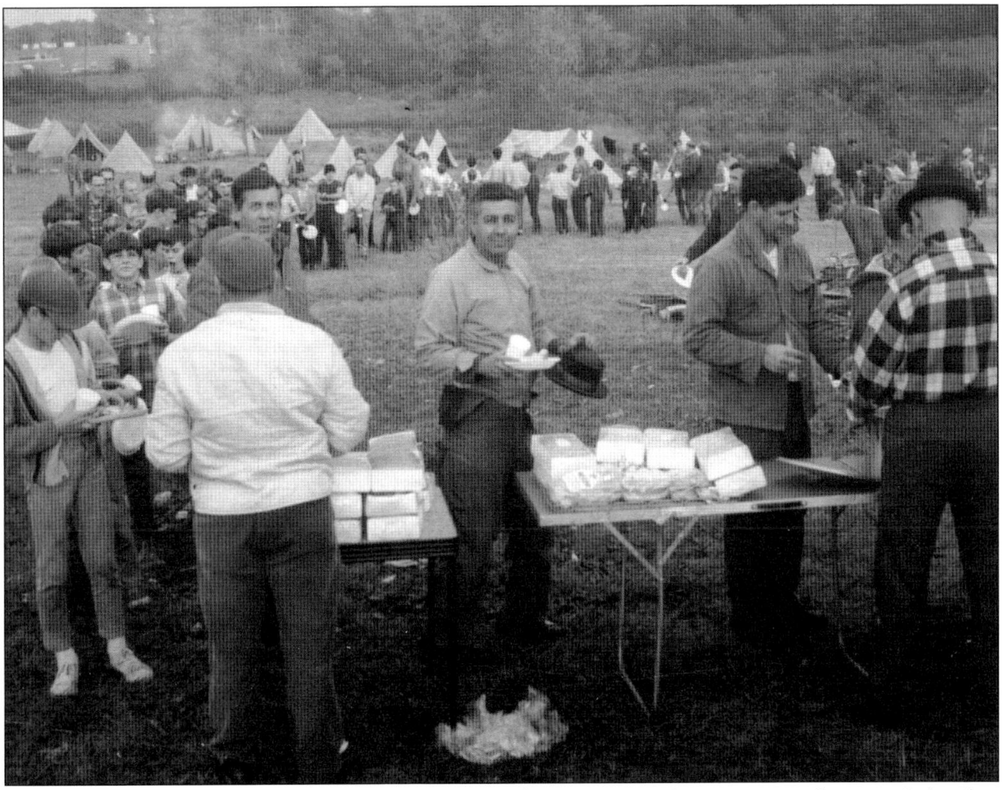

Looking east toward the Norton Plaza in 1969 is the Boy Scout Camporee in the new Columbia Woods Park. In 1974, this large encampment of young men helped to clear brush, making way for a playground, pond, gazebo, basketball and tennis courts, and pavilions.

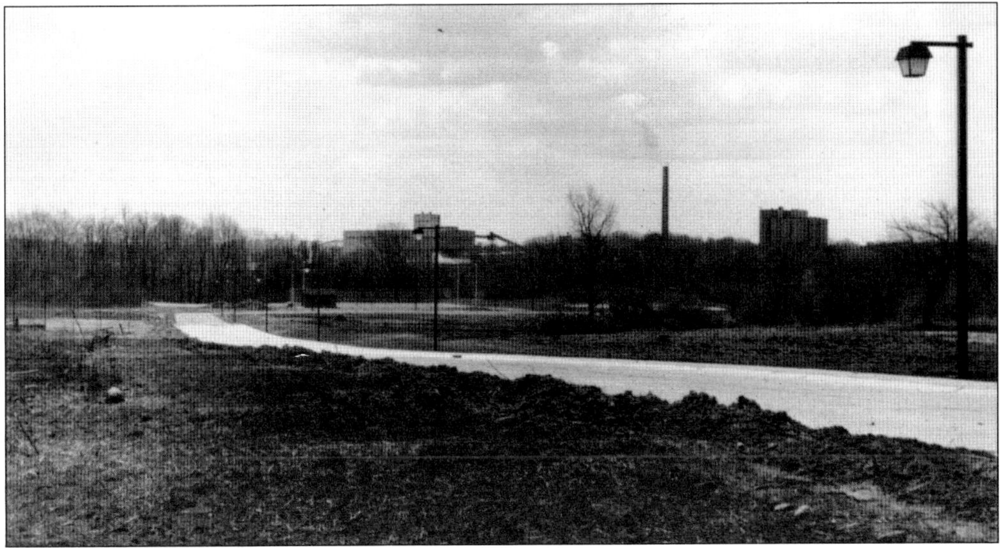

In 1963, PPG Industries donated 14.5 acres of land to the City of Norton, dedicated in June 1970. The park was named Columbia Woods Park in honor of PPG Industries Columbia Chemical Division. Seen in the distance are the buildings for the PPG limestone mine operations and the newly installed tennis courts.

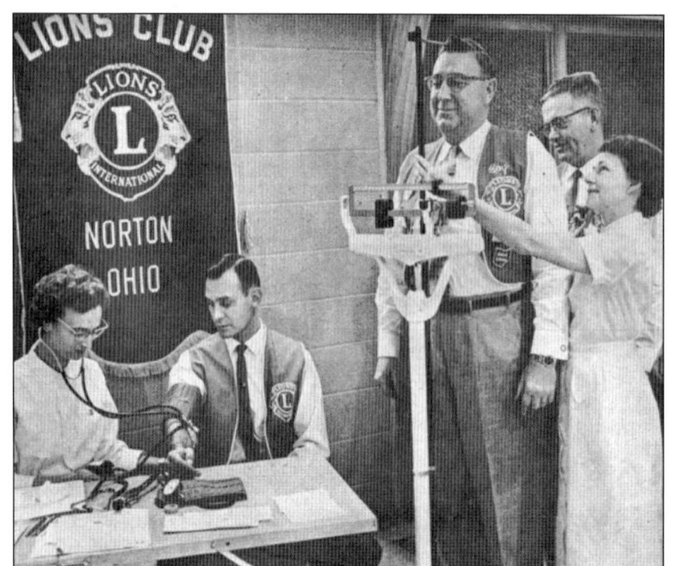

In December 1961, the Norton Lions Club took on the look of an Army induction center as members went through checkups. In the production line is Doris Minnick checking the blood pressure of Bill Wetzel. Ray Snyder gets his weight checked by Mrs. Cordrey while Jackson Cordrey looks on. The Norton Lions Club started in May 1956, with Pearl Smith as the newly elected president. The Lions Club is the world's largest service club organization. (Courtesy of the *Akron Beacon Journal*.)

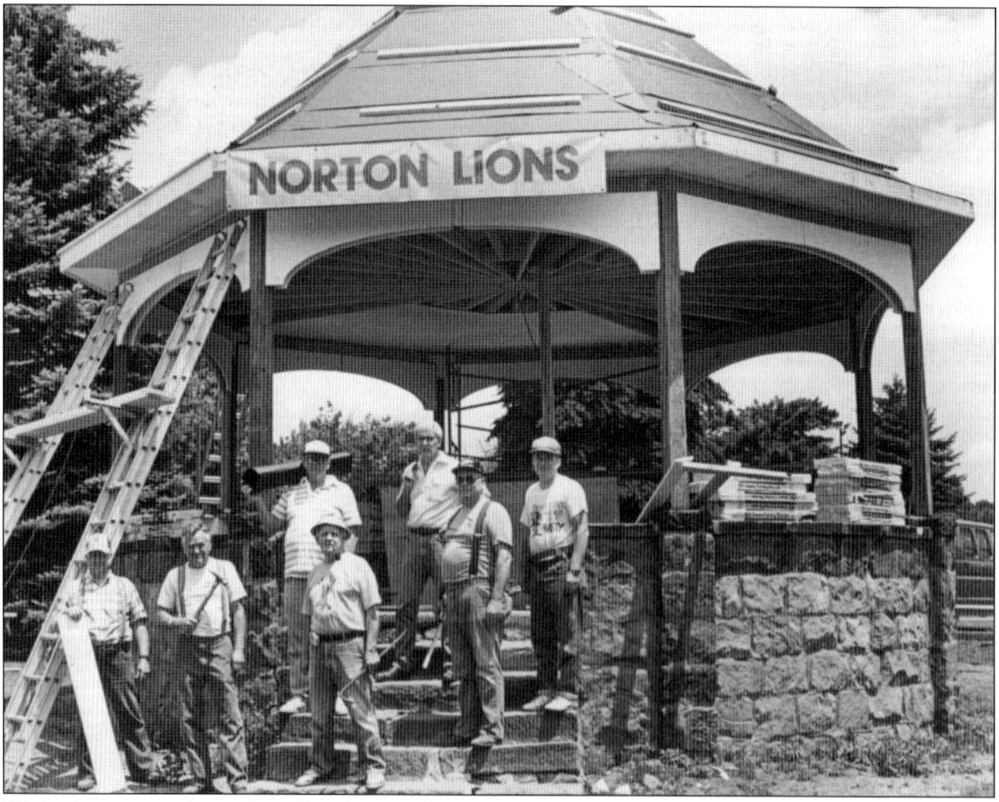

With the money from the sale of two schoolhouses in Western Star in 1935, a grandstand was built on the northeast corner of Greenwich and Cleveland-Massillon Roads. In 1992, a roof was added, and in the spring of 1993, the Lion's Club of Norton completed the project that was left unfinished in the 1930s, by adding a copper weathervane. Norton Lions Club members in 1992 are, from left to right, (first row) Al Miller, Jim Cook, and Jim George; (second row) Bob Kurt; (third row) Howard Hamilton and Don Weygandt; (fourth row) Bob Seely.

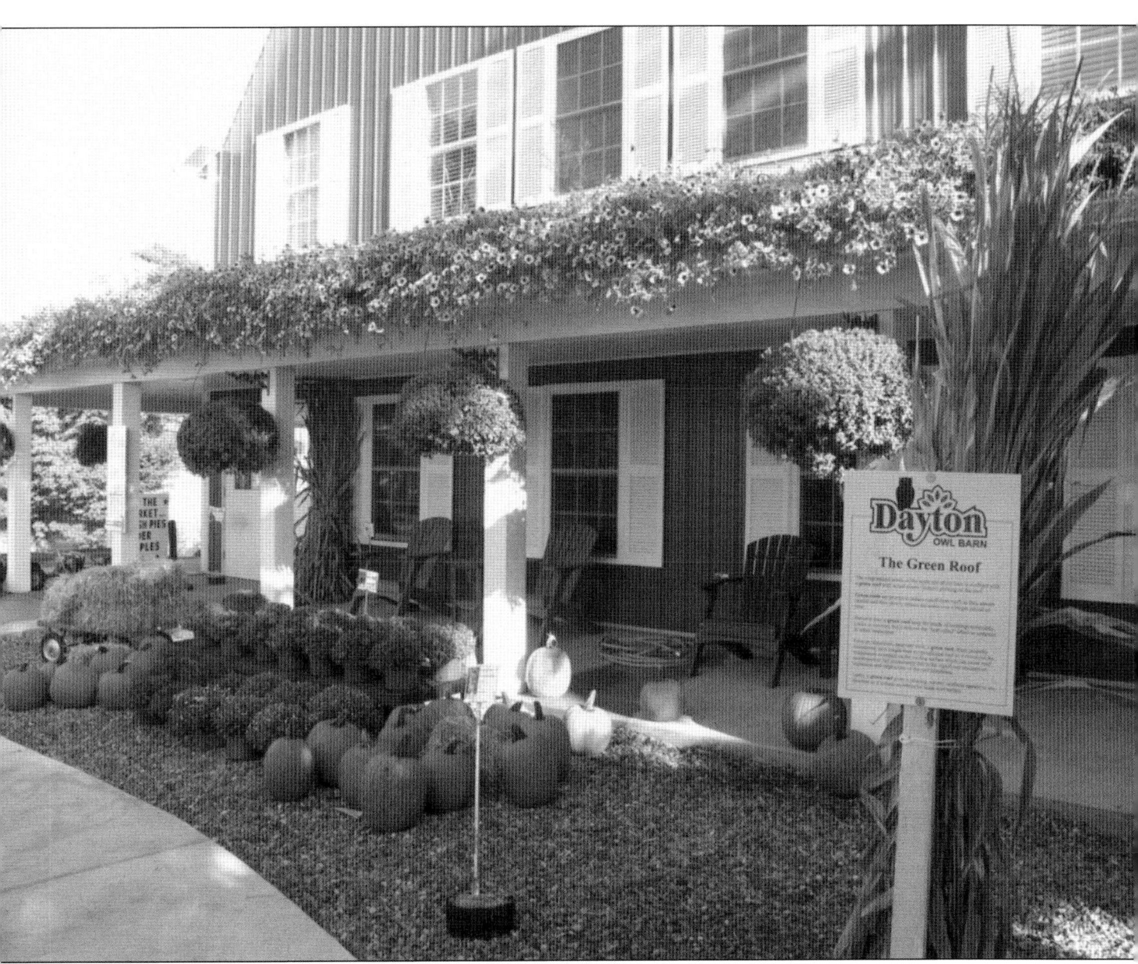

The Owl Barn at Dayton Nurseries is a composite of many 100-year-old barns that gives it the look of a Wisconsin dairy barn. This barn is similar to the one that burned down on the property in 1963 and nearly on the same location. The barn is decorated inside with tongue-and-groove pine siding that covers the walls, and the peak of the ceiling rises 26 feet from the floor. The rainfall striking the gambrel roof is drained to an irrigation lake about 800 feet east of the barn. The barn features a green roof on the south and west sides of the porch, which helps to reduce water runoff and provide cooling to the porch roof in the summer. The barn is used for educational seminars, flower shows, and a summer produce market. It features gift items and an entrance to the Wolf Creek Botanical display garden. A lovely view can be seen from Cleveland-Massillon Road in April, which includes 15,000 daffodils and 200 creeping phlox. (Courtesy of David Snowden.)

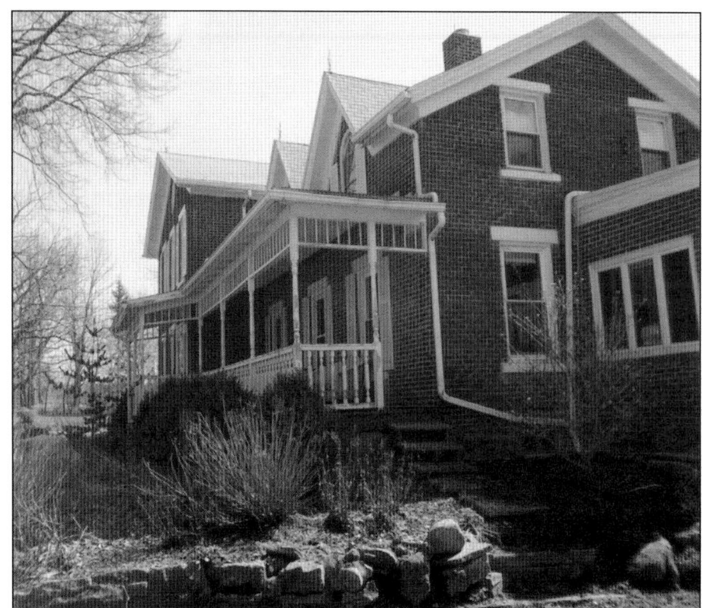

Traveling by horse teams in 1810, Samuel Green and his wife, Lucy Bailey Green, headed West from Connecticut, finally coming to live in Norton and settling on a tract of land in 1811. Now, the H&H Farm at 4162 Akron-Wadsworth Road is owned by Glen and Joellen Hoffman. Today, it is much like it was in the past, with cattle, chickens, pigs, turkeys, eggs, hay, and straw. (Author's collection.)

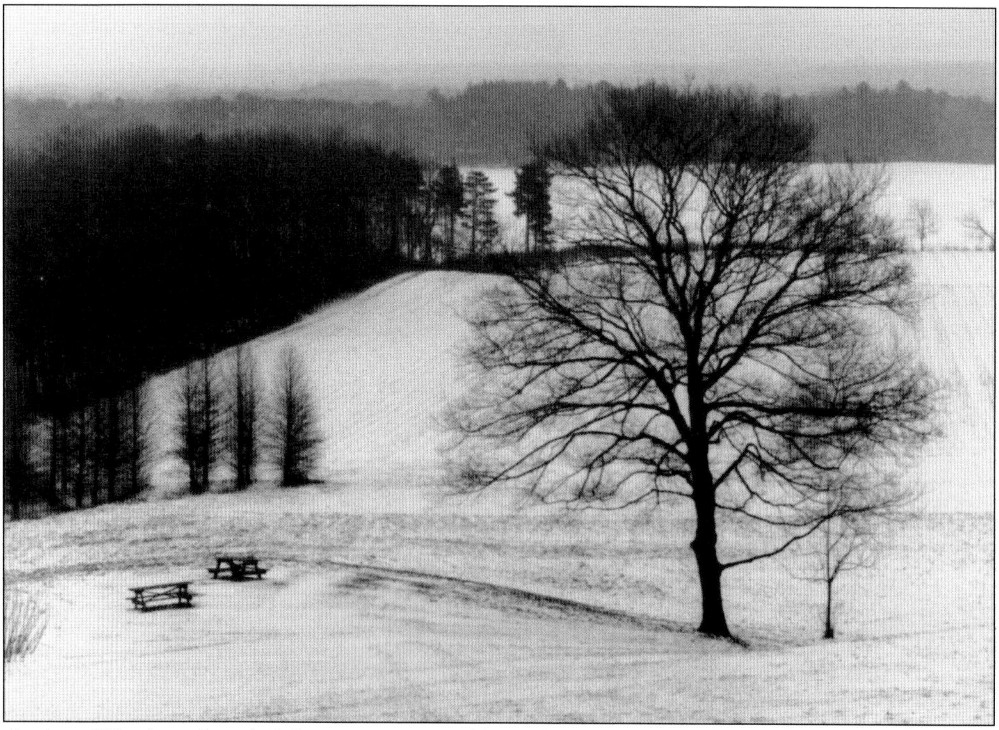

Andrew Wineberg founded the Winery at Wolf Creek in 1980 at 2637 Cleveland-Massillon Road. The winery overlooks the Barberton Reservoir, which was created as a water source for the city of Barberton. In 1984, the original cellar was created by blasting with dynamite into the rocky hillside. The first bottle of wine sold in June 1985 and the first three wines released were Seyval, Vignoles, and Sweet Revenge. In 2002, after the untimely death of Andrew Wineberg, the wine operation was purchased by longtime vineyard manager Andy Troutman and his wife, Deanna. (Author's collection.)

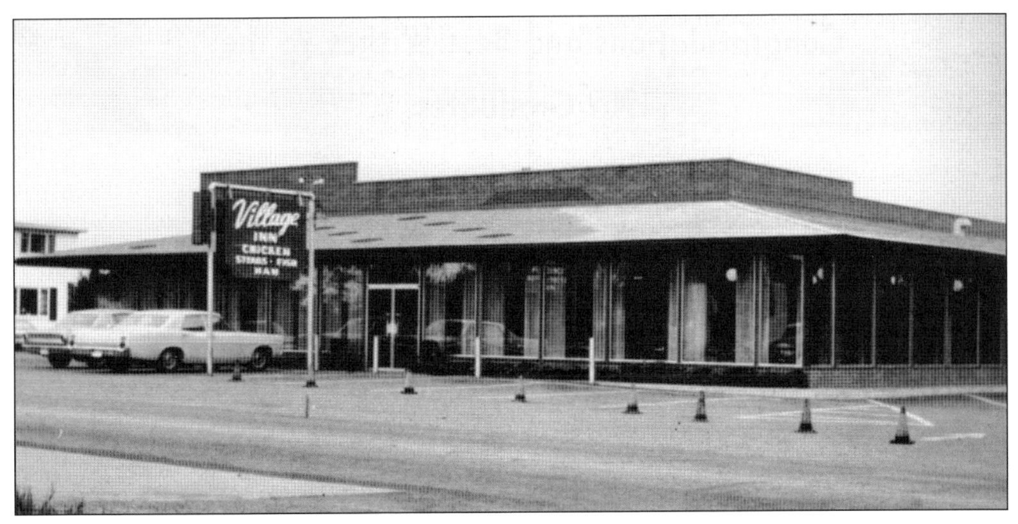

Prior to being known as Milich's Village Inn, this building was owned by the Hageys and operated as an IGA grocery store, later known as one of many houses of Barberton chicken. Milich's Village Inn, located at 4444 Cleveland-Massillon Road, was established in 1955 by Mirko and Katie Milich. The Miliches served a Serbian-style fried chicken known throughout the land, and this place was a must stop on the list of Norton/Barberton fair. The traditional Barberton chicken dinner is comprised of four pieces of chicken fried in lard with coleslaw, hot sauce, and french fries. After 60 years in business, Milich's closed in 2014. New ownership has since resumed, offering the same fare at Village Inn Chicken.

HAGEY'S Super Market

Open Every Day and Evening Except Sunday

QUALITY MEATS & GROCERIES

AT EVERYDAY PRICES

Between Norton Center & Johnson's Corners

STATE RT. No. 21 SH 1352

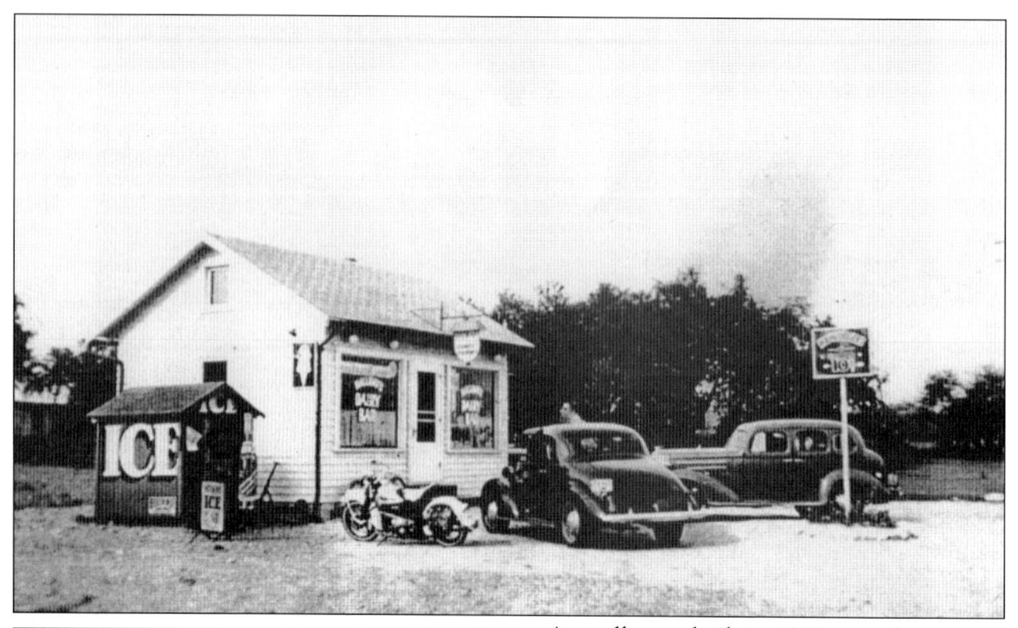

A small store built in 1937 named Hallidays Dairy Bar was situated on the northeast corner of Hametown and Akron-Wadsworth Roads. It was operated by owner William Rohlden "Rollie" Halliday, his wife Anne Houston Halliday, and their daughter Catherine.

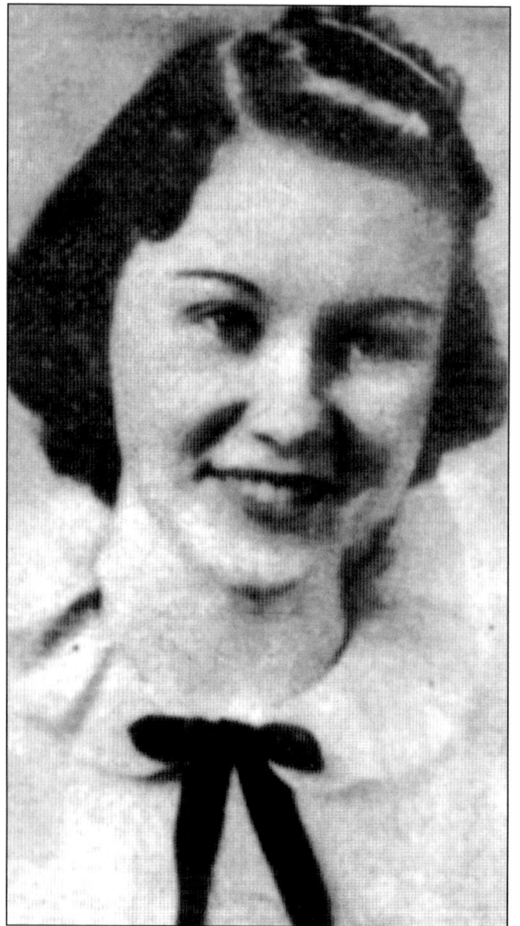

At the age of 90, Catherine Halliday Hagey, was interviewed by the author before her death in 2012 and stated that she was an only child and recalled evenings at the family store. Many locals would come in for ice cream, and at the age of 15, Catherine eventually began working for the supplier of their ice cream, Willowbrook Dairy. She married Arville Hagey, and together, they were the owners and builders of the IGA grocery store on Cleveland-Massillon Road, which later became Milich's Village Inn. Pictured here in 1922, Catherine was said to be one of Norton's youngest businessmen as she worked to raise funds for her college education. Five days a week, she opened Hallidays store next to the Halliday home and also did the buying and accounting.

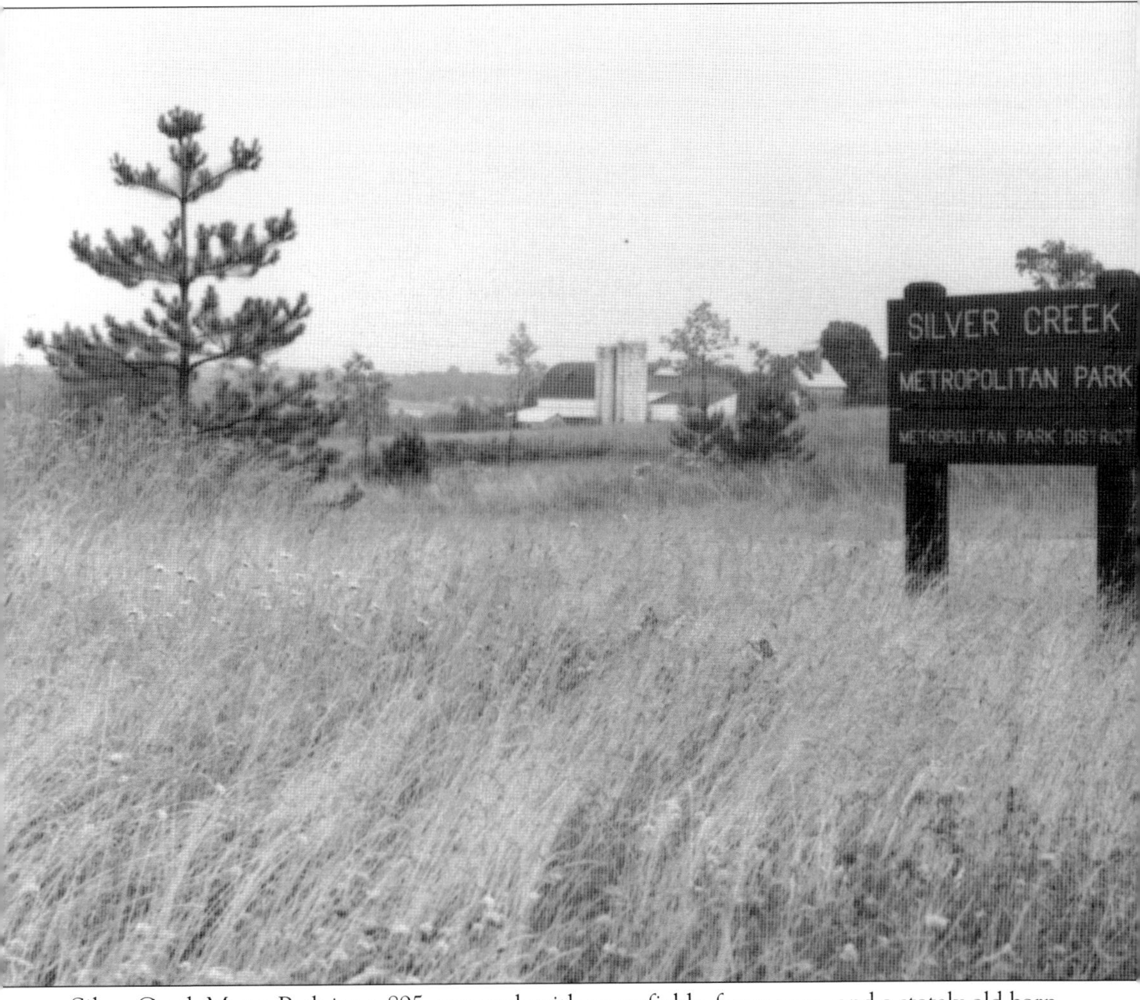

Silver Creek Metro Park is an 895-acre park with open fields, fence rows, and a stately old barn, part of which dates back to the Civil War. The park's former life was as the Harter Dairy Farm. Buried beneath the surface is a maze of tunnels and shafts that are remnants of 19th-century mining operations. Metro Parks acquired the land in 1966, and they planted thousands of trees and added a bathhouse and a 50-acre lake fed by a spring from an old mine. Iron-laden water from the mineshafts feeds into Silver Creek, coating the bottom of the stream with reddish brown iron oxide, yet fish, frogs, and other animals thrive. The open fields are home to woodcocks, meadowlarks, and Eastern bluebirds, while many butterflies flutter among the flowers and grasses. Tall sycamores grow in soggy areas, and hickory woods grow in drier spots. The beech-maple woods contain spring wildflowers. One of the largest red oaks in Summit County, which is 20 feet in circumference, stands in this park. (Courtesy of Summit County Metro Parks.)

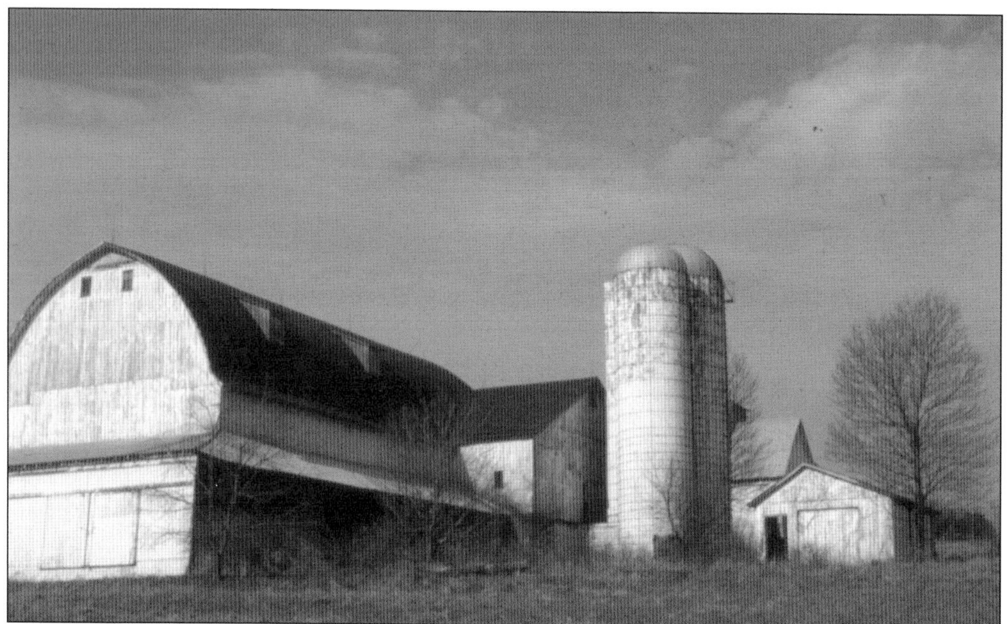

The Harter Family Dairy Farm is now in the hands of the Summit County Metro Parks as part of Silver Creek Park. Bert and Fred Harter, a former state senator, combined their Belle Isle Dairy with Reiter Dairy to become the Reiter and Harter Dairy in 1954. The barn complex was built around 1855. The outer buildings, silos, other barns, and granary were constructed in the mid-1940s. (Courtesy of Summit Metro Parks.)

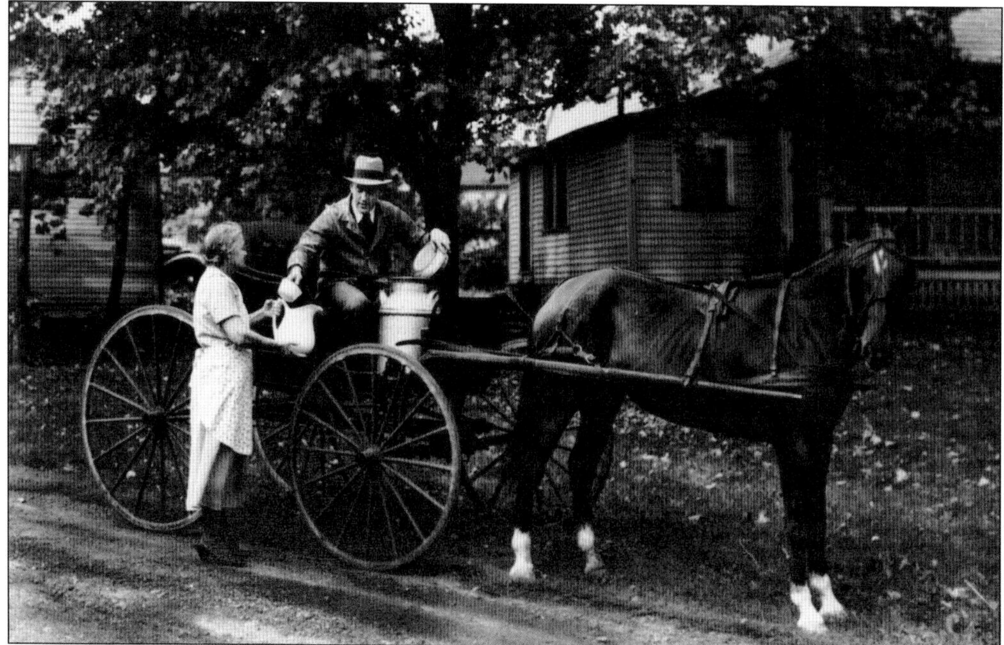

Daily milk deliveries were common in Norton and area communities because the lack of good refrigeration meant that milk would spoil quickly. Here, an unidentified man ladles milk into a pitcher for a woman. This photograph was taken in the hamlet of Sherman. (Courtesy of Mauri O'Brodo.)

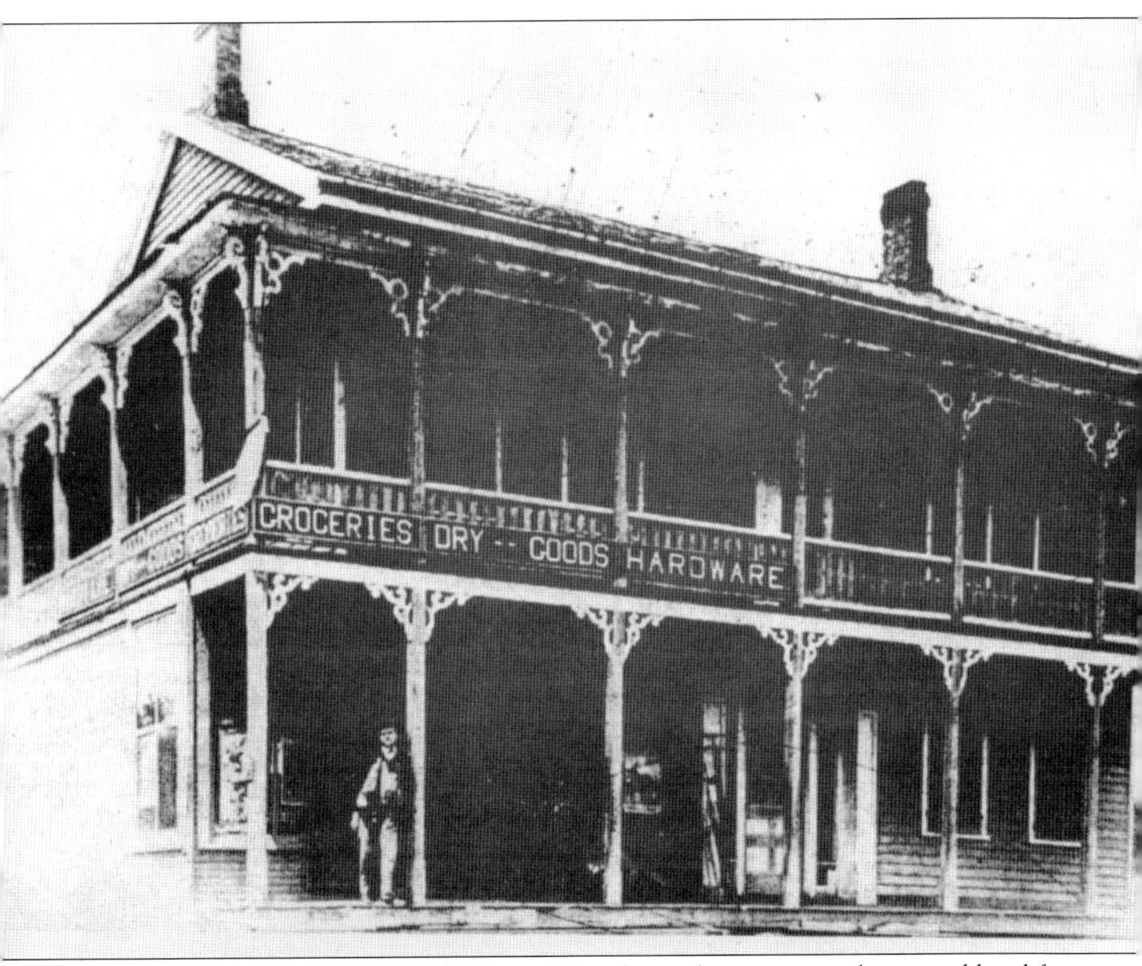

The Loyal Oak Country Store was built in 1824 and served as a stagecoach stop and hotel for wagons traveling from Cleveland to Marietta. Adzed timbers were cut from local oak trees with building stones cut and squared at a local quarry, likely Winter Green Ledges.. The attached one-car garage was the first fire station and housed two water tanks and a hose mounted on a trailer. The building had a tavern and a kitchen on the first floor and grand ballroom on the second, which was later converted into living quarters. It once had shingle siding, but it has since been removed and replaced with thick clapboards. In 1922, Lawrence V., also known as "L.V." and his wife, Edythe Theiss Bowers, purchased the property. Five daughters lived upstairs, and all worked in the general store and gasoline station. Furnace Brand, later to become Borden Ice Cream, was served there. It became a popular place for the locals to congregate on The long porch in front of the store became a popular place for locals or potential suitors for L.V.'s daughters to congregate.

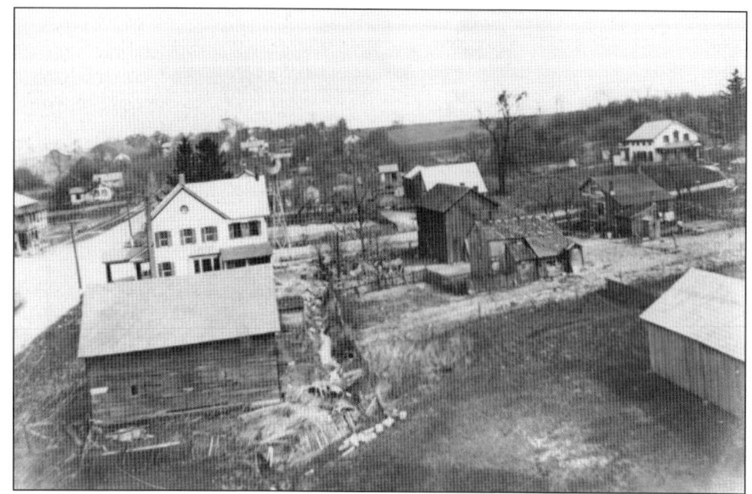

This view from the bell tower of the Lutheran church in Loyal Oak around 1910 captures the country store, tavern, and Flickinger's blacksmith shop and home. In the far-right corner is the Hoertz/Snyder farm. The two structures in the forefront appear to be barns or sheds, but they are no longer in existence.

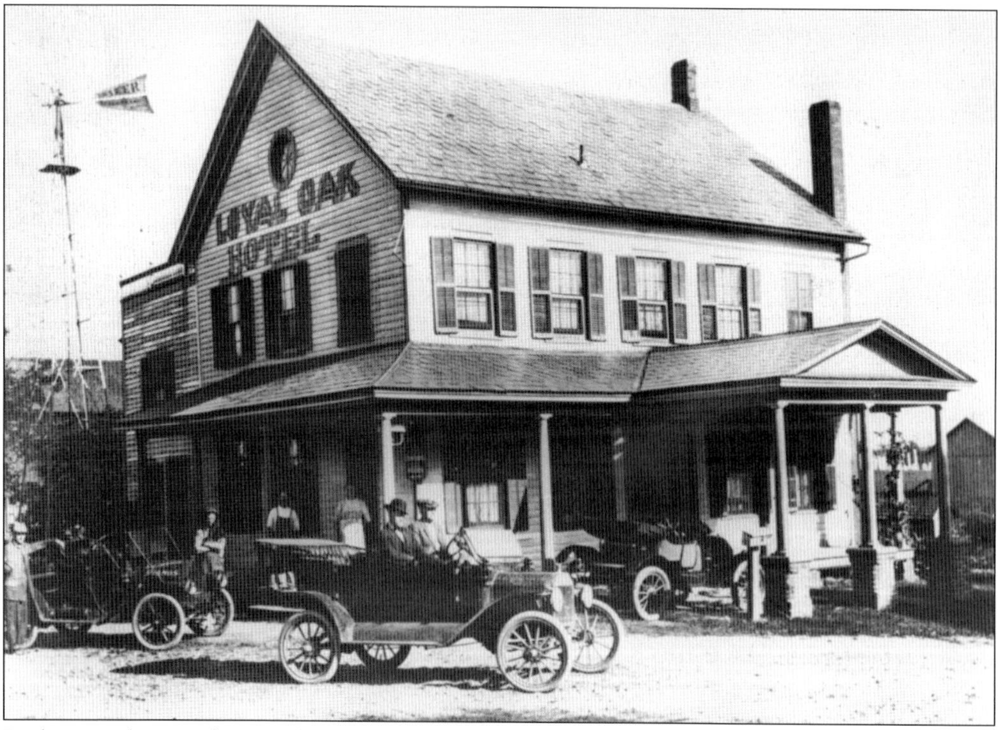

Built around 1840, the Loyal Oak House was originally a hotel before becoming a cabinet shop in 1858. In the 1930s and 1940s, it was known as Adam's Place, named after owner Adam Pinter. Old-timers tell of beer cooling in an underground stream in the basement, in which the original half-log bar is still in the wall dating to the 1930s. Rumors abound that this was once part of the Underground Railroad, with a tunnel leading from this location to the country store. Bootlegging was also a possibility. The establishment has been a restaurant known as the Loyal Oak Tavern and is currently owned by Shane and Amy Cook Moore as the Wolf Creek Tavern.

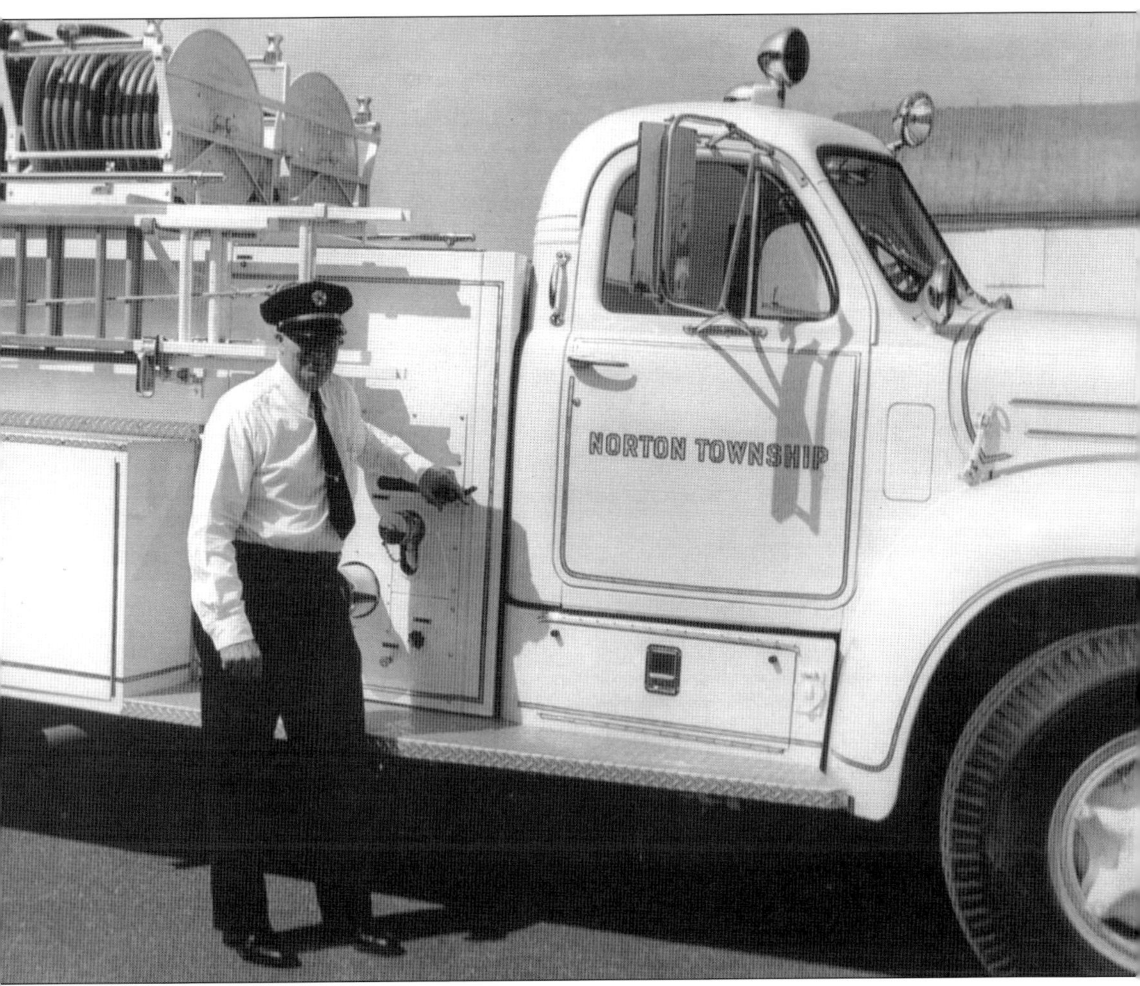

Norton Township had 14 men lined up for the first fire department in 1944, and the first fire chief, Glenn O. Kee (pictured), served from 1944 to 1975. The federal government was giving away skid pumps to communities for civil defense use, and Norton obtained one. With a used truck, the men built the first piece of equipment using the truck and pump. In 1945, the city trustees agreed to purchase a new fire truck and completed their first state firemen's training course. The first fire station was in the basement of the old town hall, a newer fire station was built on Greenwich Road in 1950, and a second station was completed in the hamlet of Sherman. In 2011, a state-of-the-art building was completed just west of the old location on Greenwich Road. This station is complete with three advanced life-support units, three engines, one tanker, and two grass-fire trucks. The station has approximately 30 firefighters, medics, and EMTs. The fire chief is Mike Shultz.

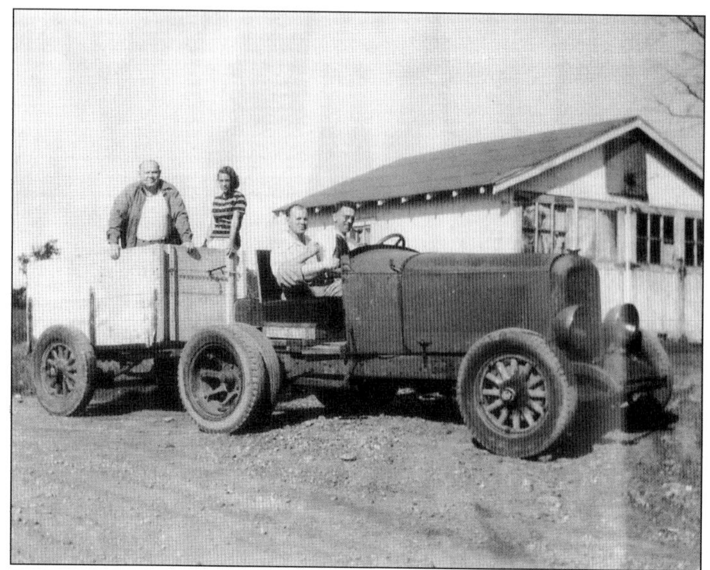

From left to right, Earl Russell Diefendorff with daughter Edna Mae, son Everett Harold, and friend Loyal Sauer are seen at the Diefendorff family farm in 1954. Earl lived in Loyal Oak with his wife, Edna Melissa Harris, and worked for the Goodyear Tire and Rubber Company in Akron as a supervisor before retiring in 1967. He and his wife had four other children: Russell, Wilma, Howard, and Donald. (Courtesy of Cliff Diefendorff.)

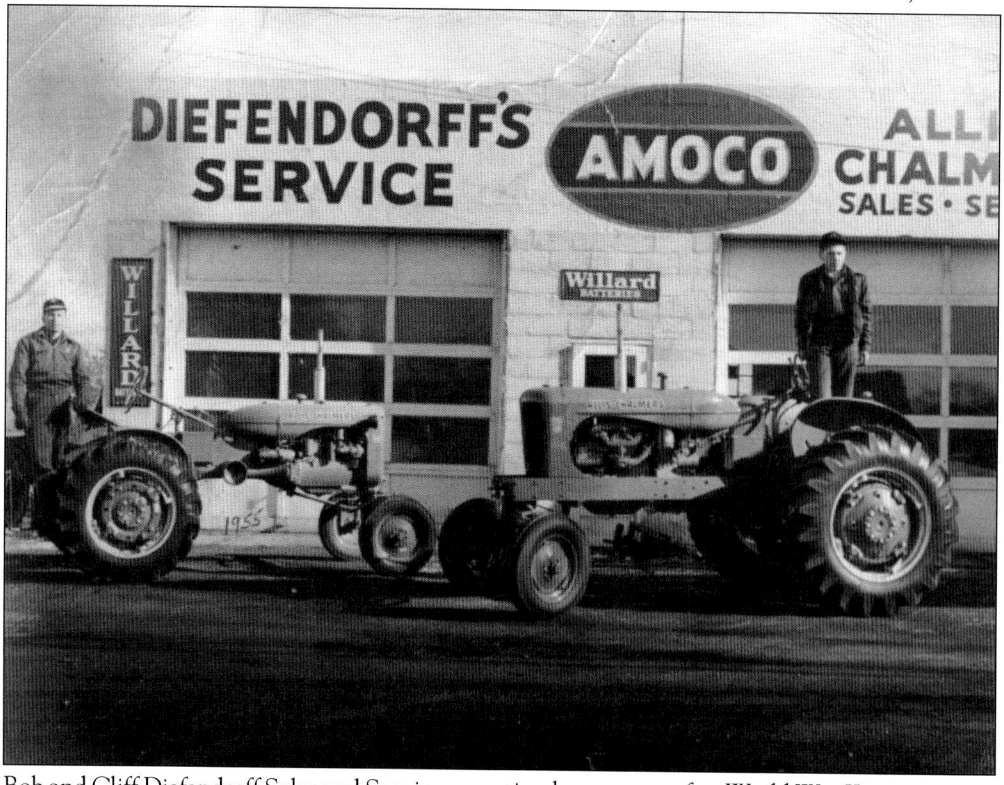

Bob and Cliff Diefendorff Sales and Service operation began soon after World War II, operating as a filling station and tractor implement dealer. Pictured here in 1955 are Cliff Diefendorff Sr. (left) and Bob Diefendorff. The original building burnt to the ground in the late 1950s and reopened in the early 1960s as a Marathon gas station and tractor dealer. Many Norton High School boys worked the gas pumps at this full-service gas station. Today, the service center is located at 3873 Cleveland-Massillon Road and run by Cliff Diefendorff Jr. It is a full-service repair shop with three bays and three mechanics. (Courtesy of Cliff Diefendorff.)

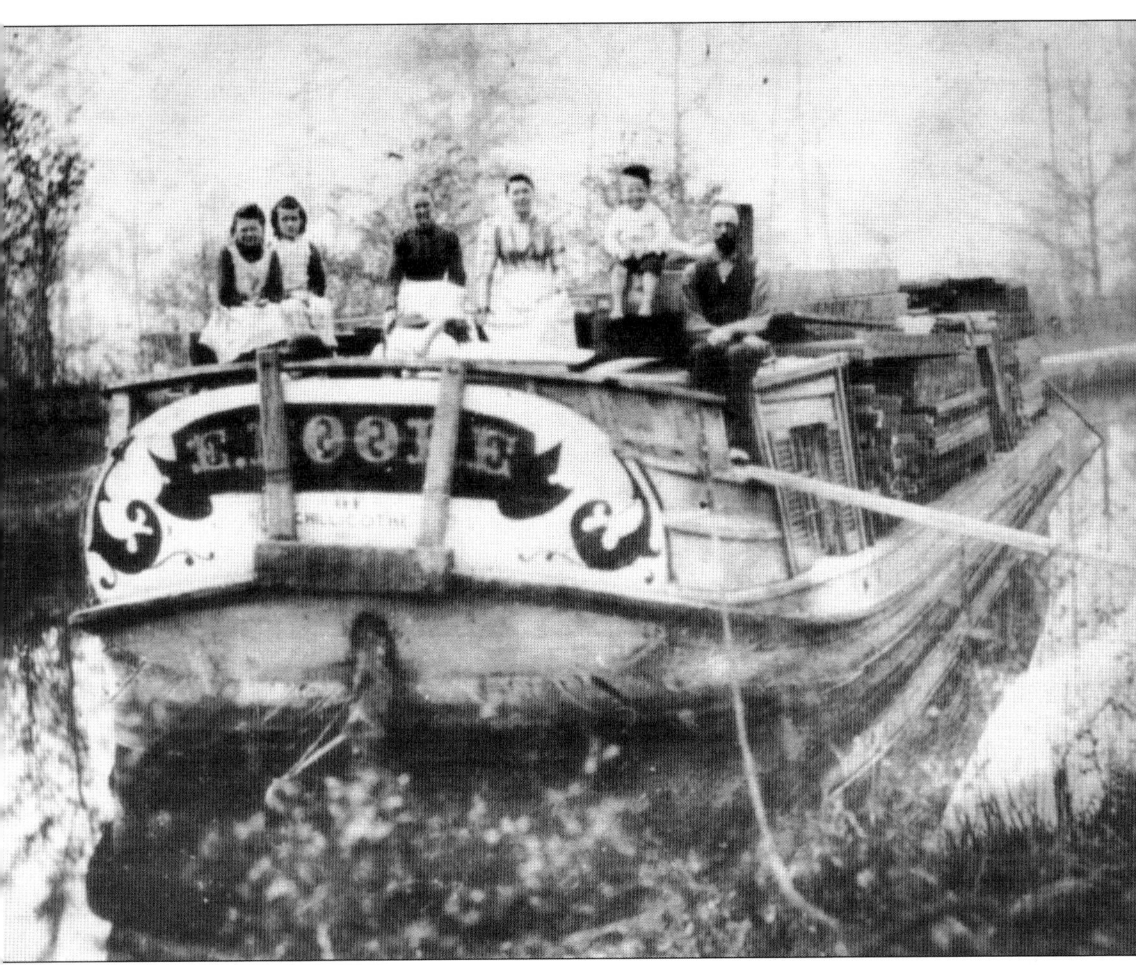

The opening of the Ohio and Erie Canal in 1827 was an important event in the history of Summit County. Providing a direct shipping route to Lake Erie and the Ohio River, the canal had a major effect on the state's economy, taking it from near bankruptcy in 1820 to the third-most economically prosperous state by 1840. In Norton Township, the canal followed the banks of the Tuscarawas River. A system of locks along the length of the canal, completed to the Ohio River in 1832, controlled the water levels through changes in topography. One of these locks was constructed at the mouth of Wolf Creek prior to 1827. Not long after, enterprising merchants located stores carrying groceries and boating supplies adjacent to the lock. Above is the Reichard family on the canal boat *E.E. Moore*. From left to right are Gertrude, Viola, Mary Ellen, Mary Ann, John Jr., and John Reichard near Wolf Creek, about 1883. (Courtesy of Lois Matney.)

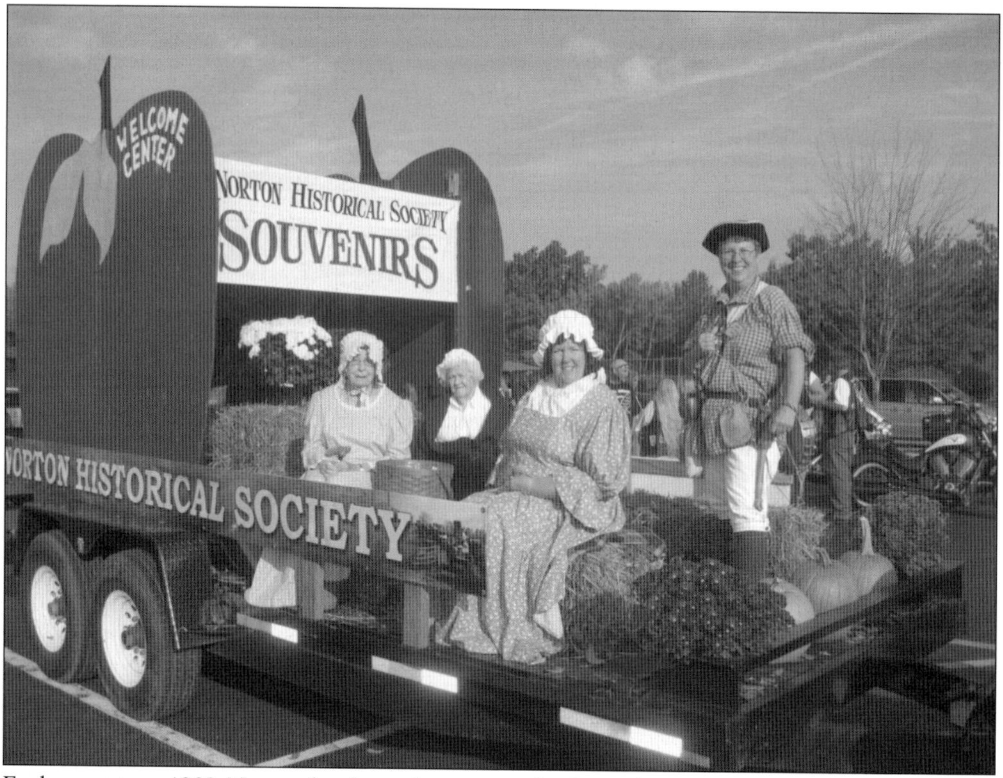

Each year since 1989, Norton has hosted its own cider festival. Started by the Norton Merchant Association and the Norton Lions Club, it was originally held at the site of the Crawford-Knecht Cider Mill and called the Loyal Oak Cider Festival. The event was moved to the Columbia Woods Park and renamed the Norton Cider Festival. The festival includes a parade, games, music, food, fireworks, craft vendors, and contests. Shown here is the Norton Historical Society parade float in 2013, which won for best original design. From left to right are Dorothy Floyd, Lillian Blackburn, Patricia Snyder, and Lisa Merrick. (Courtesy of Kim Nevling Zita.)

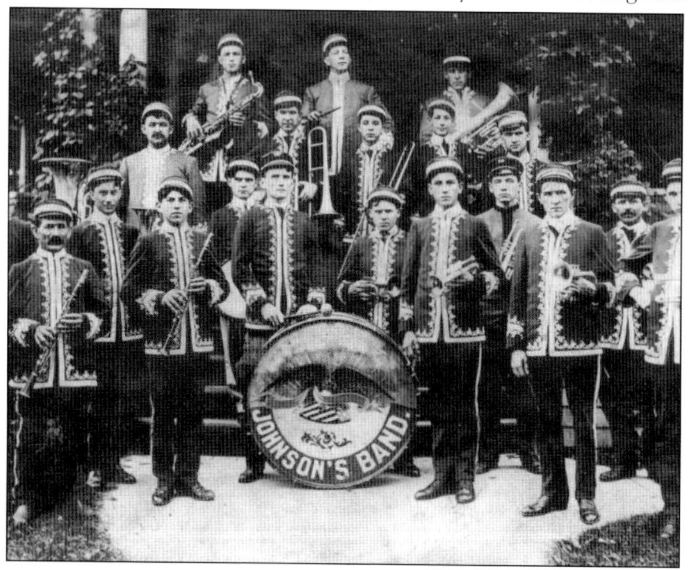

Members of the Johnson's Band in Johnson's Corners pose here in 1898. A few of the band members have been identified. On the front far left is Jacob Langguth, and to his right is Jake Langguth; both men were clarinet players. The gentleman to the direct right of the drum is Walter Smith. (Courtesy of Lori Lewis Pfahler.)

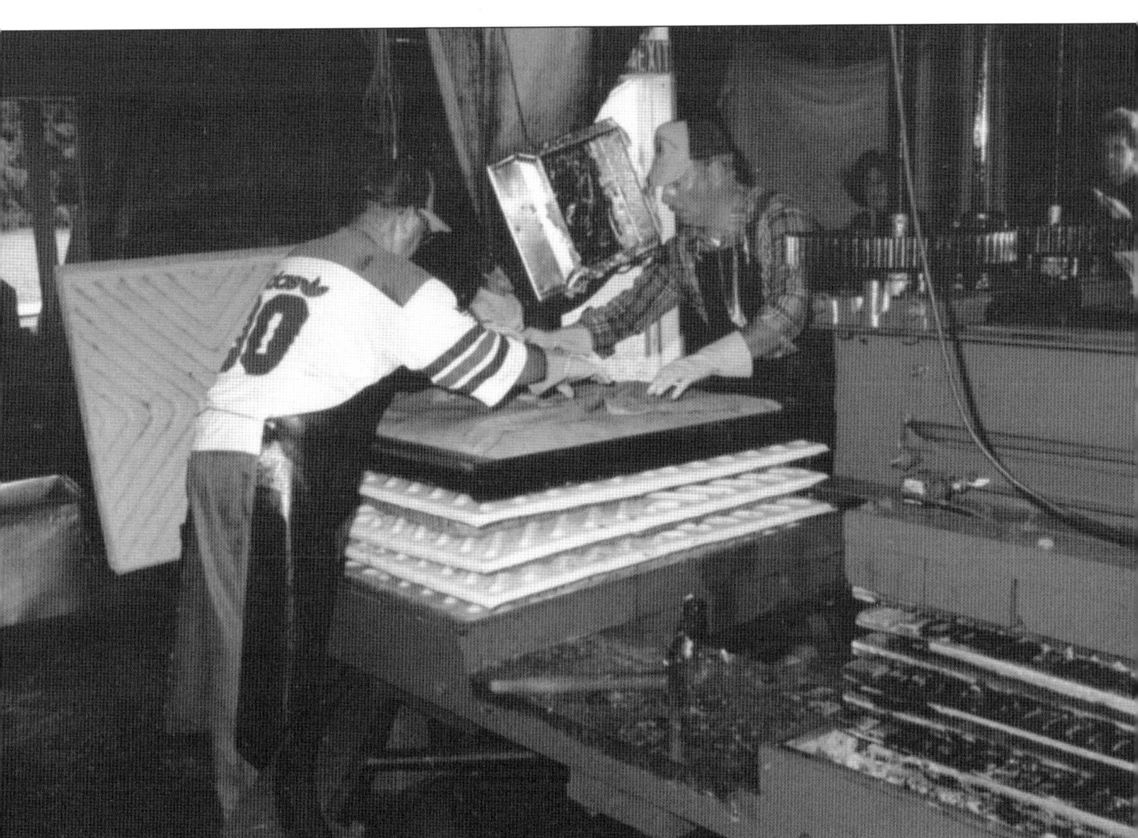

Apples were loaded into a hopper, ground up into small chunks, conveyed inside the Loyal Oak Cider Mill, and dropped between layers of thick canvas in the center of the press. The apples were then spread out evenly with a rake. When a layer reached the desired depth, workers folded the canvas up and over the edges, and then another canvas was put on the press. This went on one layer at a time until the stack was high enough to press them all. A lever was pulled, and big belts, some 20 feet long, moved pulleys that made the center screw turn and press a platform down on the stack of about six packed sections. As the top platform moved slowly down toward the bottom one, the liquid was squeezed out through the canvas, and it ran into the bottom catchment well, which drained off into a tank. Pictured here is the original mill press; Loyal Oak also produced peach and apple butter and tomato juice. (Courtesy of Tim and Debbie Crawford.)

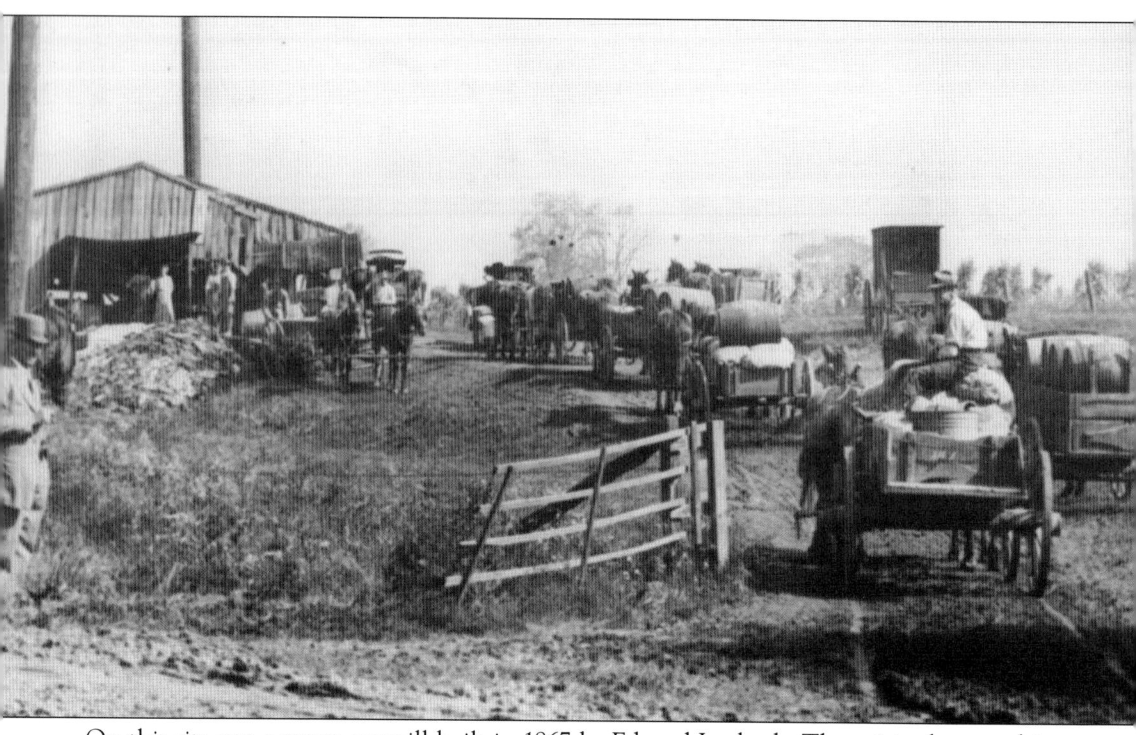

On this site was a steam sawmill built in 1867 by Edward Laubach. The original steam-driven belt and gears of the 100-ton German-built press are still intact. The mill burned down and was rebuilt and sold in 1879 to John J. Knecht, who then converted it into a cider mill. This 1913 scene depicts the comings and goings of customers waiting to have their apples turned into cider. The press went out of business in 1960. It was resurrected for a period of time in the late 1980s to coincide with the Norton Cider Festival but has remained silent since 2012.

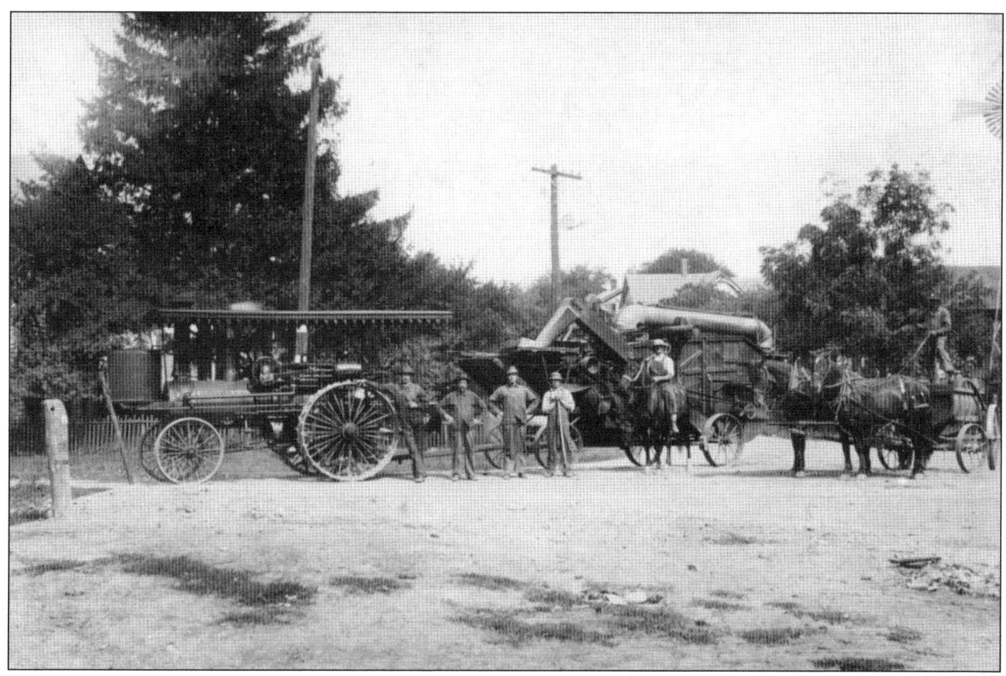

This photograph was taken in Loyal Oak as crews of threshers came to farms after grain had ripened sufficiently in shocks and was ready to be threshed in preparation for farmer to sell it. Pat Laubach Stano, a recently deceased longtime resident, grew up on a farm and said that the women at the farmsteads would provide lunch to the fellows who came to town to do the threshing. It was an exciting time of the year.

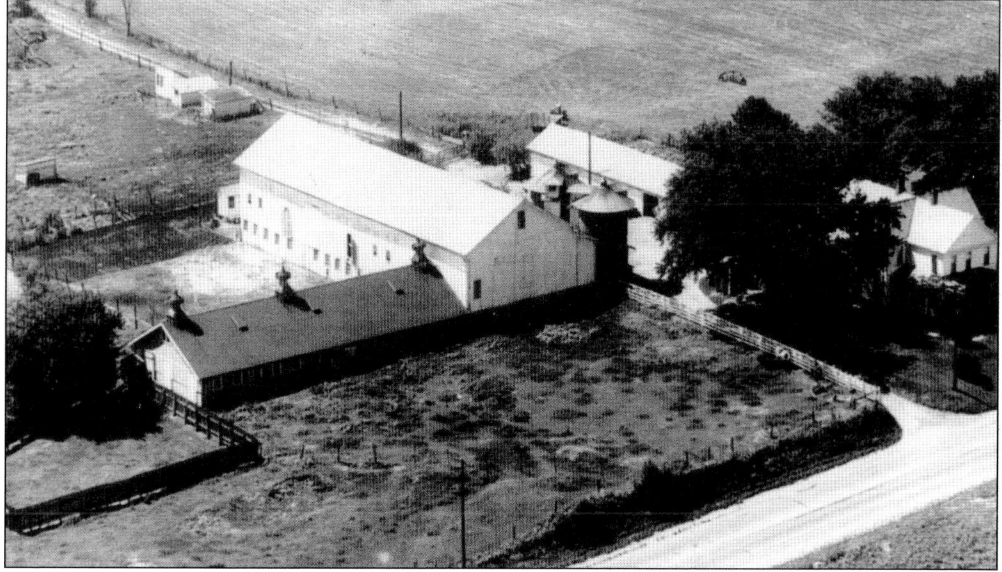

This photograph, taken in 1955, showcases the Walter and Lillian Seiberling farm, purchased in 1923. The farmstead at 3856 Greenwich Road was originally a dairy farm built by John Seiberling, son of Nathan Seiberling. In the mid-1950s, a major highway was built next to the farm to the west, which removed the farm fields in the upper-right corner. Junior, the son of Walter and Lillian, eventually purchased the farm after their passing. (Courtesy of Rodger Ramsthaler.)

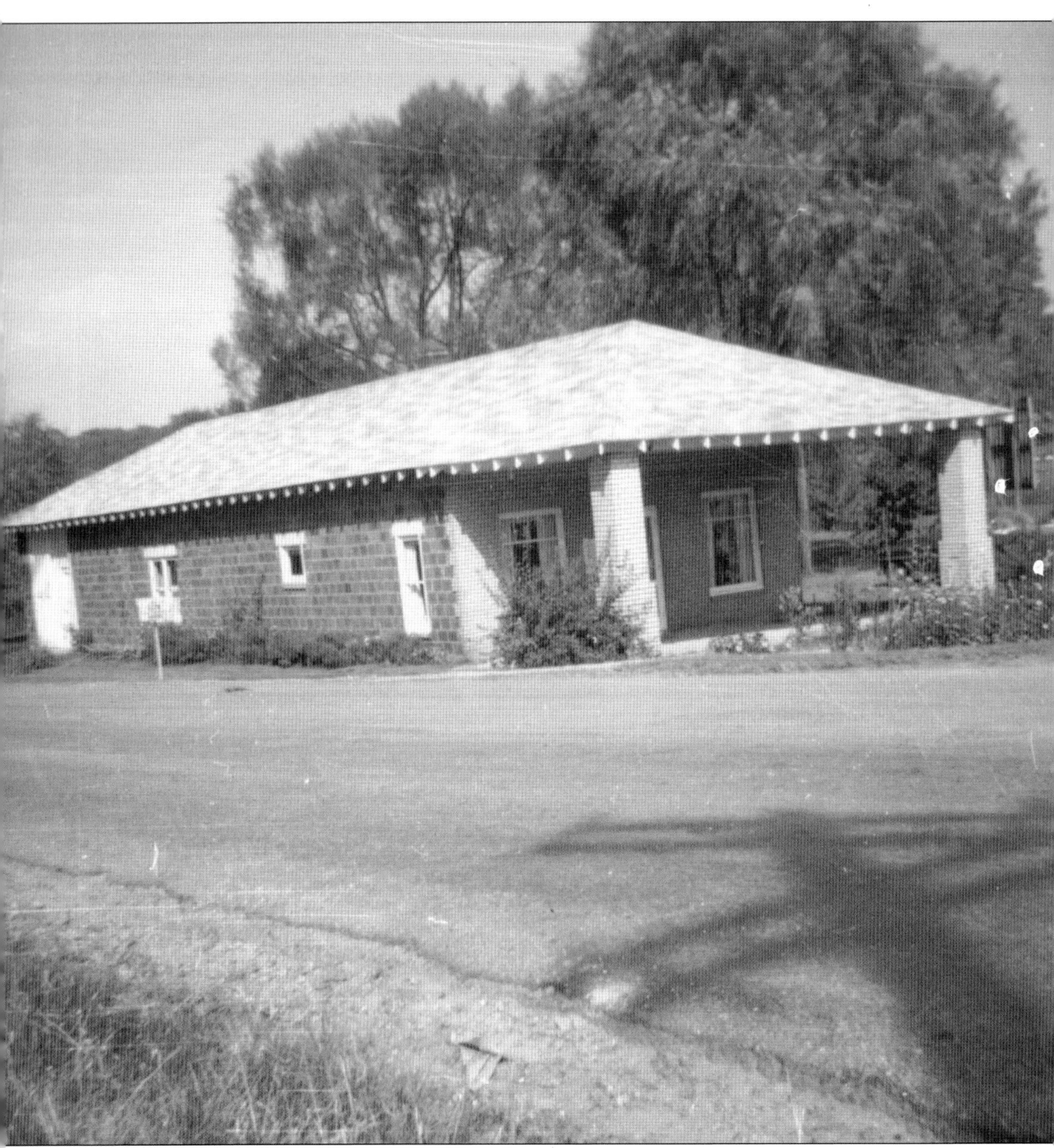

Bigelow Chapel was a church that existed in the early-to-mid-1800s on this lot of land. Not much is known about its existence other than it was named after a Reverend Bigelow. The cinder block building erected later as a gas station was constructed by Earl Sheets during the Great Depression, in 1929. It was later rented out as a dance hall with a wooden floor in a portion of the building. It was said to have been a speakeasy, and many bar fights and shootings took place there. The crawl space underneath has questionable purposes and a trap door. For a while afterward, it was privately rented as a home and then became a missionary church for a period of time, with an outside toilet, one light bulb, and cardboard to separate the rooms. In 1958, Dr. John Toth, a veterinarian, bought the building and worked there until his retirement in 1994. Toth said that during some renovations, they discovered a natural spring and a coal mine on the property. (Courtesy of Doctor John Toth.)

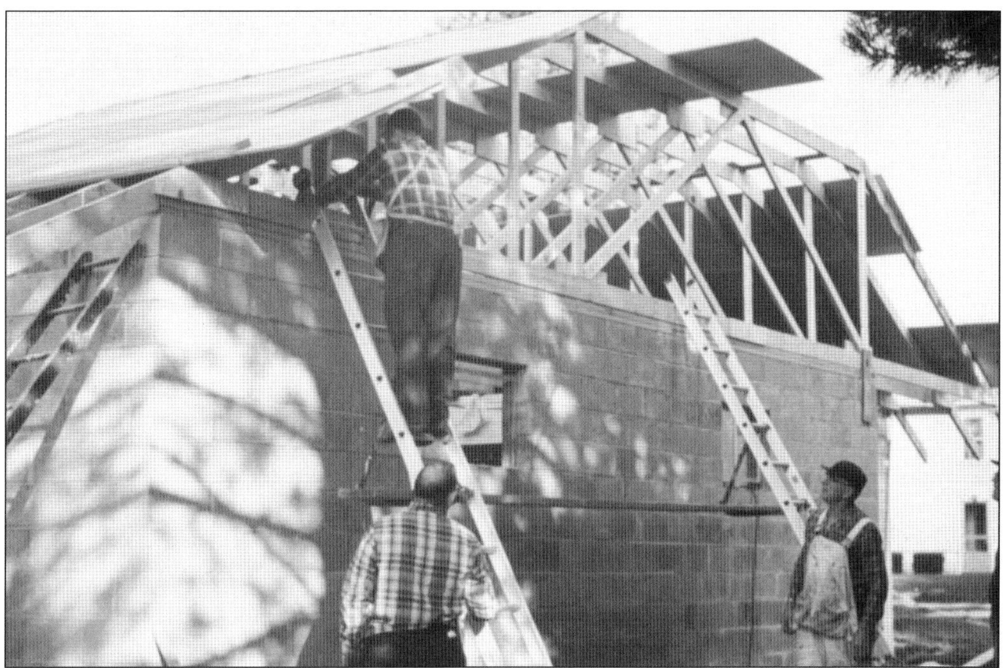

In 1968, the one-room Norton Branch Library on Cleveland-Massillon Road across from the high school stadium opened with money raised during Norton's sesquicentennial. With the help of civic groups, citizens, and remaining funds, another room was added in 1971. Here, that addition is being made for the library by Glen Long (on the ladder) and Chalmers Albright (left), Cal Tritt, and Don Diefendorff (not pictured.) A mill levy passed in 1984, which made it possible to build a new library just north of the old location. A dedication was held on May 1, 1988. (Courtesy of the Norton Library.)

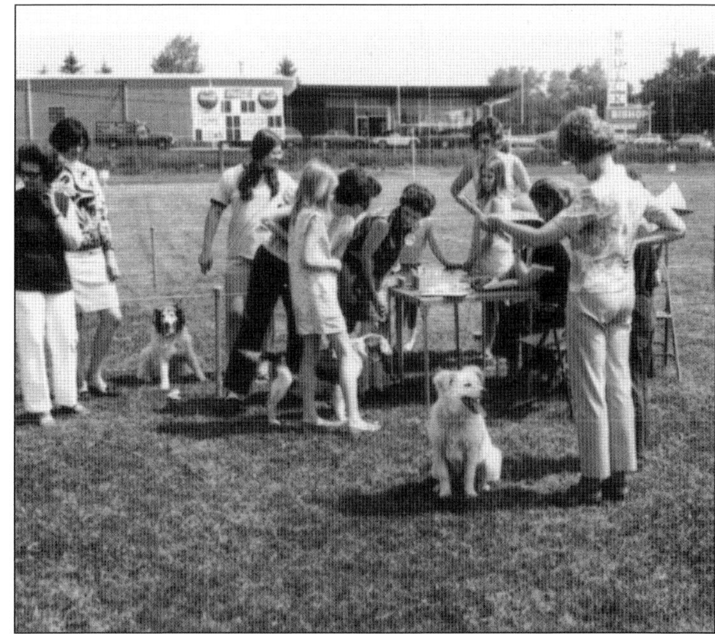

The annual library fundraising mutt show was held at the Norton High School stadium in July 1971. Dogs paraded in a ring, and judges awarded prizes, some of which were for the prettiest eyes, longest and shortest tails, longest ears, most handsome, best groomed, shaggiest, homeliest, best of show, and "muttiest" puppy. In the back of this image is the Bishop Buick dealership, started by Eugene F. Bishop in 1967. (Courtesy of the Norton Library.)

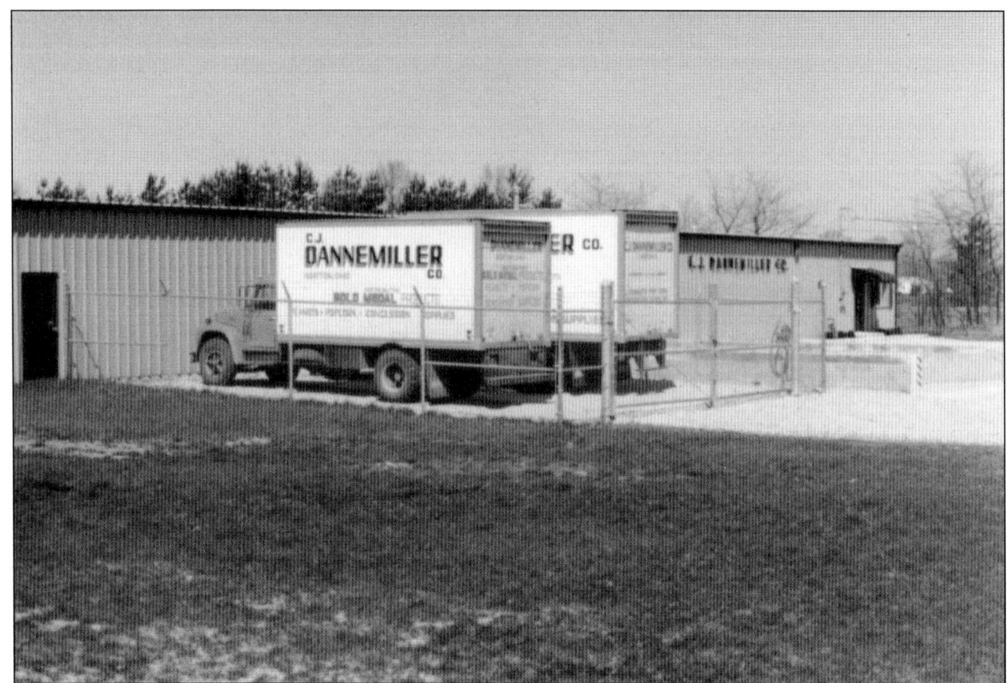

In 1935, Clarence J. Dannemiller raised popcorn in his home garden, packed it into one-pound packages, and sold it door to door in Barberton and Doylestown. This humble beginning grew into one of the major distributors of popcorn, peanuts, and concession supplies in the state of Ohio. In 1974, a major fire leveled much of the warehouse in Doylestown, and the business was moved to 5300 Hametown Road in Norton. C.J. Dannemiller Company offers concession equipment and supplies and snack foods wholesale and in-store. (Courtesy of Thomas Dannemiller.)

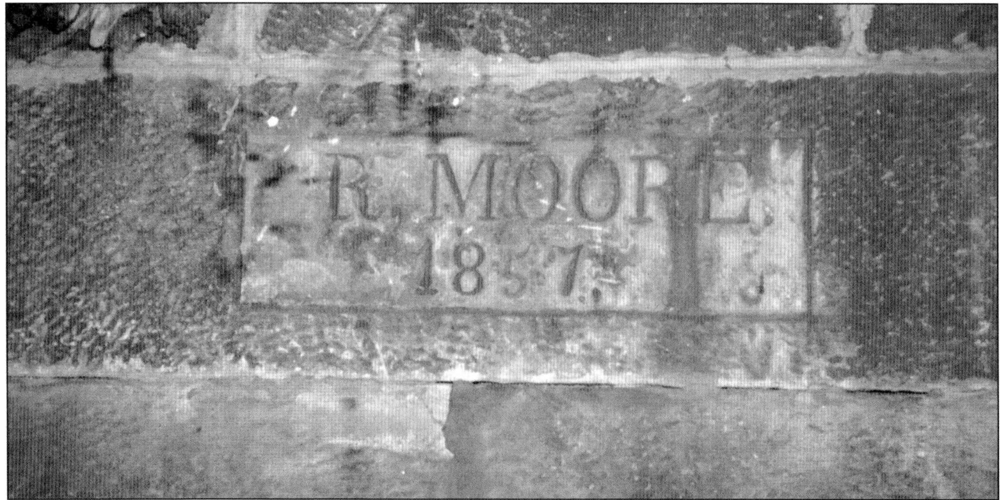

An obscure location in Norton holds local history as told by Ronald M. Shaffer, owner of Unicorn Enterprises, a fabricating and machining business located at 1689 Wadsworth Road. The setting was once a large barn built in 1857, and the foundation of the barn is still in existence, although the wooden structure burned to the ground. Over the years, the barn was home to a union organization, tavern, and dance hall and used to raise goats. This is a carving into the sandstone wall of the basement by the first owner, who lived across the road. (Author's collection.)

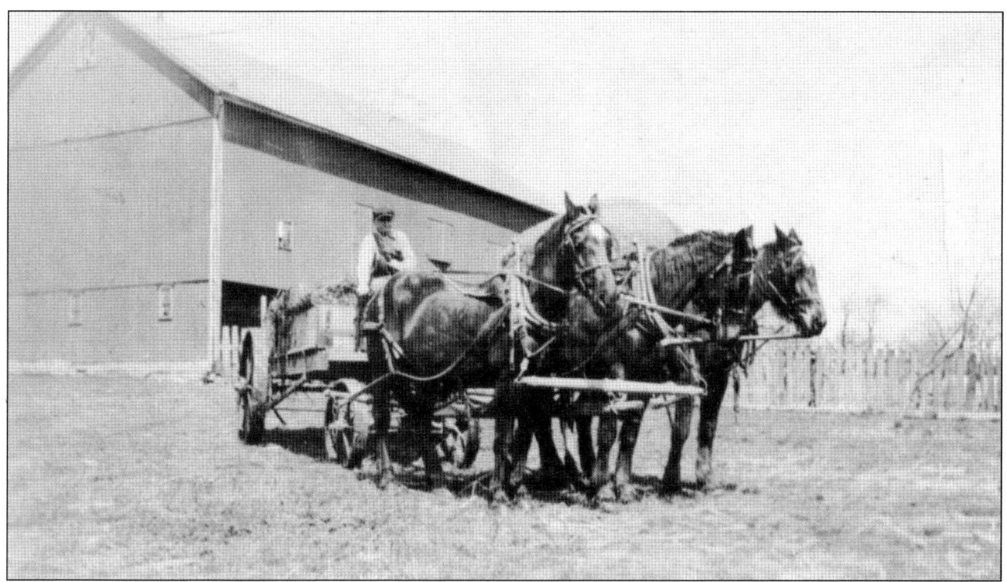

In the 1930s, Loyal Oak Golf Course was constructed on the Stump farm on Cleveland-Massillon Road. Merle R. Paul, manager of Tam O'Shanter Golf Club started construction on the new course with five tractors, five teams, and 20 workmen. The course was originally 6,450 yards in length, with bent grass greens and blue grass fairways. The plans called for a lake hole, and water around several other holes where a creek flowed through the property, rolling fairways, woods holes, and other features. In 1949, an adjacent property was purchased, and the course was expanded from 18 to 27 holes. The golf course had four different ownerships over the years, with the current owner being Katherine Gruber. The photograph is of the original Stump family homestead at 2909 Cleveland-Massillon Road, which is still is in use today as the golf course clubhouse. (Courtesy of Betty Bodo.)

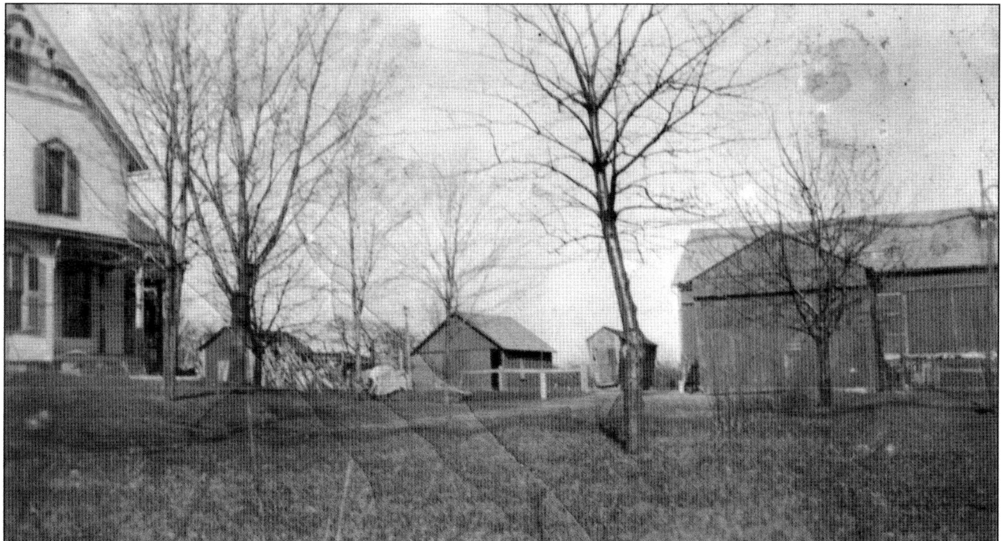

George Stump is leading a team of horses on his farm around 1920. Stump also drove a school bus for the Norton School district. (Courtesy of Betty Bodo.)

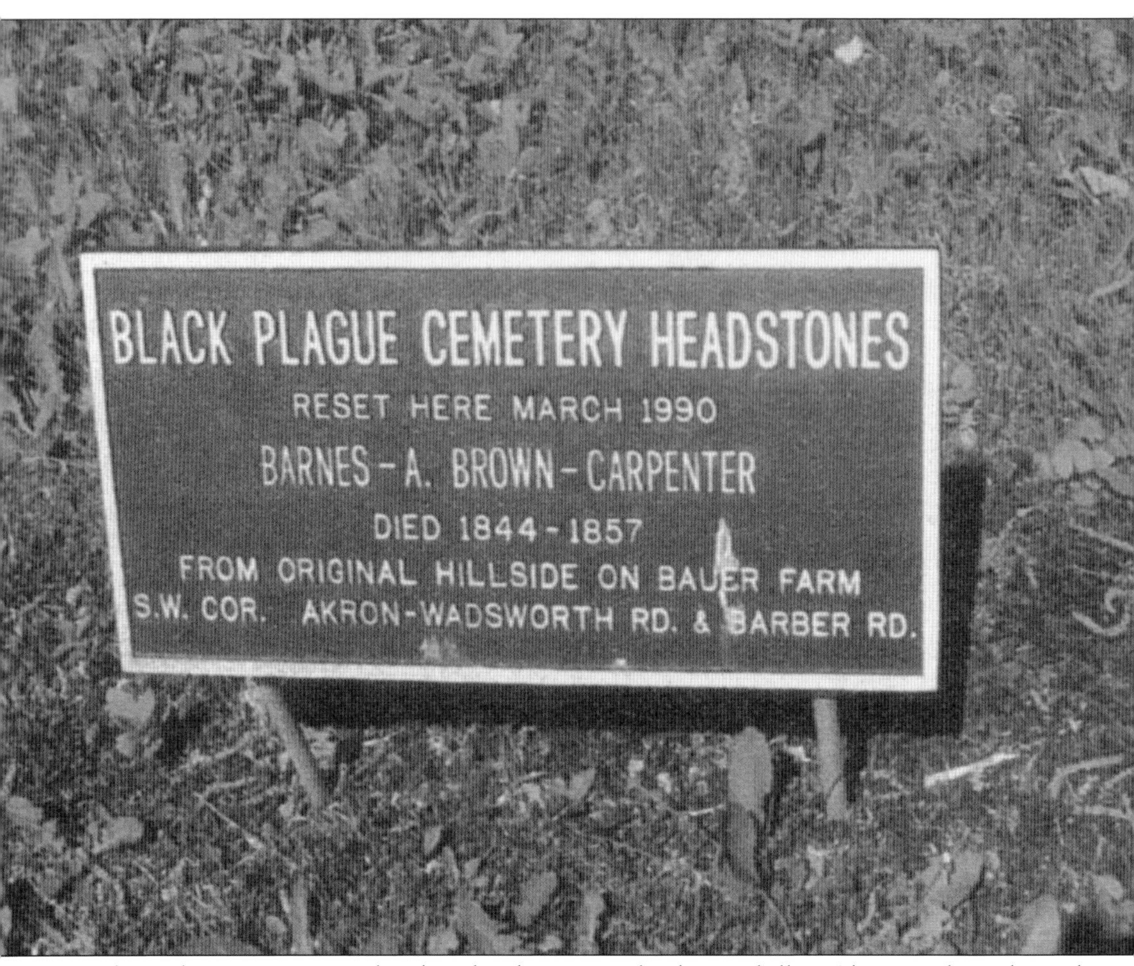

This verboten cemetery is abandoned and on private land atop a hill on Akron-Wadsworth Road. It originally was on the farm of Dennison Barnes, later known as the Bauer Farm. The origin of the name is unknown and has been handed down for generations. It is possible that an epidemic of the black plaque, also known as diphtheria, may have caused the deaths of at least some of those buried there. The Barberton water tower built in the 1930s stands at the top of the hill nearby the cemetery. During construction, this may have displaced some gravestones, others were vandalized, and many pushed over the hillside. In 1989, the Norton Cemetery Board removed the four largest headstones still in existence and reset them in the Norton Center Cemetery. It was thought there were at least 20 markers at one time. The names on the recovered stones are Abigail P., Lovewell, Phineas Barnes, Abraham and Freelove Brown, and Charles L. and Mary E. Carpenter.

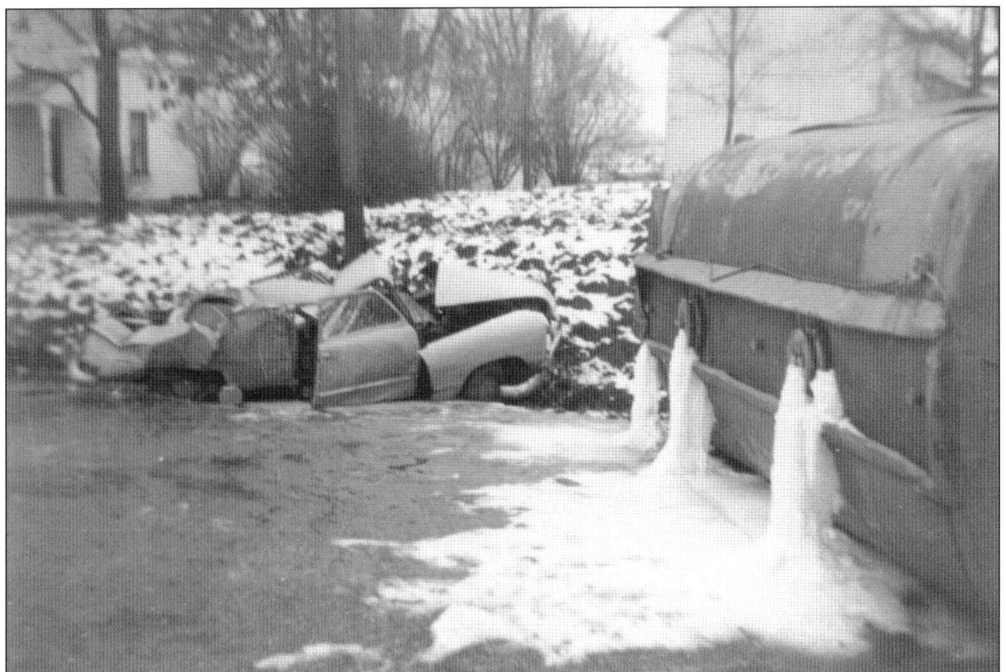

This 1950 four-door Ford sedan driven by Edward Kuba of Akron was in a spectacular accident at the corner of Hametown and Greenwich Roads (Route 224); 6,900 gallons of industrial liquid Benzol dumped on the road from an overturned trailer-tanker truck that collided with the Ford. Kuba was pinned for a time under the tanker, and his car was completely demolished, but he miraculously survived with only cuts and bruises. Because of the winter temperatures, the Benzol froze to the road surface and was eventually dissolved with portable steamers. (Courtesy of Rodger Ramsthaler.)

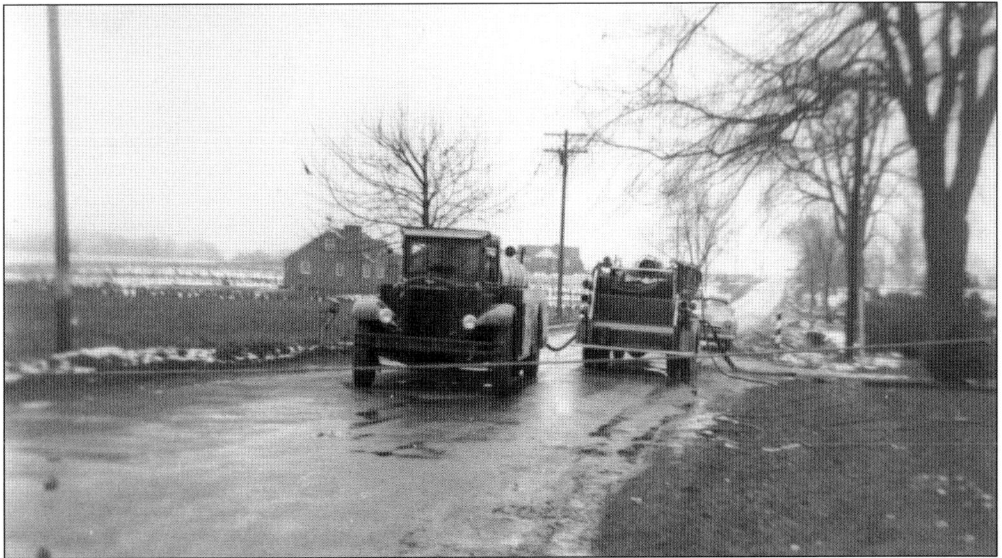

The Norton Fire Department had been newly built about the time that they assisted on the scene of this crash. The south-facing photograph was taken on Hametown Road and shows a 1946 Mack truck facing away and the water tanker facing forward. (Courtesy of Rodger Ramsthaler.)

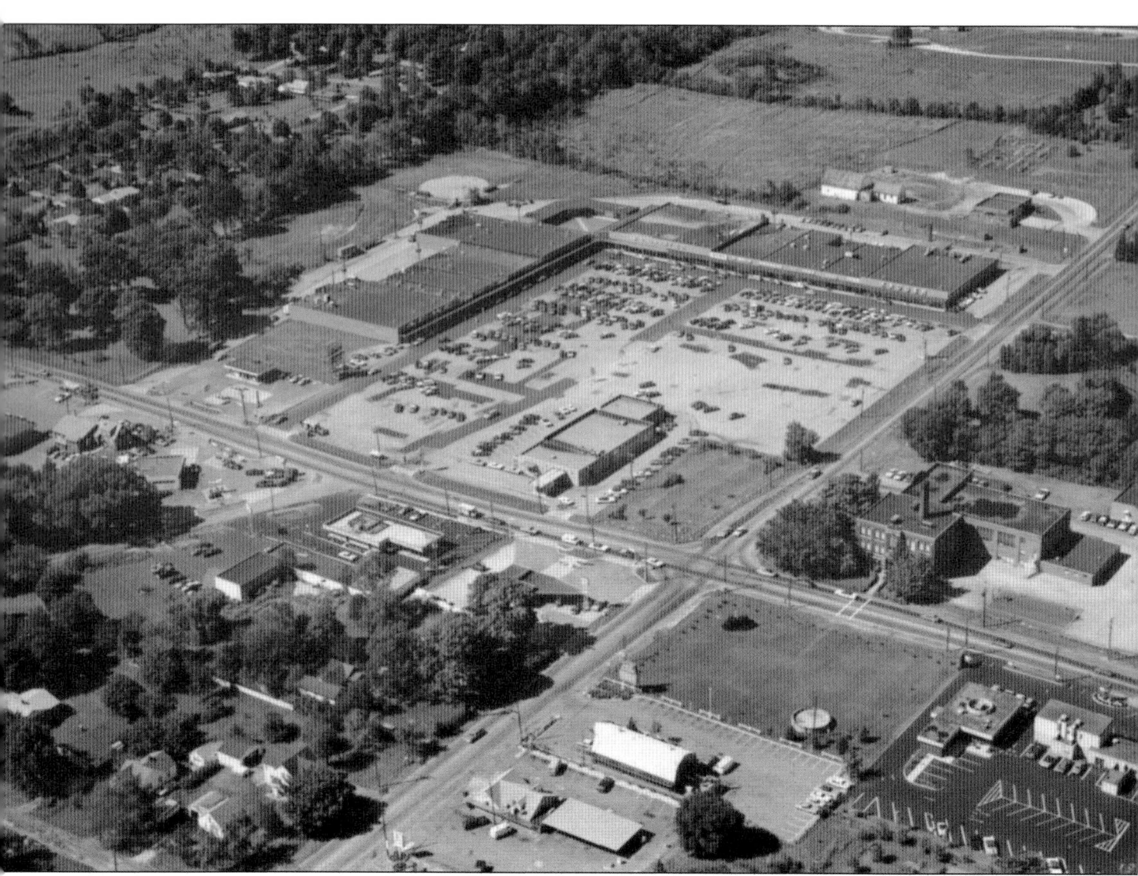

The center of Norton appears here in an aerial view in 1960. In sight are many buildings and residences that are no longer in existence. The original administration building, service garage, and fire station are clearly visible in the top right-hand corner and have all since been replaced. In the foreground is the Red Barn Restaurant, the place to hang out after football games, and next door is the fondly remembered Jimbo's where one could get the all-favorite gravy fries. The main focus is the Norton Plaza Shopping Center with its anchor store, Acme, owned by the Fred Albrecht Grocery Company. In the lower right-hand corner is the junior high school and gazebo that was a bandstand prior to getting a roof.

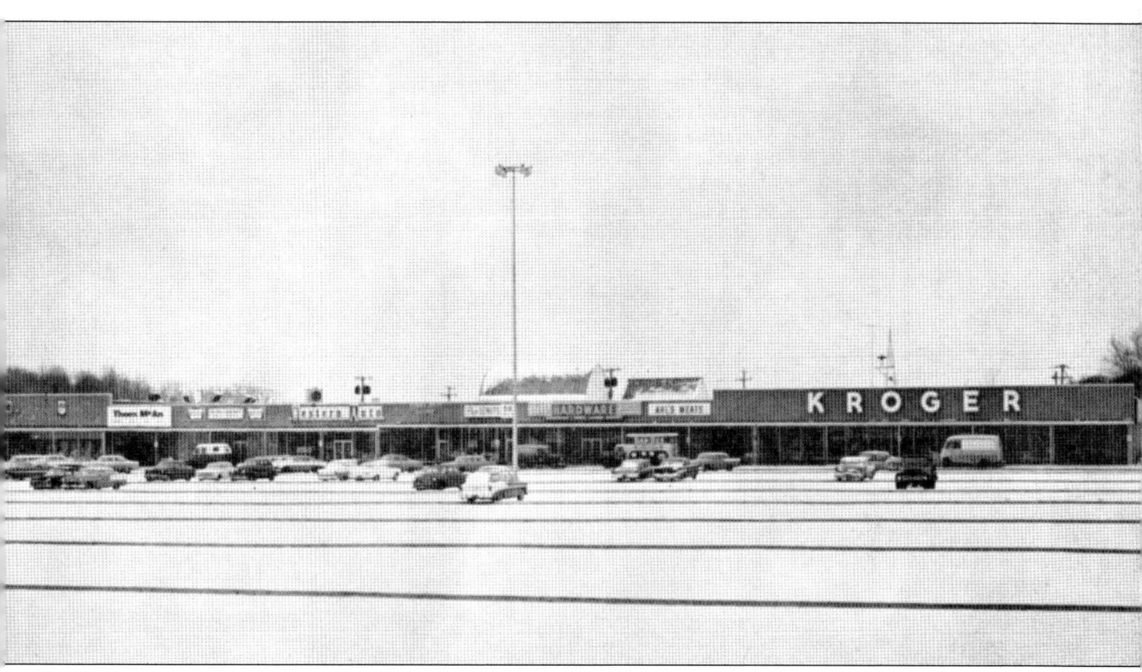

The Norton Village Shopping Center, pictured here in 1969, was under construction in 1957 and is shown here. The first official day of business was met by more than 7,000 shoppers and sightseers during a long day of ceremonies. The center actually held a weeklong program with horse shows, covered-wagon rides, and performances by a Summit County sheriff's posse and clowns.

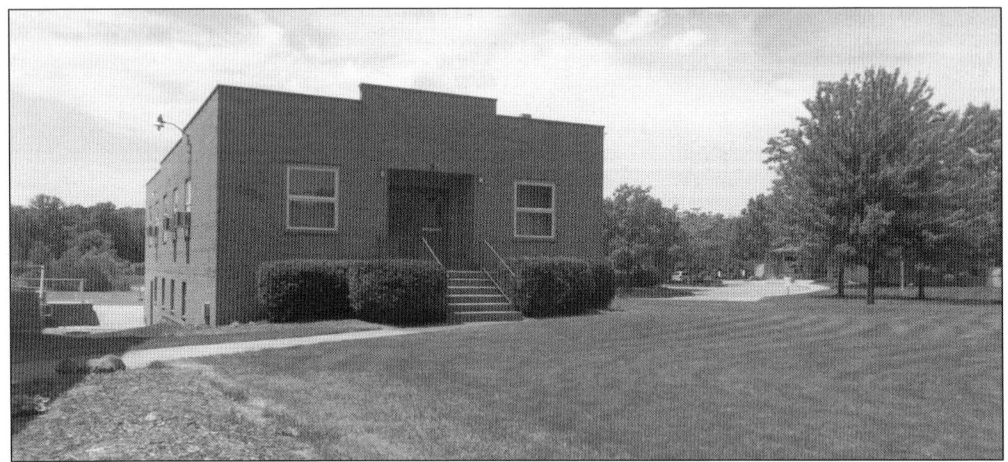

The Norton Grange No. 2566 was started in 1933—about 63 years after an act of Congress began the organization to better educate farmers, who were 97 percent of the working public at the time. After meeting at various locations, in 1962, it was decided to build a grange hall. Still active today, the organization puts its efforts toward community service. Having started with 1,200 members locally, it is now down to a meager 30 individuals with farming down to three percent of the total overall industry. In the past 10 years, the organization has donated approximately 2,000 books to the local schools. The original grange building shown here on Cleveland-Massillon Road was recently purchased by a nearby church. (Author's collection.)

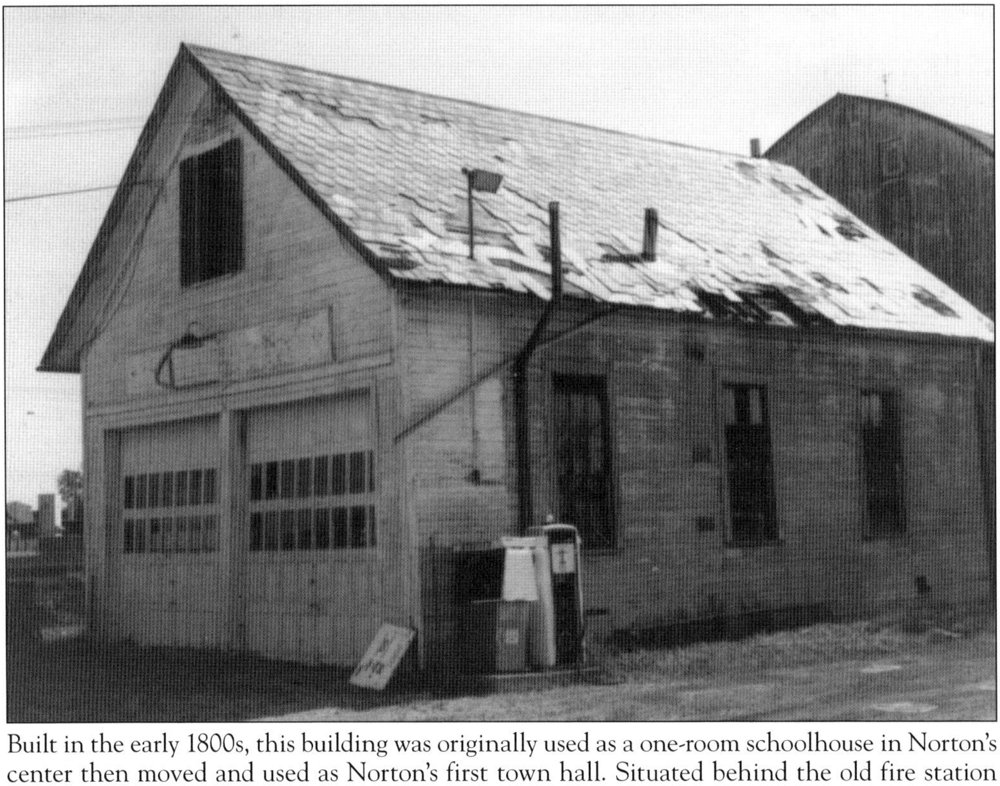

Built in the early 1800s, this building was originally used as a one-room schoolhouse in Norton's center then moved and used as Norton's first town hall. Situated behind the old fire station (which no longer exists) on Greenwich Road, the structure served as a fire station with city offices upstairs. It was torn down in 1988.

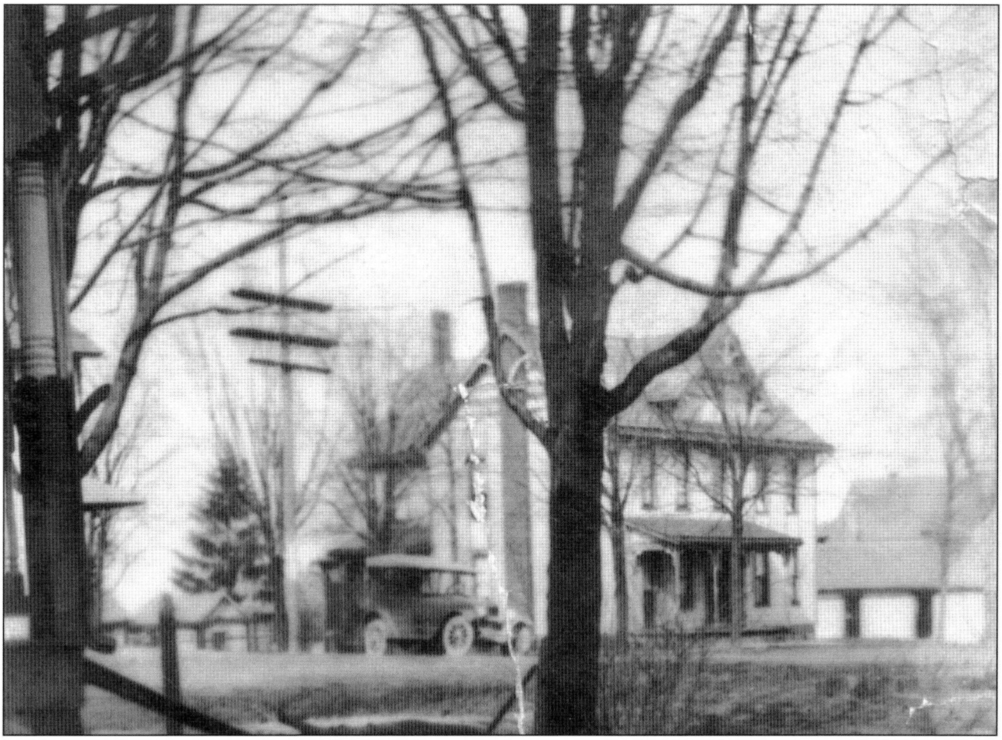

The Nash Hotel, with its 12-to-14-foot-high ceilings, was built around 1898 at the northeast intersection at Johnson's Corners. Bertha Nash kept her exotic birds upstairs. Charlie Nash opened his gas station there in the 1930s and named it Nash's Super Service. A man with many interests, including being an agent for the Buffalo Bill Show and Barnum & Bailey Circus and a noted musician, he died in 1940. (Courtesy of Lori Lewis Pfahler.)

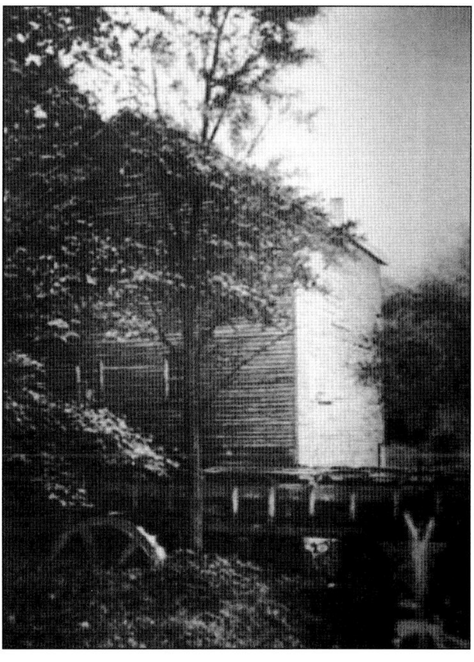

Here is one of two mills owned by Thomas Johnson, for whom the hamlet of Johnson's Corners is named. In 1830, Johnson built a gristmill on Hudson Run, near where he had earlier built his sawmill. At the raising of the second mill, it is recollected that Dennis Bates, who had offered to help put on the rafters, fell and crushed his skull, which caused nearly instant death. This image is one of the only known images of any of the mills built in Norton. Other families built mills locally, including Edward Laubach, Thomas VanHyning, Hezekiah Ward, Nathan Seiberling, and Carlos Clark.

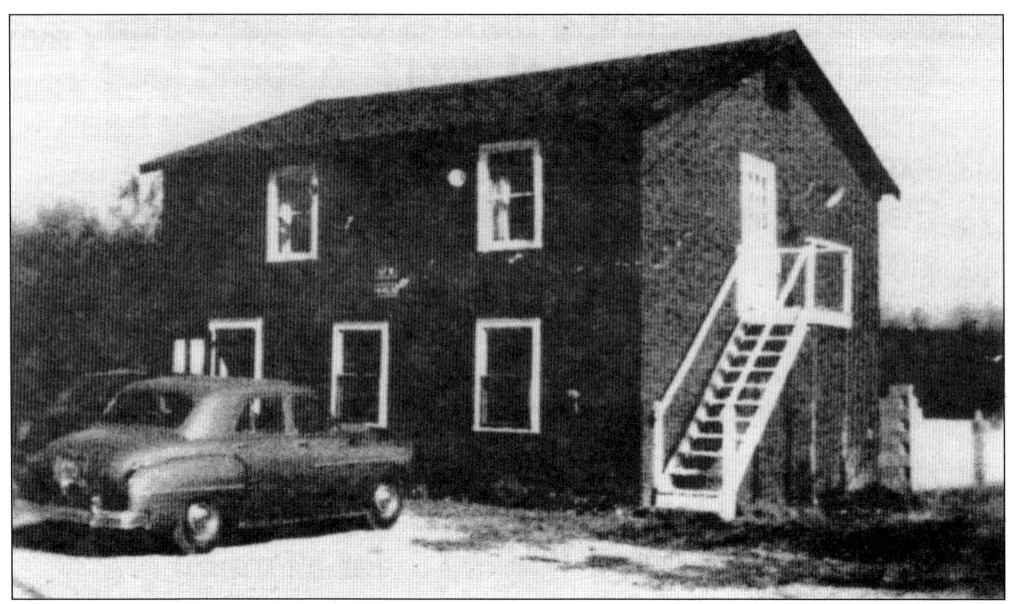

The Loyal Oak Post No. 4466 of the Veterans of Foreign Wars was formed in 1945 in an old house on the Morrison farm, located on Wadsworth Road. Shown here is a house that was purchased and used on Houston Road, which had a second-story meeting room and ground-floor social area. In 1948, the club got its liquor license, and by 1950, another addition was added. The house is gone, and the VFW closed in 2010 for lack of members. Now there is the Huston Pub and Hall, a social hall, restaurant, and bar owned by Charlie Shook.

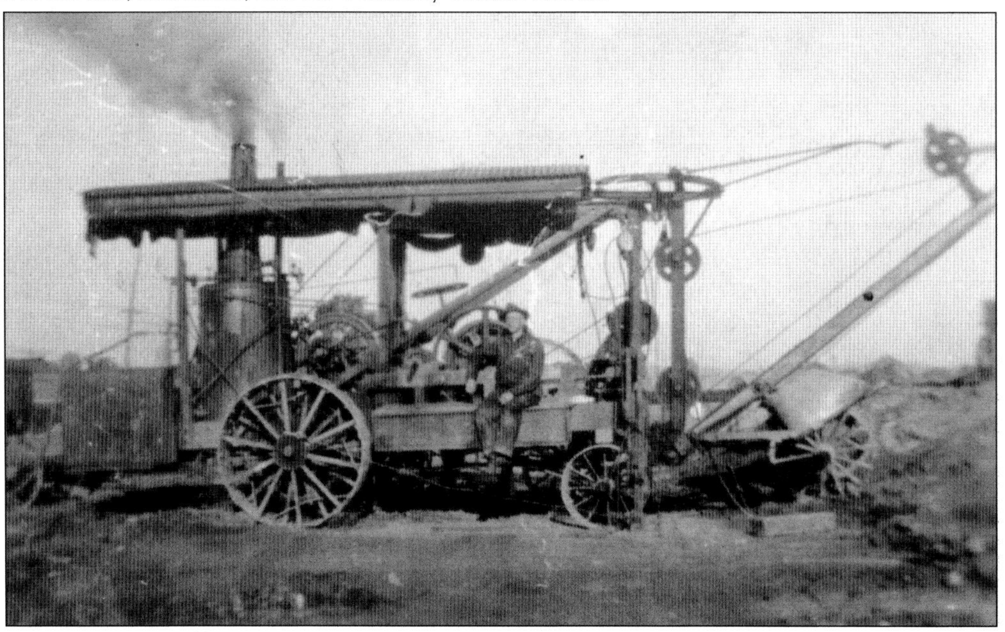

This Keystone Driller Company excavator was being used in the 1920s to build roads in Norton. Here, it is shown with an unknown man building Dorothy Avenue in Sherman. The boom is laid out flat to dig, and it digs by pulling the bucket outward along the ground. When the bucket is full, the boom is raised and swung to where the bucket is to be dumped. The operator pulls a rope to release a catch, and the bottom of the bucket drops open.

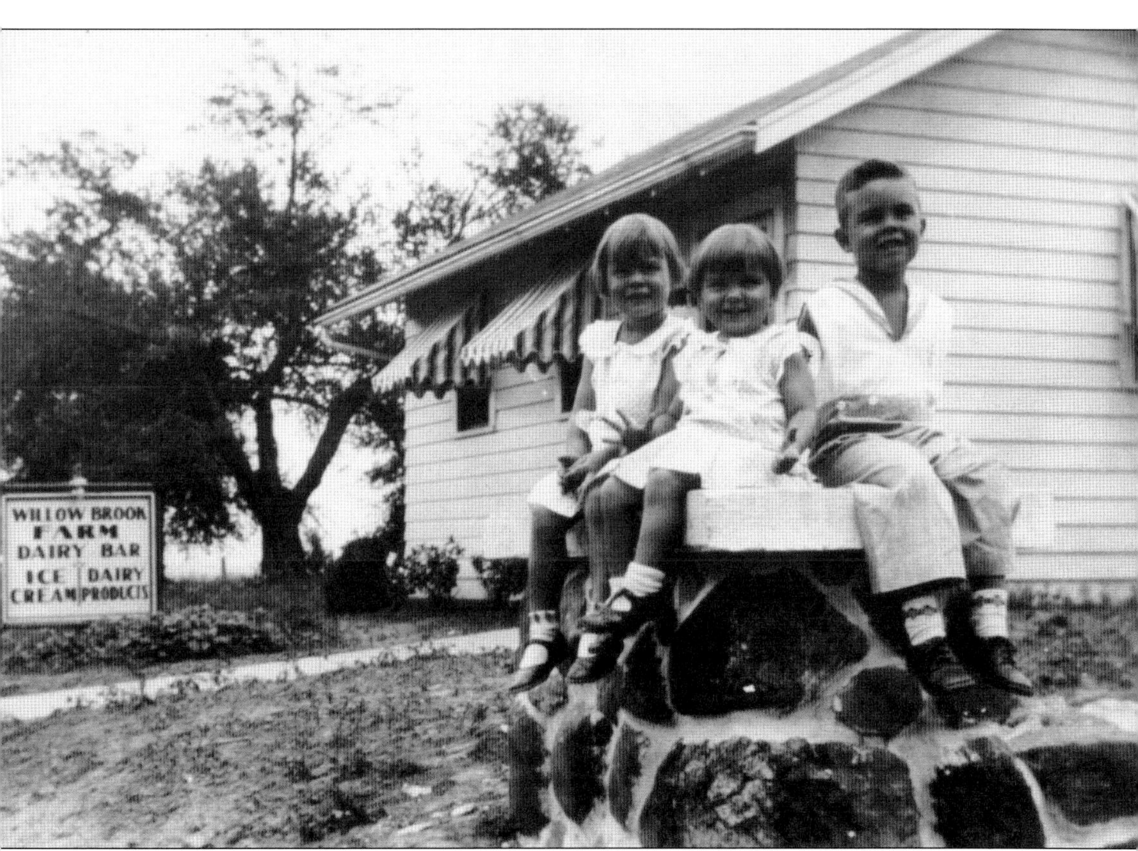

The Willowbrook Dairy Farm on Greenwich Road was owned and operated by Ernie Seiberling. This photograph, taken in 1932, depicts three of the Seiberling children; sitting from left to right are Marcene, Jane, and Dale. Having been on a main truck route at the time, truck drivers made this establishment a regular stop for lunch or just ice cream and refreshments. Marcene recalls working there at the age of 11, waiting on customers, making cones, sandwiches, and sundaes, and operating the cash register.

PUBLIC SALE.

The undersigned will offer For Sale at his residence, One Mil
Vest of Loyal Oak, on

THURSDAY, February 22, 1883.

The Following Property, To-wit:

One Good Family Horse,

3 COWS, 7 HEAD OF YOUNG CATTLE,
SEVEN SHOATS,

One Excelsior Mower and Reaper, Combined

One Two-Horse Wagon, 1 Three Spring Buggy, 1 Top Bugg
Wheel Cultivator, Pair of Bob-sleds, 1 Hay Rake, Plow an
Drag, 2 Corn Cultivators, Hay Rack, Buggy Harness, 1 set
Double Heavy Harness, 1 Set of Double Light Harness (new),
Single Harness, Double harpoon hay fork rope and pulleys, Son
Carpenter Tools, 2 Iron Kettles, 1 Copper Kettle, hay by the to

Household Furniture,

AND OTHER ARTICLES TOO NUMER
OUS TO MENTION.

Sale to Commence at Ten O'clock.

Terms Made Known on Day of Sale.

Nathan Oplinger.

LEVI NASH, Auctioneer

Here are two sale signs that appeared in Loyal Oak; one in 1883, and the other in 1932. Sarah Jane Miller's husband had died, and she sold the property to move in with her son. The home was purchased by the family of Anthony Wayne and Nellie Pearl (Hall) Ault.

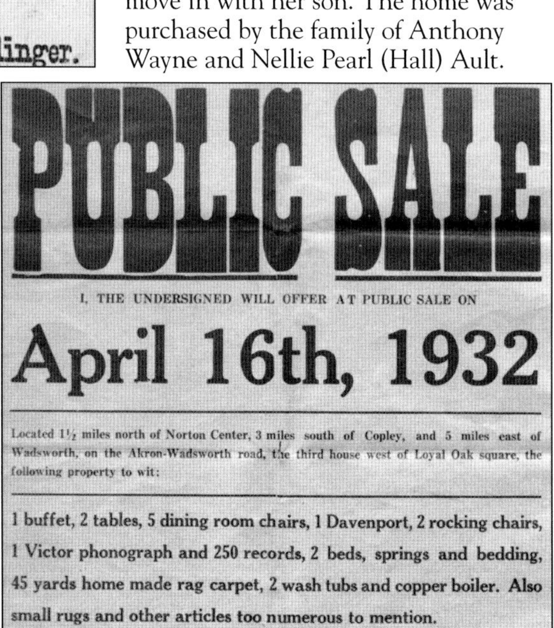

PUBLIC SALE

I, THE UNDERSIGNED WILL OFFER AT PUBLIC SALE ON

April 16th, 1932

Located 1½ miles north of Norton Center, 3 miles south of Copley, and 5 miles east of Wadsworth, on the Akron-Wadsworth road, the third house west of Loyal Oak square, the following property to wit:

1 buffet, 2 tables, 5 dining room chairs, 1 Davenport, 2 rocking chairs, 1 Victor phonograph and 250 records, 2 beds, springs and bedding, 45 yards home made rag carpet, 2 wash tubs and copper boiler. Also small rugs and other articles too numerous to mention.

TERMS OF SALE CASH

Sarah Jane Miller

E. P. LAUBACH, Clerk

J. F. MENTZER, Auctioneer

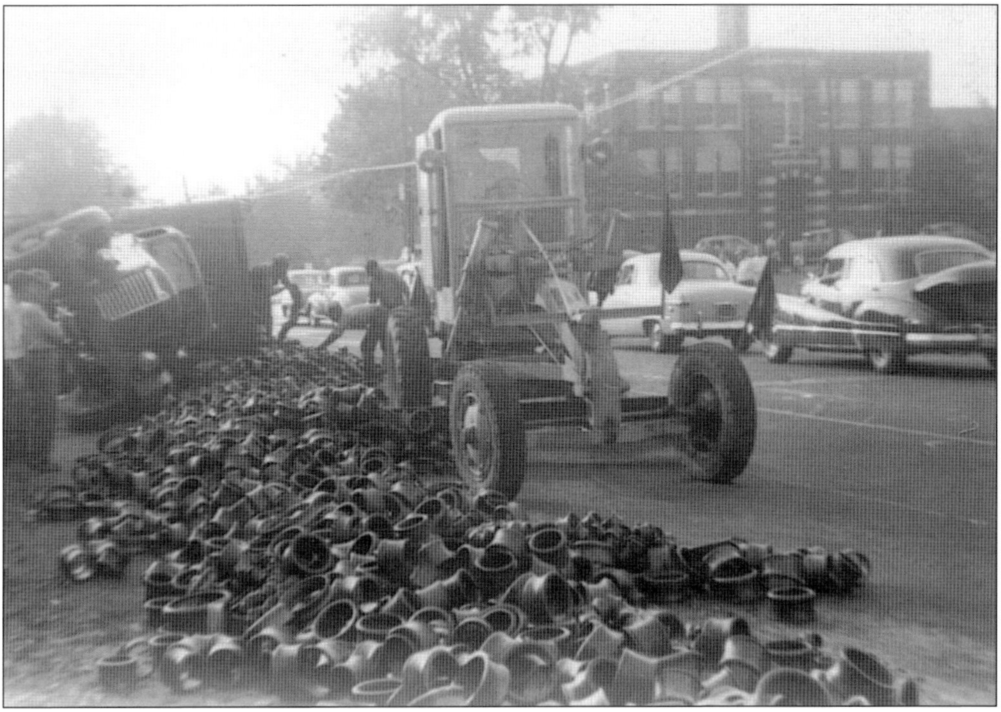

In the 1930s and 1940s in Norton Center, the traffic light was operated by trip pads in the approaching lanes about 100 feet from the light. Truck traffic was busy especially with those hauling coal from the south to the steel mills near Cleveland. These trucks coming north would attempt to get through the green light before it was tripped by east-west traffic or just go on through the light if it suddenly changed. This accident was a result of a car tripping the light from the east, proceeding into the intersection, and being struck by a truck going north. The victim was thrown from his vehicle and run over by the truck. The state eventually changed the traffic light to a timed system, and the number of accidents declined markedly after that. (Both, courtesy of Chuck Miller.)

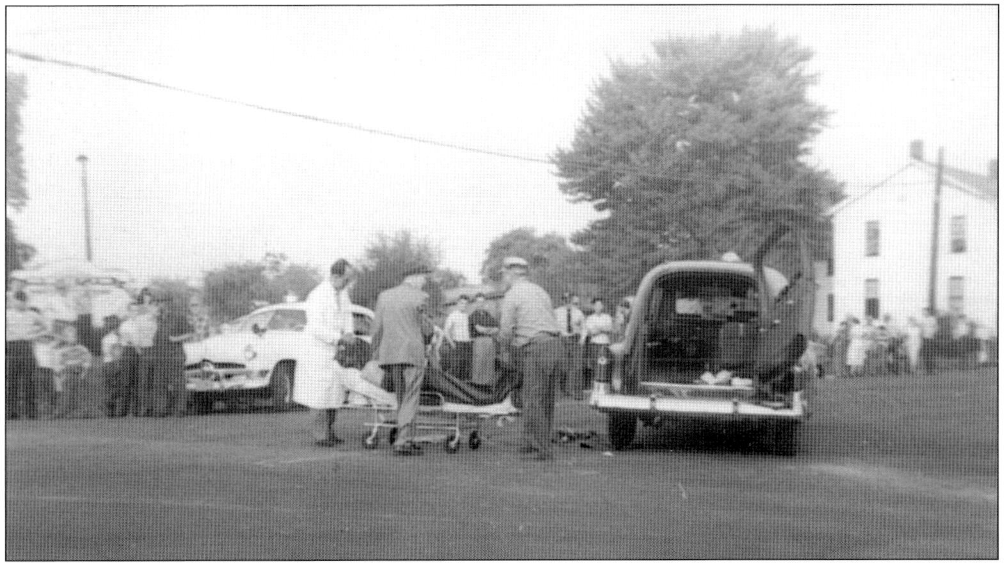

Consistent with our mission to preserve history on a local level, this book was printed in South Carolina on American-made paper and manufactured entirely in the United States. Products carrying the accredited Forest Stewardship Council (FSC) label are printed on 100 percent FSC-certified paper.

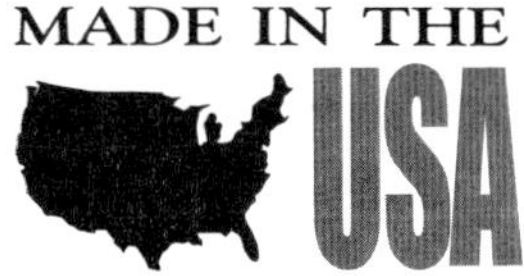